THE ANCIENT
IRELAND GUIDE

THE ANCIENT
IRELAND GUIDE

by robert emmet meagher and elizabeth parker neave

INTERLINK BOOKS

First published in 2013 by

INTERLINK BOOKS
An imprint of Interlink Publishing Group, Inc.
46 Crosby Street, Northampton, Massachusetts 01060
www.interlinkbooks.com

Library of Congress Cataloging-in-Publication Data
Meagher, Robert E.
The Ancient Ireland Guide / by Robert Emmet Meagher &
Elizabeth Parker Neave.
p. cm.
ISBN 978-1-56656-914-9 (pbk.)
1. Ireland--Antiquities—Guidebooks. 2. Antiquities,
Prehistoric—Ireland—Guidebooks. 3. Christian antiquities—Ireland—
Guidebooks. I. Neave, Elizabeth. II. Title
DA920.M43 2003
936.1'5—dc22
2003014325

Selections from *Early Irish Myths and Sagas*, translated by Jeffrey Gantz,
and from *Life of St. Columba*, translated by Richard Sharp, quoted with
the kind permission of Penguin Books, LTD.

Selected verses from Thomas Kinsella's translation of the *Prayer of
Manchán of Liath*, quoted with the kind permission of Thomas Kinsella.

Printed and bound in Korea

This book is warmly dedicated to

Patrick Sarsfield Meagher

And to the people of Ireland—

Those who left,

Those who didn't,

Those who returned,

Those who didn't,

Loving the land they came from

And longing for peace.

"Some people don't like the Irish,
but we're very popular among ourselves."
—*Brendan Behan (1923–1964)*

"Where there is sorrow, there is holy ground."
—*Oscar Wilde (1854–1900)*

PREFACE

Some will be surprised by the very notion of a guide to ancient Ireland. For many, "Old Ireland" is the Ireland of thatched roofs and clay pipes, not the Ireland of megaliths and promontory forts. On further, more reaching, reflection, Patrick and the saints may come to mind, and before them the druids. But often it stops there, with Celtic and Christian Ireland, as if they were the points of origin, the beginning of the story. Far from it. The Celts are latecomers to Ireland, and Christianity even more so. Indeed, if being Irish means being Celtic and Christian, then we simply have to concede that there was a time, a very long time, when Ireland wasn't Irish.

Indeed, most visitors to Ireland come looking for the quaint, not the ancient. Those inclined or addicted to ruins choose, one might suppose, Egypt, Mesopotamia, or more frequently Greece. Until recently, Irish antiquity has been a well-kept secret, while Greek antiquity has been a household word. The truth is that we explored and wrote about ancient Greece well before we discovered and considered writing about ancient Ireland. It was only after years of writing the Frommer's guides to Ireland that we realized that what fascinated us most about the motherland was off-track Ireland, the all-but-forgotten Ireland of the Neolithic, Bronze, and early Iron Ages. This realization of ours converged, as it happened, with a much more widespread, international rediscovery of, and resurgence of interest in, remote antiquity. Coincident with this movement is the ever-growing postmodern hunger for an innate or at least primeval spirituality rooted in the earth and tangibly located in sites still charged with indescribable power and poignancy. Two, if not *the* two, epicenters of this new spirituality are indisputably Greece and Ireland. In both, the "sacred" first referred to the earth. The first sacred sites were caves and mountains and rivers and wells or springs, whose eventual temples or tombs only marked the site as sacred. In other words, sacrality was not an artifact but a discovery. Artifacts eventually fall to ruin, but the spot—the organ or limb of mother earth—that inspired them often survives and retains its power. In short, there is more to Greece than beaches, and there is more to Ireland than pubs.

Year after year, in European Union polls, the Irish and the Greeks vie with each other for first ranking in national loyalty and pride. Why, we might ask, would these two— the land of rain and the land of sun—find themselves in such a contest? On reflection, they indeed have much in common: stone houses with traditional lace curtains, keys left in kitchen doors, annual tourist invasions, rock walls everywhere, abandoned monasteries, crumbling ruins, legendary hospitality, vital folk music, a passionate love of poetry, spectacular landscapes created by the convergence of sea and mountains and home to communities often hanging onto existence by a thin and resented touristic thread, and national drinks appreciated only as an acquired taste (stout and retsina).

But the kinship between these two peoples runs far deeper than this. Despite their illustrious past—Greece as the ancient crèche of western civilization and Ireland as its western conservator in the "dark ages"—both peoples have been conquered and humiliated for most of their histories, only regaining their full freedom and independence in the last century, an independence still disfigured by territorial amputation. The Irish, like the Greeks, have known in that same century the shame and agony of civil war; and both have entered the next century with an open wound— Cyprus for the Greeks and Northern Ireland for the Irish—and an uneasy truce with an enemy with whom they have lived and slept and eaten and worked and fought for so long as to become all but inseparable. As Aristotle pointed out long ago, most hate eventually turns to love, and vice versa. Both the Greeks and the Irish have endured centuries of poverty, in which to have dreams for their children meant sending them off to distant lands, most notably Australia, Canada, and the United States. Both countries' diasporas remain vast, in each case far out-numbering the population of the motherland; and they have in common an Odyssean longing for *nostos* or return.

The point of these reflections on Greece and Ireland is

not to talk anyone into skipping Ireland and traveling instead to Greece. Our purpose here is twofold: first, to explain how our love of antiquity and its treasures, material and spiritual, led us from Greece to Ireland; and, second, to make the point that Ireland, every bit as much as Greece and perhaps even more so, is a land of archaeological treasures and spiritual power. Most succinctly, we might even propose that Ireland is Greek, with the added benefit of reliable rainfall.

A book without collaborators and friends is a book never finished. What we know and share here is what we have learned from others—from reading what they have written, listening to what they have said, and looking where they have pointed us. To list our sources and enumerate our debts would add another chapter to a book that is already pushing the limits of a pocket-portable guide. We will limit ourselves to a few of those who have most directly and personally assisted us in putting this volume together. As always, in all of our Irish adventures, we are indebted to our dear friends John and Jean Dillon, and John and Lyndall Luce. Additionally, Peter Harbison has been a special guide and mentor, in print and in person, to this effort. With his vast knowledge and contagious enthusiasm, he is indeed a national treasure. We are thankful too for the on-site and on-the-mark insights of Joe Fenwick, and the vast photographical knowledge and resources of Tony Roche. As is their wont, Tourism Ireland and the Northern Ireland Tourist Board have been again gracious with their assistance. On the home front, here in western New England, our publisher and friend Michel Moushabeck has been warmly supportive of this project from the start; and Pam Thompson and Juliana Spear, with all of their precision and artistry, have polished our would-be gemstone until it may just shine. Last, and in fact least, we send an affectionate pat to the inimitable Benson, a beloved terrier with no concept of his own size or importance, who did everything in his power to assure that this book would never be written. Our deep thanks to one and all, especially those readers who will entrust their Irish holiday, or a portion of it, to our guidance. We hope in advance not to have broken that trust.

—Robert Emmet Meagher and Elizabeth Parker Neave
The Clearing

ENVISIONING AND PLANNING YOUR TRIP

Exploring Irish Antiquity

The modest scope and sharp focus of this volume are by design. The aim here is to address a specific gap in current Irish travel literature and thus to meet a particular need. There are, to be sure, scores of excellent books on ancient Ireland, both for scholars and for general readers; and there is certainly no shortage of informed and useful guidebooks for first-time or veteran visitors to contemporary Ireland. Surprisingly, we know of no guide, however, which confronts in detail the practicalities of exploring ancient Ireland on the ground, on one's own, despite the already substantial and ever-growing interest in early Irish history and prehistory. Every planned adventure is lived three times over: first in anticipation, then one bend in the road at a time, and finally in memory. This volume, we hope, will prove useful to its readers in all of these moments—inspiring their plans, guiding their steps, and evoking their memories.

You would never know from most tourist guides that Ireland is a prime destination for anyone seriously engaged or just plain fascinated with the ancient human past. While millions of tourists visit Ireland every year, most drive right past Ireland's ancient treasures. The common conception remains that Ireland's lure lies in such truisms as the verdure of its hills, the joy of its music, and the charm of its people. Seldom does the general public associate Ireland with its antiquities. Egypt has the pyramids, France the painted caves, Greece the Parthenon, Italy the Eternal City—and Ireland… ? All too hastily the popular imagination leaps to thatched cottages, quaint villages, and seasoned pubs. While Ireland itself is no secret, it still has its secrets; and prominent among them is its profoundly rich and remote past, available to be read not only in books but also across its landscape. Dig almost anywhere and you will discover something startling. Anyone who would explore the ancient Irish past is indeed spoiled for choice.

Every county—in fact nearly every farmer's field—in Ireland contains some tangible token of lives played out here not only hundreds but thousands of years ago. Voluminous catalogues of ancient field monuments contain, county by county, all that there is to see—tombs, royal and ritual sites, stone circles, hill forts, early monastic settlements, holy wells, and much more. To give more than a nod to every registered and annotated site would consume years, let alone a week's holiday. Priorities need to be set, decisions made, and preparations put in place for anyone to explore the Irish past, behind the wheel and on foot, with reasonable economy, coherence, and satisfaction.

This said, it is only fair to issue a warning: ruins—the inevitable condition of most authentic antiquities—are addictive. They are to the imagination what aerobic exercise is to the heart. They get the blood flowing and clear the lungs. Archaeologists and long-distance runners have at least this in common—they often get lost in thought. The finish line fades and it is all about the indescribable expansion of the present. The simple and obvious truth awaiting anyone who plunges into human antiquity is that the past is not past. It is, instead, as Augustine realized already in the 4th century, merely a dimension of the mind, waiting to be revived in the imagination, waiting to be remembered.

Since the past is never truly past, it is always bumping into what we call the present. Many of the greatest "finds" in Ireland have occurred by accident—when a plow blade breaks on an ancient embankment or a new motorway, under construction, suddenly intersects an ancient crossroads. Less dramatically, en route to and from ancient sites, today's explorers get hungry and weary and concerned about where they will spend the night. After all, they are also on vacation and, as the saying goes, you can't eat the scenery, ancient or modern. What's more, many will have junior explorers in tow, whose enthusiasm for remote ruins will wane more rapidly than their parents' and will tug in other more immediate directions. Consequently, while retaining our focus here on the distant past, we have kept in mind the primacy of a well-planned and well-rounded holiday, providing a handful of considered suggestions for lodging, food, side-trips, and activities for families with children.

Itineraries into the Irish Past

Most visitors to Ireland spend at least a week here. This is all the more true of those who bring with them a burning interest in one or other aspect of Irish life and culture. It makes plain sense, then, to divide the exploration of ancient Ireland into seven-day slices, which may be expanded at will and at any point by divergings or lingerings to trace roots, chase the sun, rest the feet, or whatever. In mapping out the itineraries detailed in this volume, we have had a number of aims in mind. Each of the three intineraries is focused on one or other epoch in the ancient Irish past. An effort has also been made to point the several itineraries towards different corners of the Irish landscape, as some visitors' preferences will have more to do with the compass than with chronology. Always in our minds, as well, has been to include in each itinerary as many prime and pertinent sites as possible. Each of the resulting itineraries, then, is a product of compromise. It cannot be otherwise. Give me a suitable lever, boasted Archimedes, and I'll move the world. In a more modest vein, our boast might run something like this: give us a week, and you'll want more.

The itineraries then follow one upon the other across a span of time from 10,000 years ago to the late 12th century C.E., defining "Ancient Ireland" as that period beginning with the first human settlement and ending with the Norman Invasions. More precisely, they are:

Itinerary #1: Pre-Celtic—Neolithic and Bronze Ages—4000 B.C.E.–700 B.C.E.
Itinerary #2: Pre-Christian Celtic—Late Bronze and Iron Ages—700 B.C.E.–400 C.E.
Itinerary #3: Early Christian Celtic—Irish Golden Age and Early Medieval—400 C.E.–1200 C.E.

Although, in fact, not all visits to Ireland begin on the same day of the week, our itineraries begin, in theory, on Sunday, allowing for weekend travel and for an initiating

ANCIENT
IRELAND
4000 BCE – 1200 CE

Grianan of Aileach
DERRY

ULSTER

Emain Macha

Inishmurray
Céide Fields
Creevykeel
SLIGO
Carrowmore
& Carrowkeel

WESTPORT
Croagh Patrick
CONNACHT

Loughcrew
Brú na Bóinne
Hill of Tara
MIDE
Clonmacnoise

DUBLIN

Dún Aonghasa
GALWAY
Burren
Lough Derg

Glendalough
Wicklow Gap

Shannon
LIMERICK
LEINSTER
Kells
Lough Gur
Rock of Cashel
Jerpoint Abbey

Gallarus Oratory
DINGLE
MUNSTER
KILLARNEY
Ardmore
Skellig Michael

ITINERARIES
PRE-CELTIC · NEOLITHIC & BRONZE AGE
PRE-CHRISTIAN CELTIC · LATE BRONZE & IRON AGE
EARLY CHRISTIAN · IRISH GOLDEN AGE & MEDIEVAL

tour of the National Museum, closed Mondays. To reduce confusion, however, we refer throughout not to days of the week but to "day one," "day two," etc. We've also assumed in our recommendations of accommodations, restaurants, and other suggestions that these itineraries are best undertaken between the beginning of April and the end of October, as they are in general the most inviting and accessible times for visiting Ireland, especially ancient Ireland.

Some potential users of this guide may rankle at the very notion of an itinerary and see it as a thinly disguised guided tour. Fair enough. Perhaps it will help if we admit that our itineraries are indeed drawn with "rulers," measuring out time and distance in ways that never quite match their experienced flow. Maps and watches need to be set aside and rules are made to be broken. All the same they serve many a purpose, all too clear once anyone gets behind the wheel and sets out to touch the past in real time.

The fact is that ancient Ireland is hardly amenable to "tours," especially bus tours or invasions of any sort. This is true for a pocketful of reasons. First among them is that many or most of the ancient sites in this volume are "sacred" in one sense or another. Like any place of profound human struggle, suffering, revelation, or triumph—places of immeasurable darkness or brilliance—they are permanently "charged" with the past or, some would say, the timeless. At some "open sites," namely those without fee or noticeable supervision, such as the passage tombs at Loughcrew and Carrowkeel, visitors are likely to find votive candles, flowers, or other token offerings—evidence of others' heartfelt reverence for and resonance with these remarkable places. The same sites are on occasion the scene of demonstrative rituals conducted by contemporary druids, wiccans, and spiritual seekers of many stripes, as well as those whose uncommon thirst and respect for the human past are more elusive though no less strong. All this is to say that even under the influence of a fast-paced itinerary it is essential to linger now and then; for much of what these sites have to offer requires some stillness and pause to discern. It also goes without saying that any littering, defacement, souvenir-hunting, or disrespect is not to be tolerated. The vulnerability of these sites is startling.

Carrowkeel

Some of the world's finest examples of stone-age art and architecture lie unprotected on Irish hilltops; so the burden is clearly on their fortunate visitors not to do anything that puts these monuments at further risk.

Next, it is important to keep in mind and plan ahead for the fact that **"Ancient Ireland" is more or less synonymous with "Outdoor Ireland,"** which in combination with the notorious unpredictability of Irish weather calls for some degree of preparedness, discretion, flexibility, and—on rare occasions—resignation. After all, most of the destinations and sites in this volume lie scattered across the Irish countryside and a number are accessible only by boat. Not only a certain level of fitness but also a certain willingness to confront obstacles is likely to be asked of the "explorers" for whom this guide is written. Of course, individual explorers will set their own limits and find their own way; but sturdy, supportive boots with a good grip, warm socks, waterproof anoraks, sunscreen, etc. are a good bet for all. It's best to pack for every season Ireland has to offer, from biting winter rain and damp to brilliant summer sun, any one of which might appear at random, keeping in mind that **layers are best** and that Ireland is at this point accustomed to quite casual attire, especially on visitors.

CONCERNING COWS

Cows have been an integral part of the Irish landscape from ancient times to the present and advice given by farmers to field walkers has been the same for as long as the mighty bovine has trod the sod.

First there's the bull. Find out if there is one in the field you plan to walk in. Ask a local person if they happen to know, and they often do, and always check out the creatures you see in the field. It's all in the undercarriage. A cow has multiple teats on her udder and a bull is "udderly" teatless. All of his interesting features are centrally located seemingly under his belly. If there is a bull in the field you plan to walk through, absolutely and without question, do not go into that field! If you start off and confront a bull, get out of that field as calmly and quickly as you can. Bulls are very bad company and they can kill you.

Cows are big but not bad like the bulls. They will happily share their field with you. Cows are curious about people and will often moo and stare and sometimes meander or trot over to see you. They can gather around you and sniff and stare and as you greet them with friendly hellos in kind tones they realize all is well and you can gently be on your way walking. Most cows just look up, moo, stare and get back to eating. We just walk on. Running creates a follow-the-leader atmosphere, and some cows like to run along behind. So walking is best.

The final point to make about cows and bulls alike concerns what they leave behind them in the fields. Most of the time you are walking through fields, you will be avoiding cow pies with remarkable diligence. But when you find a clear patch of green, do remember to look up and admire the view and remember, you are one with the ancients in all of your interludes with cows.

P.S. Sheep attacks are about as rare as meteor strikes. All you need fear from them is their obliviousness, which may hurt your feelings.

You will also want a reliable, reasonably detailed map; and we strongly recommend the most recent **Michelin map of Ireland**, with a scale of 1/400 000. This is the map we have used throughout this volume to assign coordinates to each listed site. For individual areas there is no equal to the Ordnance Survey Ireland Discovery Series 1/50 000 maps; but a full set comprises 89 individual maps, whose total cost is prohibitive. The Survey's *Official Road Atlas of Ireland* is also well worth purchasing.

Launching Your Expedition

Although Ireland, North and South, offers several international airports and a still wider array of regional airports, our itineraries all begin in Dublin and come to an end in either Dublin or Shannon. Dublin is, of course, also directly accessible by ferry from Britain and Wales. Overland access to Ireland ceased sometime before 6000 B.C.E. Information regarding air carriers, schedules, and prices are best researched on the internet, beginning with www.aerlingus.com and on to fare-search sites such as: www.air-fare.com, http://flyaow.com, and www.expedia.com. The one-stop on-line source for virtually every sort of information regarding travel to and within Ireland is that of the now coordinated Ireland and Northern Ireland Tourism network: www.discoverireland.ie. For Northern Ireland alone, go to: www.discovernorthernireland.com.

We recommend that you book not only your flight but also your accommodations well in advance of your departure. Ireland is itself a prime travel destination and the lodgings recommended in this volume are also very much in demand. Airline seats and beds can become scarce and are best reserved weeks if not months ahead. It is also preferable to negotiate and **reserve an auto rental in advance** of your travel. Bargains are seldom available in the arrivals hall of Dublin airport, and you may also find yourself with a car a good deal larger than you may have preferred. Although Irish roads can be extraordinarily narrow, we recommend a class B or C auto for the sake of safety and because they normally have closed trunks or boots to better conceal your luggage. Cars and vans larger than class C, when driven on Ireland's more abridged country lanes, often demand surgically precise maneuvers beyond the skills or nerves of novice left-side road pilots. Keep in mind that you will pay a premium for automatic shift autos, as well as for additional drivers. To economize, decide on a designated driver either already skilled in or willing to practice driving stick shift. Several large international car rental companies operate in Dublin, including Hertz (www.hertz.com) and Budget (www.budget.com), as well as an array of Irish companies. Among the latter, Dan Dooley (www.dandooley.com) is a reliable pick. A U.S. agency working with Irish car rental companies to provide both short-term car hire and long-term leases at reasonable prices is: Auto Europe (www.autoeurope.com). Make no mistake, **you will need a car** to explore the sites and follow the itineraries in this volume, the vast majority of which are not accessible by any form of public transportation. Car rental is expensive but not exorbitant, ranging at the moment from €200–350 all-inclusive per week for a compact car in high season. You will want to check with your credit card company and/or auto insurance agent to determine whether you might be able to decline the costly collision/damage insurance otherwise mandated.

Lastly, there is one purchase you will want to make either in advance or at the very first Heritage Service site you visit. This is the **OPW Heritage Card**, which provides unlimited admissions to all national heritage sites in the Republic of Ireland for a full year for one flat fee, currently €21 for an adult. Children, student, family, or senior cards are also available. The Heritage Card pays for itself in a day or two of exploration; so we will assume that readers of this volume have one in hand. Consequently, we will not indicate the price of admission to individual OPW sites. For advance purchase or further information regarding the Heritage Card, go to: www.heritageireland.ie.

Many first-time overseas travelers from outside the Eurozone will be inclined to load up on travelers checks and begin the monetary conversion process at the airport's Bureau de Change. This strategy is both unnecessary and ill advised. Carrying travelers checks is a bit like carrying your own oxygen. They serve no discernible purpose, though some find them reassuring. Better to bring your own **ATM and credit cards**. The exchange rate will prove more favorable than that offered by local moneychangers, and often the fees are low or non-existent. Among credit cards, **Visa and MasterCard** are the most widely accepted; American Express and Diner's Club cards are frequently frowned upon or declined.

In sum, outfitted with **passports**, **drivers licenses** (no need for special international licenses), practical layered clothes suitable for all of Ireland's unpredictable seasons, sturdy **waterproof shoes** with a worthy tread, **airline tickets**, **auto rental vouchers**, **advance reservations for your lodging**, a Michelin map, **an OPW Heritage Card, a flashlight** or torch, **a compass**, and a copy of **this guide**, you are fully prepared to launch your own expedition into ancient Ireland. That leaves, of course, modern Ireland; and some people aren't prepared to go anywhere these days without a mobile phone. Unless you're coming from Europe, your mobile is not going to work here; but you can rent one by the day or week quite reasonably. To explore this option prior to your trip, go to www.cell-phone-ireland.com or www.cellhire.com.

Practical Notes and Cautions

There will be no particular order to the following remarks, nor do they pretend to be comprehensive. A good general travel guide, with which you may wish to supplement this volume, will answer many more of your inevitable questions. We will be more selective here, urging you to turn to the Irish locals for advice, directions, or answers to your quandaries as they arise. Questions and puzzlements are a good thing. Look upon them as opportunities to reach out and make contact with people whom you would otherwise pass by. Irish hospitality did not become a legend without cause. Every encounter is a potential story, and to leave Ireland without stories would be as incomprehensible as leaving Greece without a tan.

Money first, not because it is most important but because you will need it from the moment of your arrival. **The currency of the Republic of Ireland is the euro**, whose symbol is €. One euro is equal to 100 European cents. Euro notes are available in the following denominations: €5, €10, €20, €50, €100, €200, and €500. There are €1 and €2 coins, as well as 1¢, 2¢, 5¢, 10¢, 20¢, and 50¢ coins. The 1¢ and 2¢ coins seem to have been a mistake and are regarded more as an annoyance than as legal tender. As one of our itineraries extends into Northern Ireland, it is important to emphasize that **Northern Ireland**, like the rest of Great Britain, has not as yet adopted the euro and **remains committed to the pound sterling** (£) as its legal tender; so leave your euros at the border.

On to **language**. Ireland is officially bilingual. In practice this means that nearly everyone speaks English (though with an entrancing array of diverse regional accents) and that if you know some Irish you will have the opportunity to use it, especially in the Gaeltacht or primarily Irish-speaking regions. Signage is another matter. Many signs are only in Irish, for which there is no consistent system of transliteration. Other sign-postings are so thoroughly anglicized that their Irish connection or root is lost altogether. Proper names are particularly problematic, as you will be reliant on them for getting to where you are going and for knowing when you have arrived; and you may not guess, for instance, that Dún Aengus is the same site as Dún Aonghasa, or, more impossibly, that Loch Garmann and Wexford are the same county. After a while you will make enough mistakes, ask enough questions, and notice enough patterns that your brush with Babel will not be a problem for you. Here, in this guide, we will give two names for many sites: first, a more anglicized name and spelling (corresponding as a rule with the Michelin map); and second, one common Irish form of the same name (in parentheses). Remember, systematic consistency is simply not to be had; so stay flexible and give your verbal imagination a good stretch every chance you get.

A few words on **driving in Ireland** will not go to waste. Irish roads once had a well-deserved and infamous reputation for being especially hazardous, partly because they were often wet, narrow, winding, and congested; but more pointedly because too many Irish drivers were addicted to speed and took risks that people at all fond of life—their own or others'—should not take. New motorways and heightened vigilance have improved road safety in the past ten years, resulting in a 50 percent drop in highway fatalities. But caution is still in order. Perhaps the one most effective safety measure at any driver's disposal is what we call "the power of the brake." When hounded by speed junkies, just squeeze or pull over in the left lane and let them pass. You are unlikely to lose unless you play the game; and not losing is winning. Avoiding the roads after dark or after the pubs close or on bank holidays will also add years to your automotive life. That said, it is only fair to highlight an area in which the Irish authorities have enacted severe and effective legislation: **drinking and driving**. The new legal alcohol limit, enacted in 2010—50 mg alcohol per 100 ml of blood—for driving on Irish roads is dramatically lower than that in the United States and in many other countries, so low that two glasses of stout or wine will surely exceed it. Random screening is routine, and penalties are severe. If you are in an accident, whether or not you are at fault, your alcohol level will be checked; and remember that violation of this law can void your auto insurance coverage. To give an idea of how serious the Gardai or Irish police are about cracking down on those who drink and drive, they sometimes screen drivers in the morning, as anyone who drank heavily the night before will very possibly still have an alcohol level in excess of the legal limit. The simple conclusion to be drawn from all this is that you cannot both drink and drive in Ireland without putting yourself at risk. This is one of the reasons why, in our recommendations for lodging, we have favored B&B's and guest houses that also serve an evening meal, most often with an accompanying wine list. Lodgings without wine permits generally allow guests to bring their own. To bring our notes on motoring to a close, it is well to remind you that in Ireland **all traffic drives on the left** and you must always turn left into a roundabout. In our experience, straying into the right lane is not as much of a temptation as one might expect; after all, the flow of oncoming traffic in the right lane provides a convincing reminder to stay left. Speed limits, even if ignored, are posted, ranging from 75mph (120kph) on dual-carriage motorways (M1, M50, etc.) to 30mph (50kph) on smaller roads in built up areas. The Road Safety Authority online brochure entitled *Rules of the Road Online*, is available for download at www.rotr.ie and is well worth a look. On a final note, with the exercise of common sense and caution, there is no reason to be apprehensive about finding your way safely on Irish roads. We have traveled tens of thousands of miles on Irish roads without incident and wish the same well-being, if not the same mileage, for our readers.

Interpreting our Icons and Estimates

As this is not a comprehensive travel guide destined to be updated one year to the next, we have limited significantly the number of details offered here regarding days and times of opening, cost of rooms and meals, amenities such as cable television, firmness of beds, non-smoking provisions, etc. The reader should know this much about us—that we are non-smoking, semi-vegetarians with tricky backs—which means that, all things being equal, we favor restaurants with interesting vegetarian options, lodgings with firm if not orthopedic beds, and restaurants and lodgings with either moderate or strict non-smoking restrictions. Tobacco smoke was once all but unavoidable in Ireland, and pubs were virtual smokehouses. But all that changed in March 2004 and even more in May 2007, when the Irish Government enacted a blanket ban on all smoking in the workplace and in all enclosed public spaces. Additionally, hotels and other lodgings prohibit smoking in all or most of their rooms.

Now a few words more about beds, since our readers will be putting in strenuous days and will want to make the most of their nights. As one traditional measure of luxury in Ireland has been the softness of one's mattress, we have often insisted on "the punishment room," a name given by one Waterford hostess for "the room with the hard (read *firm*) bed." The moral here is that it's always safer to request a firm bed if that is indeed your preference. Another lesson learned in our numerous years of writing comprehensive travel guides in Ireland and Greece is that exactly detailed prices and schedules often give the reader a false sense of assurance. The fact is that in heavily touristed countries, in the words of Herakleitos, "all is in flux," and so most guidebook details are already out of date by the time their ink dries. Restaurateurs and guest-house hosts decide their hours and their prices according to demand, which is nearly as readable as the weather. There are exceptions to this rule, to be sure, such as the largest hotels, catering to a business clientele, and the OPW sites, which are operated as a public service and not for profit.

In the ensuing pages, the following icons will be used to assist in planning your trip. Again, we want to stress that travelers checks are about as acceptable most places as an I.O.U. and foreign currency—anything other than euros in the Republic of Ireland or pounds sterling in Northern Ireland will not do. Keep in mind that these and all price indications in this guide are accurate at the time of our writing and not of your reading. In other words, expect increases and stand in awe of any decreases.

Icons

[L#] Bracketed letter(s) and number(s) refer to Michelin map coordinates.

CC Credit cards accepted, either Mastercard or Visa or both. Best to carry both, and be sure to inform your credit card providers of your travel plans lest they put a hold on your card the first time you attempt to use in Ireland.

€/£ Inexpensive—a double ensuite room (i.e. double room with private bath or shower) per person per night including breakfast: under €45/£40; and, at dinner, main courses under €15/£13 or complete dinners under €25/£22. Inexpensive entrance prices to sites and attractions are under €5/£4.4 for adults.

€€/££ Moderate—a double ensuite room (i.e. double room with private bath or shower) per person per night including breakfast: between €45/£40 and €75/£67; and, at dinner, main courses between €15/£13 and €30/£26.4 or complete dinners between €25/£22 and €40/£35. Moderate entrance prices to sites and attractions are between €5/£4.4 and €8/£7 for adults.

€€€/£££ Expensive—a double ensuite room (i.e. double room with private bath or shower) per person per night including breakfast: over €75/£67; and, at dinner, main courses over €30/£26.4 or complete dinners over €40/£35. Expensive entrance prices to sites and attractions are over €8/£7 for adults.

Bear in mind that these are rough averages. Finally, please note that the times of opening and closing for various sites as listed here do not reflect the fact that the last admission to nearly all sites is usually 45 minutes prior to the stated closing time.

METRIC CONVERSION

TEMPERATURE
Convert °C to °F by multiplying by 1.8 and adding 32
Convert °F to °C by subtracting 32 and multiplying by .55

LENGTH, DISTANCE, AND AREA	MULITIPLY BY
inches to centimeters	2.54
centimeters to inches	0.39
feet to meters	0.30
meters to feet	3.28
yards to meters	0.91
meters to yards	1.09
miles to kilometers	1.61
kilometers to miles	0.62
acres to hectares	0.40
hectares to acres	2.47

WEIGHT	MULITIPLY BY
ounces to grams	28.35
grams to ounces	0.035
pounds to limograms	0.45
kilograms to pounds	2.21
British tons to kilograms	1016
US tons to kilograms	907

a British ton is 2240 lbs., a US ton is 2000 lbs

VOLUME	MULITIPLY BY
imperial gallons to liters	4.55
liters to imperial gallons	0.22
US gallons to liters	3.79
liters to US gallons	0.26

5 imperial gallons equals 6 US gallons

a liter is slightly more that a US quart, slightly less than a British one

A WALK THROUGH
ANCIENT IRELAND

Origins

The Irish abroad—that vast Hibernian diaspora which, if it ever set foot on the motherland, would sink it for sure—have a notorious penchant for tracing their roots. In the United States alone, over 40 million current citizens herald, at least in part, from one of the 32,559 square miles of wind-swept, rain-soaked, evergreen soil known as Ireland. The ancient Irish too were concerned to trace their roots and to tell their story. With this in mind, a thousand years ago, Irish scholars created a remarkable multi-volumed fusion of inherited prehistoric lore, recently acquired classical and Christian learning, and genetically uninhibited imagination. They called it the *Lebor Gabála Érenn*, "The Book of the Taking of Ireland," or as it is more commonly known "The Book of Invasions." It has been labeled "learned fiction," a genre not entirely foreign to anyone today who reads the newspaper, watches television, or surfs the net. While grasping threads of memories that in all likelihood strung back to actual events in the deep Irish past, the authors of the *Lebor Gabála* were at the same time imbued and enthralled with "New Age" lessons recently learned. Some authors today stare in wonder at the pyramids of Giza and assert extra-terrestrial visitation to explain their design and construction. Similarly, the early medieval Irish borrowed such items as the biblical flood and Exodus to create their own book of origins.

What the authors of *Lebor Gabála* got right, however, was that the people of Ireland arrived, as does the sea, in a succession of waves. They were all immigrants at one time or another—tracing very different paths to, and having very different designs upon, Ireland's shores. The details are less impressive. The *Lebor Gabála* lists six (or seven) depending on whether you count the reputed first settlement of Ireland by Noah's daughter, Cesair, who is said to have been sent by her father, along with fifty female companions and three suitably sturdy men, to survive the flood and to populate Ireland, starting with Waterford, their point of debarcation. The remaining six waves or "invaders" were the: Fomorians, Partholónians, Nemedians, Fir Bolg, Tuatha Dé Danann, and the Sons of Míl. These names and the elusive peoples they designate pervade the mythology and folklore of Ireland to the present day. The two "invaders" most readily matched to recognizable populations would seem to be the Tuatha Dé Danann and the Milesians. The Tuatha Dé Danann, the people of the goddess Danu, were thought by their Celtic successors to have been the once gigantic builders of the megaliths, the great mysterious mounds, deep within which they still resided as the miniature yet mighty people of the síd. The prehistoric Sons of Míl, on the other hand, stand at the very edge of historical daylight. Míl's full name—Míl Espáne—is transparently Miles Hispaniae, the "soldier from Spain." The "Sons of Míl" are clearly the Gaels or Goidels, the Continental Celts who, with strongholds in Tara, Croghan, and Cashel, were dominant in Ireland by the fifth century B.C.E. Spain, in this instance, means Celtic Galicia, where it is said that Bregon mac Bratha built a tower from the top of which his son Ith spied the southern coast of Ireland on what must have been an exceptionally clear winter's evening. As the story goes, Ith soon ventured across the sea to claim what he saw as the "Promised Land" of the Gaels and was killed upon arrival by the Tuatha Dé Danann, provoking a full-scale invasion of Ireland by the Gaels, who prevailed and founded Celtic Ireland.

As it happened, the *Lebor Gabála*'s conceit of Irish history as a series of invasions proved far more accurate and telling as prophecy than as history. Dating from the 11th or 12th century, the *Lebor Gabála* could know or say nothing of the future "invaders"—some successful, some failed, some benign, some malicious—who would shape Irish history for at least the next 1000 years: the Normans, the English, the Spanish, the French, the Scots, and perhaps even the 20th-century tourist and the 21st-century refugee. Our view here, however, looks back from the 12th century and not forward; and, fortunately, the *Lebor Gabála* is not our only lens. Archaeology, while unable to tell the whole story, allows us to see ancient Ireland with much greater clarity and proximity than either the *Lebor Gabála* or the Túir Bregoin, the lookout tower of ill-fated Ith.

History and Prehistory

When the Irish mythographers and storytellers looked back at their predecessors, they assigned to them greater and greater stature the further back they went. In their own day, for instance, the Tuatha Dé Danann reached the heights of hilltops; and even the ancient heroes of Ulster, when transformed by battle frenzy, might tower over the tallest trees. Later figures of legend, like Finn Mac Cumhaill and his all but invincible *fianna,* though they might draw upon superhuman strength and prowess, fit for the most part standard-length beds and average-sized shoes. Another measure of antiquity was the length of a lifespan. The Tuatha Dé Danann were blessed with immortality, while the Sons of Míl, according to the *Acallam na Senórach* or *Tales of the Elders of Ulster,* were "mortals with a short life." Historians and archaeologists, however, prefer a less imaginative approach and more precise distinctions.

The first distinction we need to make here is between prehistoric and historic Ireland. "Prehistoric" has to the average ear a misleading ring of the primitive, the savage, even the pre-human, whereas all it really means is pre-literate. Life without pencils is still life, and stories need not be written down to be remembered. Nevertheless, people who leave behind no written texts are fated to be known mostly by their artifacts and, especially, by their tools. Consequently, we customarily divide Irish prehistory into such periods or "ages" as the old, middle, and new stone age, the bronze age, and the iron age. Modern archaeologists are not the first to speak of human epochs in terms of raw materials. It's actually a habit that goes back at least to the ancient Persians, Greeks, and Hebrews, among others. The Greek poet Hesiod lamented having been born into the age of iron—the meanest, harshest, most miserable of all ages, as he saw it; and Plato proposed a political caste system ideologically supported by what he called a "myth of metals." The modern archaeological stratification of human prehistory, from stone to bronze to iron, carries with it no such social agenda. Rather, it simply recognizes that *homo faber*—Mr. and Ms. Fiddle-and-Fixit—worked first with stone tools and then with metal tools, trying always to make them sharper and harder. It was and is called "progress."

Archaeologists sometimes claim that ancient stones speak, and even tell stories. Actually what they do is closer to muttering. The virtually mute finds of the past are mere "givens" or data, which require the learning, imagination, and bravado of the scholar to find their voice. What they tell us is always provisional and open to question. If history needs to be rewritten by each new generation of scholars and storytellers, this is all the more true of prehistory. That said, we begin in the beginning.

The Irish Mesolithic

Actually we begin in the middle. In "Lithic" or stone terms, Ireland skipped the "Old Stone Age" or the "Paleolithic" period, since the first humans to reach her shores were already, as it were, in middle school, though probably not at the top of their class. Unlike their Continental cousins, they don't seem to have been artistically inclined, and nothing much is known of their burial practices, which suggests that they were minimalists. All the same, in then densely forested Ireland they were accomplished fishers and hunters, fully capable of clothing themselves, putting a temporary roof over their heads, and keeping themselves warm and dry and fed even in what could be daunting winters.

Between 12,000 and 8000 B.C.E., Ireland emerged from the Ice Age, shedding its glaciers and eventually playing host to a respectable array of temperate flora and fauna making its way across the last land-bridge still connecting Britain and Ireland. As the seas rose, Ireland and Britain were slowly sundered. The post-glacial water-clock was ticking on the connector; and we know, for instance, that only one form of reptile, a species of newt, made it across in time. While it has been a matter of open debate whether the first human inhabitants of Ireland arrived by foot or by boat, that has all but been resolved by two recent lines of research. Coastal core samples now indicate the disappearance or submersion of the land bridge between Britain and Ireland prior to the arrival of the first humans, while at the same time extensive DNA surveys of the populations of Europe and Ireland clearly point to northwestern Spain as the source of Ireland's earliest population. So, it seems the first Irish arrived dry-shod aboard boats launched from the Basque regions of Spain. However or from wherever they came, the truth remains that Ireland was among the last bits of what is now Europe to know the paradoxical weight of the human foot.

At first the human footprint leaves nearly no trace. Hunters and gatherers leave the land and sea almost exactly as they find it. Even so, remnants of their campsites have been found in Co. Offaly at Boora Bog; and Mount Sandel, near Coleraine in Co. Londonderry, has yielded the first examples of branch-woven round huts. These hunters and fishers, their families, and their dogs seem to have done reasonably well for themselves on a menu that included wild pig, salmon, trout, sea bass, pigeon, duck, and hazelnuts. By 5000 B.C.E. similar camps and other remains give evidence that human habitation had spread to the east, the south, and the west of Ireland in such sites as Sutton and Dalkey near Dublin, as well as Cork, Waterford, and the Dingle Peninsula in Co. Kerry.

The lasting contribution of these first Irelanders may be limited to the gene pool. What can surely be said of them is that they observed the prime tenet of the Hippocratic Oath to "first do no harm." They left the island very much as they had found it, which in retrospect rings as an achievement.

The Irish Neolithic

The Irish Neolithic, like the earlier Neolithic periods in Southeastern Europe and the Near East from which it emerged, proved transforming of the island and its population, irreversibly so. The Neolithic or "New Stone Age" marked a dramatic alteration of human habits from migratory life in small hunting and fishing bands to domestic life in settled farming and grazing communities, communities which invariably developed in size and complexity. There is little risk of overestimating the significance of the human choice to settle down and to produce one's livelihood rather than to go out daily looking for it. If there is one act which epitomizes the Neolithic "revolution" as it is often called, it would be the building of walls; and any even brief visitor to Ireland will notice that the Irish have long practiced and mastered the art. It is worth our while to think about walls for a moment.

The mesolithic hunters and fishers of Ireland, like other hunting and gathering populations, lived without walls, which is to say that they lived without drawing lines—no one builds a wall without first drawing a line—lines that are essential to other people. The line between the wild and the tame, human and animal, natural and artificial, theirs and ours, yours and mine—all these lines that map out the terrain of our lives and define our interactions with the world and with each other are marginal to meaningless until the Neolithic period. The first walls to go up, of course, are the outer and inner walls of houses and then the walls around tilled fields and penned animals. Walls and roofs separate humans from animals, the elements, and other people. Field walls separate wild plants from sown ones, separate one crop from another, and sometimes manage to keep out pests and unwanted mouths. Pens, on the other hand, keep domesticated animals in and wild animals out.

Despite rough beginnings as farmers and herders learn their arts, the settled life eventually brings leisure and surplus labor. It simply takes less people and fewer human hours to raise food than to find it, which frees up human ingenuity and energy for other purposes like art, architecture, ritual, politics, commerce, and war. We notice that walls get thicker and higher with time. Stone walls ten feet thick and forty feet high are, after all, needed for only one purpose—to keep out other human beings. Wealth and power—realities unknown before the Neolithic—must be preserved behind walls. Apart from the supernatural, man comes to fear man more than anything else. While private homes remain simple and modest, tombs, along with ritual and royal sites, become more and more massive. The individual life becomes a blur except to its owner, and the focus of society is directed more and more to the community, its deities and its leaders.

Ireland's first farmers—in what must have been a precarious passage when we consider that they shared their boats with their livestock—arrived sometime around 4000 B.C.E. and set about at once to change the face of the island. Before they could plant the seeds they brought with them, at least on any wide scale, they needed to clear the land; and so Ireland's hardwood forests began to come down, one tree at a time. A mass-produced, Neolithic stone axe, wielded by a sturdy arm, could fell a sizeable elm in an hour. Slowly the forests gave way to tilled fields and pastureland.

SAMPLE PREHISTORIC MENU
CIRCA 9000–3000 B.C.E.

Appetizers
Hazelnuts
Complimentary willow basket of Emmer wheat bread

Catch of the Day
Fresh salmon and eel

Specials
Water pit, fulachta fiadh style, boiled mutton
wrapped in straw
Roast acorn-fed pig with red deer
Smoked eel

Entrées
Roast lamb and goat
Roast and boiled beef
Shellfish on the half-shell
Ground barley porridge
Toasted barley and meat stew
Emmer wheat bake

Vegetable Sides
Freshly harvested greens and sweet roots

Desserts
Dried rosehips and crab apples
Wild strawberries in season
Dried bramble berries

All dessert selections served with fresh or fermented cow's milk.

*The foods on this menu were gathered, raised, hunted, grown,
harvested, and prepared by hard-working men, women,
and children. Bon Appetit!*

The fourth millennium has rewarded the archaeologist's spade with dramatic evidence of the presence and activities of these earliest Irish farmers, especially at Céide Fields in Co. Mayo and at Lough Gur in Co. Limerick, the two most spectacular early Neolithic sites in Ireland. Fourth millennium homes, traces of which have been uncovered at several sites, took either round or rectangular form, some with stone foundations, some with planked walls, others with walls of wattle-and-daub, and thatched roofs. While these houses often appear isolated one from another, instead of grouped in villages, there is also evidence of collaboration on a significant scale. For example, at Céide Fields over four square miles of forest were communally cleared, divided, and laid out for tillage and grazing, with many miles of stone boundaries dividing crops and livestock. It is estimated that these walls comprised a quarter of a million tons of local stones, dug up, hauled, and set into place. To grasp the antiquity of this exhausting endeavor, it is helpful to note that these fields were deserted before work was begun on the pyramids of Egypt.

Speaking of the pyramids, they have long occupied a unique spot in the popular imagination as the supposed earliest, most dazzling testaments to human aspiration. Not so. It was, in fact, the next few waves of settled agriculturalists, the next "invasions" as it were, heralding perhaps from Brittany, that built in Ireland, not Egypt, the first "world-class" stone architecture. These new settlers were far more skilled, productive, ambitious, and communal than their predecessors. In addition to being farmers they were builders, builders in stone, on a progressively grander and grander scale. While their homes remained modest, leaving very little trace, their megalithic monuments startle us even today. Their houses, like the lives lived within them, proved ephemeral. Their tombs and ritual sites tell a different story.

In actual fact, the picture sketched above needs to be made less clear in order to be more accurate. Ireland's earliest monumental stone architecture can no longer be traced with any confidence to the "passage grave builders" whose arrival in Ireland was once placed as late as 2500 B.C.E. Quite recent claims by the Swedish archaeological team excavating the stone age cemetery of Carrowmore in Co. Sligo for the past several decades have called radically into question the most widely accepted chronologies of European megalithic architecture. One of these claims is that mesolithic hunter-gatherers in Co. Sligo were building roofed, free-standing, stone tombs surrounded by stone circles as early as 5400 B.C.E. Regardless of whether we accept this claim, and many or most do not, it is no longer a given that the first emergence of monumental stone architecture in Ireland necessarily marked the arrival of new immigrants bringing such skills and aspirations from either Britain or the Continent. These skills and aspirations may be, at least in part, more "home-grown" than previously imagined. Put most boldly, the open question seems to be whether Irish builders are best seen as the heirs or the originators of the megalithic movement.

Debates regarding who built what first, as well as where and when the builders arrived in Ireland—debates in which no stone will be left unturned, or unthrown—are likely to rage for the foreseeable future. Meanwhile, the monuments of the Irish Neolithic builders will continue to bring the unsuspecting visitor to a sudden and stunned silence. The most impressive of Ireland's megalithic monuments are the passage tombs, numbering roughly 300 in all, the earliest examples of which are concentrated in three extensive, ancient cemeteries: Carrowmore and Carrowkeel in Co. Sligo and Loughcrew in Co. Meath. The culminating achievement of Ireland's megalithic architects is, however, to be found at the "bend of the Boyne" in Co. Westmeath. This is Ireland's "Valley of the Kings," where three major passage tombs stand out among the numerous burial mounds comprising a vast 5,000-year-old necropolis. These three are Dowth, Knowth, and Newgrange. While all three mounds have roughly the same outer dimensions, each is inwardly unique; and only Newgrange has been near fully excavated and restored. Entering the Newgrange cairn and descending the 62-foot-long passage to its cruciform core, where a central vaulted chamber is illumined by the rising sun at each year's winter solstice, is as profound a detour as Ireland offers. Newgrange's other and older name—*Brú na Bóinne*—provides a clue to the world entered here. A *Brú* is an abode, and legend has it that this was first the abode of the Dagda—the god who was "good for everything"—and his wife Boann, and their son Oengus, of the Tuatha Dé Danann.

Altogether, over 1,200 great stone tombs, dating from at least the Neolithic period, have been identified in Ireland—court tombs, passage tombs, wedge tombs, and portal tombs—all abodes of the dead, the long silent dead. Many of these tombs are adorned, even covered, with abstract engravings, as elusive as they are intriguing. If a picture is worth a thousand words, then these carvings would speak volumes, were we only able to read them. Most attempts and claims to bring them to voice only amount to ventriloquism. Sometimes it is better to meet silence with silence. The truth seems to be that we will never truly know these people of Ireland's Neolithic; so, if we still crave stories of them, the Irish mythological cycle remains a privileged and entertaining source from which to slake our thirst.

The Irish Bronze Age

The truth is that the study of Bronze Age Ireland is largely an indoor pursuit, for there are very few significant field monuments dating from this period. Most of the clues to the Irish Bronze Age reside today in museums, notably the National Museum. The movements and lives of these peoples must be read from their graves and the artifacts they left behind or sought to take with them.

Unlike the passing of years or lifetimes, the line between one "age" and another cannot as a rule be drawn with precision. The most we can say is that the Irish use of metals—beginning with copper, soon hardened with the admixture of tin to make bronze—occurred sometime before 2000 B.C.E. Copper and then bronze axes appear, followed by new lines of weaponry, including daggers and halberds. With time, the blades of these daggers become longer, sharper, and harder, which may have as much to say

Newgrange chamber
Photo: "Duchas, the Heritage Service," Dublin

about increased hostility as about upgraded technology. To account for violence, after all, we need only to uncover opportunity, means, and motive. The opportunity is always there; the means were becoming more advanced and available; and new signs of personal wealth—lunulae of hammered river gold—may speak to the matter of motive.

These were, however, only some of the changes indicating both progress at home and the ingress of newcomers. New pottery types—Beaker, Food Vessel, and Urn—are in evidence and have given their names to their makers. In archaeological circles, populations are commonly called after pots or other everyday artifacts. During this same time, single inhumation burials, nearly all male, in cists (below-ground stone chambers) increasingly replaced shared grave sites. Then, inexplicably, single cist graves and Bronze Age pottery, known mostly from burial deposits, drop out of the archaeological record sometime around 1400 B.C.E. Otherwise, the most common type of Bronze Age field monument is the stone circle, of which there are notable concentrations in central Ulster and in the southwest of Ireland, in West Cork and Co. Kerry.

The next major page in the Irish Bronze Age is turned a century or two later when striking new wares appeared on the Irish scene. Bronze cauldrons, swords, spear heads, shields, horns, and axes became commonplace; and gold ornaments, while not likely found on every wrist, hand, or neck, were far from rarities. It is a fact that dating from this period more gold crafts have been uncovered in Ireland than in any other country in western or northern Europe. Again we find a likely correlation between walls, weapons, and wealth; for during this same period, as the island (or portions of it) gleamed with gold, weaponry proliferated and became more lethal, and architects turned their talents from tombs to hilltop forts. More specifically, near 700 B.C.E., as production of bronze wares and gold ornaments reached its zenith in Ireland, the hilltop complex of Emain Macha, soon to be the royal site of the most powerful tribes in Ireland, was being developed. Not surprisingly, with much of worth to sell and the means to purchase, this too was a time of significant overseas commerce for the Irish, whose trading partners included Britain, Spain, and most likely Scandinavia. On another day, of course, the

Scandinavians would acquire a great deal more of Ireland's treasures in what could be described, I suppose, as a "fire sale"; but that episode awaits us.

Celtic Ireland

It is difficult to say when the Irish became a Celtic people. Nothing so dramatic as conversion or conquest or even colonization adequately describes the process. In retrospect, studying an illiterate though skilled people in terms of its "stuff" rather than its texts or genes, we assume that new styles and techniques of production mean new hands, new people at work. The first dramatic line of Celtic "imports" reveal Hallstatt influence from Central Europe. Then, in the late 1st millennium B.C.E., the proliferation of highly sophisticated Celtic metalwork and stone carving in the elegant, abstract style named after its motherland in La Tène, Switzerland, is assumed to signal not only the presence of Celtic products but also the presence of Celtic peoples in Ireland. Many scholars are skeptical, however, of any easy, exact answer to when "the Celts" came to Ireland. To understand their skepticism, while the analogy is not precise, it may be helpful to consider the decisive sweep of the U.S. auto market by the Japanese, beginning in the 1960s, and realize that archaeologists thousands of years from now, studying this phenomenon, i.e. digging through landfills and finding a remarkable cache of Japanese cars, might well conclude that the United States was colonized by Japan sometime in the last third of the 20th century, a conclusion supported by the profusion of Japanese electronic goods, woven black and brown karate belts, karaoke clubs and sushi bars dating from the same period. While there is little doubt that Ireland became increasingly Celtic in the late bronze and early Iron ages, there is, it is fair to say, considerable debate regarding exactly when and how that process unfolded. The National Museum in Dublin today displays a great deal of the most eloquent evidence regarding that transforming episode in Irish history. Put to those objects your most precise questions, listen closely to them, and you will find that they mostly only mutter back what they have to say about who made them and what Irish life was like then. It's the best they and we can do.

The Celtic Iron Age • The Age of the Heroes

What is unique about ancient Ireland is that it never came under Roman domination. Surely the Romans knew about Ireland for centuries, spied it from Britain, and more than likely had designs upon it. There is even some evidence that the Romans made some expeditionary sorties, commercial and/or military, onto Irish soil. But they seem never to have invaded Ireland and surely never seized any portion of it. What this means is that in the lst century C.E., when Ireland's by then decisively Celtic culture had taken root and was flowering, every other Celtic territory, with the exception of the Highlands of Scotland, lay under the Roman *imperium.* What's more, Celtic Ireland remained free of foreign invasion and rule for over a thousand years, from the early Iron Age to the Viking incursions beginning in 795 C.E. and the more decisive Norman Invasion in 1167–1169. During this Celtic millennium Ireland enjoyed an enviable insularity which, however, did not isolate it from European influence. It simply meant that Ireland was able to absorb that influence, including Christianity and the classical culture embedded in it, on its own terms, in its own way. In a word, the evolution of Celtic Ireland was a process more metabolic than metamorphic.

The Iron Age—it comes as no surprise—marks the slow but sure eclipsing of bronze by iron as the principal raw material for tools, weapons, and household metalware, that is, everything from swords and axes to cooking pots. Hill forts and hilltop enclosures serving as royal inauguration sites, such as Emain Macha and Tara, are constructed throughout this period, sometimes in close proximity to, even incorporating, the great burial mounds of the Neolithic. These hilltop sites point to there having been "kings of the hill" in what must have been regional tribal societies. Some cliff-top promontory forts, ringforts, and crannogs may also date from this period, though all of these are more characteristic of the later Christian era.

The profile of Iron Age Ireland available from the material record pales, however, against the vivid images provided by its written record. The Iron Age is also the Age of the Heroes; for we know these peoples, their lives and exploits, from more than their wares. We know them from their stories, as well. That's the good news. The bad news is that the earliest texts of those stories date from many centuries later. The reason for this is a story in itself. The first form of writing introduced into Ireland was the so-called "tree alphabet" or *ogham*, each of whose 20 characters bears the name of a tree. While clearly influenced by the Roman alphabet, *ogham* was nowhere near as functional as its Latin mentor and was better suited to brief inscriptions than to extended texts. It was not until Christian clerics brought Latin and thus the Roman alphabet to Ireland that the Irish oral tradition could find its way onto the page. Then, even after many of the stories of ancient Ireland had been written into books by dutiful Christian monks, the vast majority of those books were destroyed by notoriously unbookish Vikings. Most Irish books were made and kept in monastic settlements, and these settlements were favorite targets of Viking raids. The Vikings, however, unable to read or appreciate the Irish manuscripts, coveted only their ornate and often quite valuable covers. Consequently, the books' pages were burned or discarded, never making their way back to Denmark and eventually into modern libraries or museums. To sum up, the stories we have today from ancient Ireland, are likely very old, while the texts that preserve them rarely predate 1000 C.E. These texts are mostly copies of copies of stories representing threads of oral memory woven across centuries; and, of course, the monastic copying process was far from photographic. Corrupted and fragmentary as it is, though, the surviving narrative record of pre-Christian Iron Age Ireland, the Age of the Heroes, is undeniably entertaining and arguably informative.

Crannog Huts

Ogham

Ireland was learned but illiterate for all of its early Celtic period. Wisdom of all sorts—skills, laws, stories, genealogies, visions, spells—were spoken and remembered from one generation to the next. The *filid*, the poets, were mortal arks, assuring that life as they knew it would survive the always rising waters of oblivion and change. Among their patrons was Ogmios, the god of learning and speech, sometimes portrayed as a bald, peripatetic teacher whose younger disciples are bound to him by chains proceeding from his mouth to their ears. Ironically, the invention of writing, which would break those chains forever, was attributed to him, and was called *ogham*.

This first form of writing in Ireland was more enchanting than practical. The number 5, a mighty number in the Celtic psyche, figured highly in the conception and arrangement of the *ogham* alphabet, which divided its characters into 5 groups of 5. The first 3 groups of 5 represent consonants, while the 4th group of five stand for vowels. The last five, regarded as later additions, are supplementary letters, or *forfeda*.

The blank "page," most often a pillar stone, was first inscribed with a center line, the *fleasc*, as a rule vertical, like a tree. Each character or letter was then carved along that line, generally from bottom to top, either to the right or left of the *fleasc* or intersecting it. Indeed, according to the Scholar's Primer, *Auraicept na nÉces*, *ogham* is to be read as a tree is climbed. This metaphor of text as tree is reinforced by the fact that each of the essential *ogham* letters bears the name of a tree. For example, the letter "b" *beith* means "birch," and the letter "d" *dair* means "oak."

The 15 consonants—represented by lines, which meet or cross the *fleasc*:

The 5 principal vowels—represented by notches along the *fleasc*:

The oldest surviving heroic tales of ancient Celtic Ireland herald from Ulster and are known as the Ulster Cycle. They comprise roughly 80 sagas, poems, and narrative bits recording and commenting on births, deaths, courtships, sieges, battles, voyages, banquets, visions, invasions, elopements, and much more—the everyday stuff of early Celtic imagination if not life. One common story-type is the *táin bó* or the cattle raid. Thirteen such stories of cattle raids have survived, but the mother of all cattle raids, as it were, was the *Táin Bó Cuailnge* or the Cattle Raid of Cooley, whose focal figure and preeminent hero is Cúchulainn, the Irish Achilles. Several times larger than any other ancient Irish tale, the *Táin Bó Cuailnge* or, more simply, the *Táin,* is the nearest any ancient Irish text comes, in scale and stature, to the classical epic genre. It is, with a grain of salt—or a glass of Guinness—often called the Irish *Iliad.* Whether or not it provides a reliable window into the age of heroes traditionally set in the 1st century C.E. provokes passionate debate. Before we dismiss the *Táin* altogether, however, as learned fiction or anachronistic fantasy, it is well to recall that the *Iliad* too, not all that long ago, shared these same labels, whereas scholars today concede that much of the *Iliad* rests on historical bedrock.

The image of ancient Ireland that survives in these tales is that of an aristocratic tribal society, thickly settled with royalty, warriors, druids, prophets, maidens, gods, and ghosts. Loyalty, particularly kin-loyalty, courage, honor, hospitality, and romance are the virtues and values which make this world go round and occasionally stand it on end. Shame is worse than death, and love defies it regularly. Love often comes on with the suddenness of a storm, at first sight or even first hearing, burns with fierce brevity, and then brings a sorrow that breaks not only the hearts of the lovers but of all who hear their tale. Indeed, W. B. Yeats may as well have been describing any number of ancient Irish heroes and their bards when he wrote: "Being Irish, he had an abiding sense of tragedy which sustained him through temporary periods of joy."

Christian Ireland • The Age of the Saints

The Irish 5th century was not one of business as usual. In a single century Ireland crossed from "paganism" to

Christianity and from prehistory to history. Both might be and were soon seen together as a passage from darkness into light. In a text composed centuries later about this axial moment in Irish history, Cáilte, the last of the *fianna,* the warrior band of Finn, is baptized by none less than Patrick himself, to whom he says "before you came there was a demon beneath every single blade of grass, and now there is an angel." In other words, Ireland had changed forever. Not all of this, however, can be attributed to Patrick, who, whatever his larger-than-life stature in later cult, neither began nor completed the task of Ireland's transformation into a Christian culture. It seems a priest named Palladius, ordained in Rome by Pope Celestine, became Ireland's first bishop in 431, sent there to minister to those *credentes in Christum,* Ireland's earliest Christian community. Clearly the conversion of Ireland was well underway by 432, the date cited in the *Annals* for Patrick's arrival as a missionary. Ireland's very first missionaries remain anonymous. They most likely came from Cornwall or Roman Gaul in the late 4th or early 5th century. Wherever they came from, it is more significant that the first clear effort to structure and to organize the church they founded came directly from Rome. It is important to note that Ireland was the first European country to be proselytized by the Roman church beyond the borders of what had been the Roman Empire. Patrick and his legends served well this effort to assure that the Irish church would be Roman first and Irish second. Within a hundred years Ireland's Christianization, though not complete, was guaranteed. Its Romanization, on the other hand, had only begun and was far from a sure thing.

As most every ancient text describing the Christianization of Ireland was written by monks, not just Christians, it is impossible to know with any confidence just how this major metamorphosis unfolded. It seems that many of the Irish embraced the Christian faith with enthusiasm, while others succumbed to it as an inevitability. Not many in the end resisted the new religion, which promised to alter nearly everything that was Irish except the weather. It is truly remarkable, given the depths of its roots and the legendary violence of its ways, that the threatened and soon-to-be eclipsed Gaelic civilization—its kings, warriors, and priests—gave the Christian interlopers not a single martyr. The other side of the arrangement reached was that many of the old ways remained intact, so many that one might wonder whether on this particular island Celts became Christians or Christians became Celts. There are some even today who would claim that Irish Christianity was and is no more than a veneer, an imposition that will one day be peeled off as were the British. Even if that were the case, the Church, like the Crown, would still have left its indelible mark.

Patrick sought to pattern Church organization in Ireland after that of the Roman Church, which in the first centuries of the Christian era had followed a Roman imperial model of civil administration. This called for dioceses and archdioceses, presided over by bishops and archbishops named and often sent from Rome. This Roman model presupposed an urbanized society well-accustomed to accepting highly centralized rule. All this was quite foreign and contrary to Irish habits. Ireland was at this time without a single town or city and was divided among as many as 150 tuatha or tribes, whose tangled alliances made a messy sight. As Ireland became Christian, its Christianity became Irish, which is to say that the Irish, as they have nearly always done, took their own path. By the 6th century, Church organization was largely monastic not diocesan; and, by the 7th and 8th centuries, Irish monasticism had all but erased the diocesan structure drawn by Patrick and his followers. What this means is that Church politics, like Irish politics, had gone local. Within the Church each monastic settlement was self-contained and self-governing, often practicing within its walls a radical "democracy" whose very existence challenged and offended the Vatican. Outside the monastic enclosure, the abbot and his monks exercised a regional jurisdiction in spiritual matters not unlike that of local chieftains in temporal matters, though these two wires could and did occasionally cross.

Irish monasticism drew from two principle sources— one for its "body" and the other for its "soul." Its administrative autonomy and egalitarianism mimicked the monastic settlements in Gaul, Aquitaine, and northern Spain, while its ascetic severity was inspired by the desert monks of Egypt, Syria, and Iraq. The unique

Clonmacnoise

native hybrid that came to be Irish monasticism truly shaped Irish Christianity for two centuries and had an even more profound and enduring impact on western European piety and culture. One of the first of these monastic foundations, attributed to St. Declan, was at Ardmore in Co. Waterford, followed by Clonard in the east, Clonmacnoise in the center, Bangor in the north, and Lismore in the south. These early monasteries were seedbeds for Ireland's new breed of warriors, warriors not of the sword but of the book. St. Finnian, Abbot of Clonard, for example, was the spiritual father of both St. Brendan the Navigator and St. Columba, who rivals Patrick as the father of Christian Ireland.

Deprived of "red martyrdom" by an early form of Irish hospitality, the first Christians of Ireland sought a substitute in "white martyrdom," which was how they saw the monastic life. A kind of "living death" in the later words of Bernard of Clairvaux. An even more extreme form of monastic denial was undertaken by those who forsook not only secular Ireland but Ireland itself as *peregrini pro Christo,* voluntary exiles for Christ. These monks took to the waves in search of remote off-shore outposts, sea-bound crags of uninhabited and all but uninhabitable land where they would give over all of their days and much of their nights to prayer and a range of prescribed disciplines. The remnants of such settlements may be visited today on Skellig Michael off the Kerry coast, and on Inishmurray, four miles from the nearest land in Co. Sligo. There were those too, like St. Brendan, who just kept going, setting course to the furthest edges of the earth to do battle with demons and to find the Land of Promise, or Columba and Columbanus who, together with their disciples, left Ireland to found monastic settlements abroad, in Britain, Switzerland, Gaul, Germany, and Italy. Indeed, Columbanus may justly share with Benedict the title "father of western monasticism."

View of the Kerry Coast

Martyrdom, however, was not the sole paradigm for the saints of Ireland. Their own Celtic warrior heroes provided models as well. The dazzling feats of strength, bravery, and prowess performed by Cúchulainn and Finn Mac Cumhaill as well as their magical weapons were mimicked and matched by the wonders of the saints—their demon-defying valor and their often miraculous powers. The early lives of the Irish saints are, in fact, transparent both to the Christian Gospels and to the Irish sagas. Male saints, for example, change water into wine and enjoy the "warrior's light," while a female saint, Brigid, embodies aspects of Celtic goddesses as well as of the Virgin Mary.

Monasteries were not only about ascetic denial, however; they were also about learning and culture. Both were pursued with passion. With Christianity came Latin and with Latin, and eventually Greek, came the riches of the ancient Mediterranean. Soon Latin and its verse forms were adapted to make possible the transcription and preservation of vernacular Gaelic or "Old Irish" learning and lore. St. Columba, for one, was a friend and protector of the *filid*, the Irish bards, whose stories were written down as much for entertainment as for the heritage they represented. Irish monks were notorious at home and abroad for their devotion to learning, not only book learning but also art and architecture. It was in monastic scriptoria and workshops that the priceless literary and artistic treasures of the Irish "Golden Age" were created, including the Ardagh and Derrynaflan chalices, and the *Book of Kells*. In the words of John Henry Newman, the Irish monastery was "the storehouse of the past and the birthplace of the future."

By the end of the 8th century the balance of power and influence between the two Church administrative systems—the Roman episcopal and the Celtic monastic—had shifted. It is more difficult to say why. The growing concentration of power in the hands of the Eoganacht dynasties in the south and the Uí Néill further north were changing the political landscape and pointing to a future that would not favor fragmentation and local autonomy. At the same time, Celtic monasticism had lost some of its early passion and purity. Not every scholar was a saint, and not every monk was either one of these. The Roman church saw in the Celtic church deviations in doctrine and discipline that it was less and less inclined to tolerate. The enhanced status of women in the Celtic church, the disproportionate power of abbots, permissiveness regarding concubinage and divorce, and the celebration of Easter on a date different from that set by Rome were all among the irritants provoking the Roman church and its Irish adherents to take control. Early and multiple Viking raids on Iona, the mother-house of the Celtic church in Ireland, Scotland, and Britain, may also have contributed to the decline of the Celtic church. The south of Ireland was the first to accept the Roman Order and the north fell into place by the 9th century. The primacy of Armagh—the seat reputedly founded by Patrick—was again without rival; and the similarly ascendant Uí Néill in control of Ulster, the most powerful kingdom in Ireland, whose ancient royal site, Emain Macha, lay only two miles from the Patristic church at Armagh. Church and state, so entangled in the Roman church since Constantine, were beginning to come to terms in Ireland as well, which led to new levels of secularization in the church and, eventually, to ecclesiastical reform.

Viking Ireland

Ireland's former trading partners to the north and east—the "Ostmen" as they called themselves—returned to Irish shores at the close of the 8th century with plunder, not commerce, on their minds. Their inaugural raid was on Rathlin Island off the Antrim coast in the North Channel. This was to be followed by two centuries of mayhem. At first the Norsemen confined their attacks to islands and the Irish coastline. They hit and ran, leaving slaughter and devastation behind them. Matters became a good deal more grim, however, when in 837 Viking fleets made their way up the River Boyne and the River Liffey (sixty ships in each) to assault the interior of Ireland. Four years later the invaders founded Dublin in 841 as their base of operations on the Irish Sea. A visit to the Viking exhibits in the National Museum, as well as to Wood Quay on the south bank of the Liffey will help to bring alive the transforming turbulence of the Viking era.

Under the leadership of their notorious king, Turgesius, the Vikings brought systematic devastation to the Irish midlands. Not surprisingly, monasteries were their prime targets. The monastic sanctuaries, metal shops, and libraries held objects of great value, and they were all but undefended. The Irish Golden Age became a lot less golden. Contrary to common opinion, the Irish round tower, a distinctive feature of the monastic landscape, was of no strategic assistance to the monks, neither as a watch-tower nor as a safe haven against marauding Vikings, because the worst periods of Viking violence predate the earliest recorded towers. Many monasteries were struck repeatedly. Iona, for example, the mother-house of the Columban church, was pillaged four times, the last attack accompanied by a mass slaughter of its resident monks. It was not only the monks, however, who were ill-equipped and disinclined to meet the Vikings sword for sword. The Irish kings were often as deeply at odds with each other as they were with the Norsemen. Only a united front was likely to make the Vikings take notice, and unity did not come quickly or easily to the Irish. But it did come, by steps, as when the king of Meath captured and drowned the Viking king Turgesius, and so gave to the Uí Néill kingship, seated in Tara, new unparalleled stature. There are few bonds as fierce and fragile as a common enemy.

After a nearly forty-year respite, the Vikings resumed full-scale operations in Ireland in 914. Norse fleets set up new bases in Waterford, Limerick, Cork, and Wexford, thus giving Ireland its first cities. In these new Norse cities, the native Irish and their first colonizers lived in close proximity, did business, and eventually intermarried. Eventually, the Viking grip loosened. They were distracted by other interests, and Irish resistance was mounting. King Brian Boru, Ireland's foremost Dane-fighter, stood at the center of that resistance; and, in 1005, declared himself *Imperator Scottorum,* Emperor of the Irish, in the church of Patrick at Armagh. Nine years later he died victorious in the Battle of Clontarf, defeating Norse Dublin and the King of Leinster, and bringing an end to the Viking conquest of Ireland.

In retrospect, apart from raising the bar on ruthlessness, the Norse taught the Irish a new appreciation of urban life and extended commerce, enabled by the introduction of coinage and advanced shipbuilding. By laying waste the monasteries, building cities, and in some measure unifying the Irish powers that be, the Ostmen may have also unwittingly served the cause of the Roman church, whose armies—spiritual and temporal—would soon arrive in force. The old Gaelic order, and with it ancient Ireland itself, were coming to an end.

Twilight of the Old Order

When the Vikings officially took their leave of Ireland— many, of course, remained and went native—they left in predictable disarray. Without a common enemy to unite them, the Irish again turned on each other, with a new level of brutality recently learned from their Viking mentors. At the same time, the Roman church and its Irish champions, now ascendant, decried the laxity and barbarism among the flock as well as many of their shepherds. Some of these abuses were shared with the Continent, while others were more or less peculiar to Ireland. At this point kings and clerics joined together to embrace the Gregorian reform movement sweeping through western Christendom, a movement whose point men were the monks of the Benedictine Order, most notably the Cistercians. It was

Malachy of Armagh, the most revered of Ireland's ecclesiastical reformers and a personal friend of Bernard of Clairvaux, who brought the Cistercians to Ireland. Indeed, by the time of his death in 1148, Malachy is credited with having brought all of Ireland under the discipline of the Roman church; and he, in turn, by decree of Pope Clement III in 1190 became the first officially canonized Irish saint.

Ecclesiastical politics, in short, were falling neatly into place. The chain of command was transparently clear. The Bishop of Armagh was the unrivalled Primate of Ireland, and he at the same time acknowledged the sovereign primacy of the Pope, the Bishop of Rome. Meanwhile, the civil order unraveled at will. Rivalries seethed and often came to flame. We needn't sketch in detail here the particular feud that opened the door to new invaders. It is enough to say that Ireland's inability to unify itself made it easy prey to those who had eyed it for years from across a narrow and treacherous sea. It was a man who would be king, Diarmait Mac Murchada, who solicited the Normans to set him on the theoretical throne of Ireland. Diarmait, King of Leinster, aspired to be King of All Ireland, as if such a post were truly available to him. Instead, the sequence of events he unleashed put quite another man on that throne: Henry II of England. Ironically, the Norman invasion of Ireland, which would lead in time to the Protestant suppression of the Catholic church, was blessed by the Pope, an English Pope, Adrian IV, the only English Pope in the Church's 2,000 years. With the arrival of Strongbow in 1170 and the royal visit of Henry II in 1171 to survey and claim his new domains, Ireland entered a new age, as the first colonial possession of the British Empire. It was not only Ancient Ireland that had come to an end.

TIMELINE

B.C.E.

8000–7000	Arrival of earliest humans—mesolithic hunters and fishers
4000	Arrival of Neolithic settlers—farmers and megaligthic builders
2500–500	Irish Bronze Age
700	Arrival of Celtic settlers
5c	Early Irish Iron Age—Hallstatt influence
387	Celtic sack of Rome
3c	La Tène artifacts and cultural traditions

C.E.

1c	All Celtic territories under Roman rule, except for Ireland and Scottish Highlands —traditional Age of the Heroes
432	Traditional date of Patrick's mission to Ireland
400	Ulster Cycle
500–800	Ireland's "Golden Age"
7–9c	Táin—Recension I
795	First Viking invasion
841	Norse fort on the River Liffey
853	Danish occupation of Dublin Norse settlement
988	Recognition of Dublin as an Irish city
1014	Defeat of Vikings at the Battle of Clontarf
12c	Táin—Recension II
1142	Founding of the Cisterican Abbey of Mellifont
1155	Papal Bull Laudabiliter of Adrian IV, blessing the future invasion of Ireland
1169	First Norman Invasion of Ireland
1171	Henry II visits and claims Ireland

GETTING ACQUAINTED
WITH ANCIENT IRELAND

T his chapter will comprise a bit of miscellany, all aimed at preparing you for the sites and sights of ancient Ireland by introducing you to some of the most commonly recurring terms, names, and phenomena you're likely to encounter in your exploring as well as in your reading.

Getting Your Bearings

The Iron Age, the Age of the Heroes, which roughly corresponds with the first mapping of Ireland by the Greek geographer Ptolemy around 150 C.E., was the time of the Pentarchy, when at least in theory Ireland was governed by five provincial kings. In fact, Ireland was divided into scores of often inconsequential *tuatha*, tribes or kingdoms, which tended to group into larger configurations presided over by an "over-king" or Ard Rí. The "ideal" divisions of Ireland were in accord with the cardinal points or directions of the compass: Ulster in the north, Munster in the south, Leinster in the east, and Connacht in the west. When it was that a fifth division or province formally emerged in the center or *mide* of Ireland is unclear. The Irish word for province is *cóiced* or "fifth," suggesting a possible link with a number of ancient cosmologies for which the number five is foundational. To cite one, in the *Rig Veda* we find five directions: north, south, east, west, and "here." For the Celts too, the number five pervades the architecture of the universe and of the imagination. Here, at the center, was the Hill of Mide, Uisnech, the omphalos of Ireland and the site of the annual celebration of Beltaine on the first day of May.

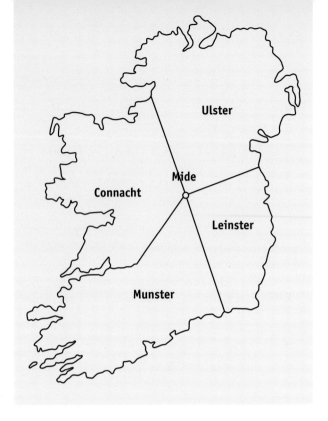

However many ancient bids were made for the always elusive high kingship of Ireland, it was the Normans who first brought centralized administration to Ireland, and with it a system of counties. By 1260 there were, apart from Dublin, already seven counties: Cork, Connacht, Kerry, Limerick, Louth, Tipperary, and Waterford, as well as six "liberties": Carlow, Kildare, Kilkenny, Meath, Ulster, and Wexford. Today there are thirty-two counties on the island, divided into "North" and "South" by a line of partition drawn by Irish and British negotiators in 1921, after the South had won its independence from the British after over 700 years as a colony. The status of "the North" or "Ulster" and of the line dividing it from the Republic of Ireland in the south is in flux. Ultimately, the people of north and south will decide by plebiscite to retain or erase the border between them.

Principal Irish Field Monuments

The story of Ancient Ireland is quite literally written in stone. This is an island abounding in stories, and unlikely ever to run out of rocks. To discover or "dig into" its past, it is often more fruitful to open a field than to open a book.

In Ireland, the past is always underfoot. When a farmer's plough blade suddenly snaps off or an earthmover simply stops moving, it is often because the past has arisen to assert itself again. The Irish landscape is strewn with such discoveries—silent, unyielding, there. To read the past is to recognize its forms, fashioned in stone:

Court Tombs

Also known as "court cairns." A series of uprights and capstones create a long, segmented flat-roofed burial gallery, divided by jambs and sills. While some court tombs have up to four chambers, the majority have only two. The unique feature here is the additional unroofed semi-circular or oval forecourt at the entrance to the first section, presumably to enclose mourners attending funeral or memorial rituals. Remains can be either cremated or inhumed. The entire chamber is covered with a mound of earth and stones. The court tomb is traditionally held to be the earliest form of megalithic timb in Ireland.

⌗ Neolithic, before 3000 B.C.E. ca. 395 known.

⌗ Examples: Creevykeel, Co. Sligo (below); Annaghmare, Co. Armagh.

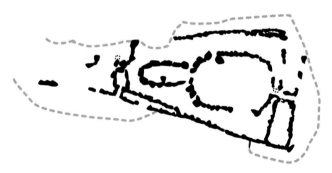

Passage Tombs

The crowning achievement of the megalithic builders. A circular earth and stone mound up to nearly 300 feet in diameter contains one or more passages (up to 130 feet in length) leading to a central roofed burial chamber (or chambers). Walls, sills, lintels, and kerbstones are often elaborately decorated with abstract ornamental carvings—spirals, serpentine patterns, triangles, lozenges, chevrons, radial motifs, zigzags, parallel lines, grouped arcs—reminiscent of the symbolic language of southeastern

Europe during its Neolithic period. Passage tombs are frequently encircled by standing stones and clustered in a vast cemetery or necropolis.

⋈ Neolithic, 3500–2500 B.C.E. ca. 230 known.

⋈ Examples: Newgrange, Knowth, Loughcrew, and Four-knocks (below), Co. Meath; Carrowmore and Carrowkeel, Co. Sligo.

Portal Tombs

A simple structure and a work of engineering genius, thought by many to have developed from the court tomb. Two upright portal stones—accompanied by as many as five additional uprights—support an often massive (up to 100-ton) capstone the front of which, as a rule, inclines upward at an appreciable angle from the ground level. Cremated ruins are placed within the chamber and the *dolmen* (from Breton for "stone table") is commonly covered with a long rectangular mound. While the cairns have mostly been removed and used for other constructions (walls, houses, etc.), the portal and capstones prove more intransigent and often survive. Folklore associates dolmens with fertility and imagines them as the beds of lovers.

⋈ Neolithic, before 2000 B.C.E. ca.175 known.

⋈ Examples: Poulnabrone, Co. Clare (below); Carrowmore, C. Sligo.

Wedge Tombs

The most numerous and widely scattered megalithic tomb form in Ireland—a long, tapered rectangular burial gallery—orthostats and roof slabs—set in a wedge or D-shaped mound. The chamber is usually wider and taller at its entrance, where there is sometimes a short antechamber. Both inhumed and cremated remains have been found. Wedge tombs are considered to represent a late phase in the megalithic tradition.

⌘ Bronze Age, after 2000 B.C.E. ca.505 known.

⌘ Examples: Island, Co. Cork (below); Lough Gur, Co. Limerick; Loughash, Co. Tyrone.

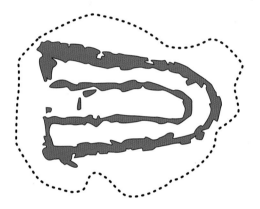

Stone Circles

The most enduring and impressive form of circular enclosure marking ritual sites from the megalithic to the Bronze Age. Orthostats or "standing stones" (numbering anywhere from 6 to well over 100 stones) form a circle or oval surrounded by or placed atop an earthen embankment. The Grange Circle in Co. Limerick extends 215 feet in diameter, and the stones of the Giant's Ring in Co. Down average 12 feet in height. Ireland's largest stone circle, 340 feet in diameter, surrounds the passage tomb of Newgrange. Circle O at Lough Gur comprises an earthwork embankment faced on either side by standing stones and an inner circle of contiguous stones, 50 feet in diameter. The largest concentrations of stone circles are found in West Cork, County Kerry, and central Ulster.

⌘ Neolithic and Bronze Age, 3000–1000 B.C.E. ca.180 known.

⌘ Examples: Great Stone Circle at Grange, Lough Gur, Co. Limerick; Drombeg Circle, Co. Cork; Piper's Stone, Co. Wicklow.

Ritual Enclosures

Circular hilltop enclosures, most often with embankments and ditches, some exceeding 900 feet in diameter, are thought to mark ritual sites. They are difficult to date and even more difficult to interpret with any confidence. The presence of internal ditches (that is, between the enclosing wall or bank and the interior space) would seem to rule out any defensive purpose. Evidence of wooden structures—concentric rings of upright timber posts—has been found at such sites as Knowth, Co. Meath; the Giant's Ring, Ballynahatty, Co. Down; and Emain Macha, Co. Armagh. Extensive hilltop complexes encompassing elaborate earthworks and enclosures are thought to have been royal inauguration and assembly sites. These include Ráith na Rí, the "Fort of the Kings," at Tara in Co. Meath; Cruachain or Rathcroghan in Co. Longford; the Hill of Uisneach in Co. Westmeath; and Dún Ailinne in Co. Kildare, which encircles 40 acres.

Hilltop and Promontory Forts

Impressively fortified occupation sites, usually encompassing at least several acres, are strategically placed on the crests of hills or, when the opportunity presents

itself, on the tips of steep promontories. Some of these mostly Iron Age forts may have had their roots as early as the Bronze Age. What most clearly distinguishes these sites from the ceremonial sites described above is their manifestly defensive design. They are either "univallate" or "multivallate,' that is, encircled with one or more ramparts and eventually stone fortification walls, all of which may have been a measure of tribal status as well as of local peril. Several, like Dún Aonghasa on Inishmore and Doonamo in Co. Mayo, sport an additional chevaux-de-frise, a stand of more or less contiguous stones serving as formidable obstacles to the onslaught of an attacking army.

⌗ Bronze Age after 900 B.C.E. and Iron Age. ca. 50 known.
⌗ Examples: Dún Aonghasa, Dún Eochla, Dún Eoghnacht, and Dún Dubhchathair on Inishmore; Rathgall, Co. Wicklow; and Grianán of Aileach in Co. Donegal.

Ringforts

In keeping with the dictum that a man's home is his castle or *cashel* in Irish, the ringfort represents the domestic consumer version of the larger royal or tribal forts described above, providing reduced security proportionate to lesser wealth and status. These are the homesteads of well-to-do farmers. In some cases the ramparts are made of loose stone

Entrance to a ringfort

and dirt, better suited to keep domestic animals in than to keep wild marauders out, while other ring-forts, like Staigue Fort in Co. Kerry, boast stone walls roughly 18 feet high and 13 feet thick. The circular living space within the walls was in this case nearly 90 feet in diameter, only half the floor plan of Caher Ballykinvarga in Co. Clare. Many ringforts, as well as some monasteries, hilltop forts, and ringforts, offered a quite remarkable defensive feature, when fleeing seemed preferable to fighting. These were the *souterrains*, of which over 2,000 examples have been noted—underground passages, some over 300 feet in length, leading either to secure subterranean chambers or to a secret exit from the enclosure.

⌘ Iron Age, after 500 B.C.E. to 1000 C.E. ca. 40–60,000 estimated.

⌘ Examples: Altagore Fort in Co. Antrim, Knockdrum Fort in Co. Cork.

Note on Nomenclature

Rath, *lios* (or lis), *cahair* (or caher), *dún*, and *caishel* (or cashel, anglicized as "castle") all designate one or other form of royal, tribal, ritual, or domestic enclosure, and remain embedded in the names of many of Ireland's modern towns, cities, and suburbs, such as Rathgar, Lismore, Cahirciveen, Dun Laoghaire, and Castlebar. Although not always used with precision, *rath* and *lios* refer mostly to earthen embankments, sometimes banked with stones; *dún* designates an enclosure of high or royal status; *caher* and *cashel* refer to forts built of stone.

Crannógs

One of the more curious Irish domestic options, crannógs were small artificial islands, created at the shallow edges of lakes and marshlands by piling up mud, stones, and brush. Access to the island was often provided by a causeway or bridge to the nearest shore, or else was simply by boat. The relative isolation of the site and an encircling palisade of wooden stakes contributed to the questionable security of these sites.

⌘ Iron Age, 500–1000 C.E. ca. 2,000 estimated.

⌘ Examples: Reconstruction at Craggaunowen Project, Co. Clare.

Irish Christian Architecture

Apart from the stone tombs of the megalithic period and the later fortresses of the Celtic and Christian periods, the Irish builders worked mostly in wood. Private homes, and even the royal ceremonial structures evidenced at Emain Macha, were fashioned of wood, as were roughly the first four centuries of Christian churches and monastic settlements. The earliest monastery buildings—chapels, libraries, scriptoria, craft shops, kitchens, refectories, monks' cells—were wooden constructions, often finely crafted but hardly designed to survive for centuries. The earliest free-standing stone architecture after the megalithic period dates from between the 5th and the 9th centuries as archaic stone structures began to replace their wooden predecessors. Principally in the west and southwest of Ireland, monks experimented with dry stone constructions such as corbelled beehive huts and what we would see as miniature sanctuaries. The monastic settlements of Inishmurray in Co. Sligo and Skellig Michael in Co. Kerry, together with the Gallarus Oratory (pictured below) and

the Church of Kilmakeador on the Dingle Peninsula provide striking examples of early Christian stone buildings. The monastic stone tower, which appeared late in the Viking period, stands out here as an anomaly. All but unique to Ireland, it is a creation whose inspiration and purpose remain elusive. Nearly 75 examples survive today in uneven condition, with those at Ardmore, Co.

Waterford and Glendalough, Co. Wicklow among the finest. It was the Cisterician monks and the Norman invaders who first introduced major stone architecture to Ireland. (The Cistercians arrived at Mellifont, Co. Meath, in 1140 and the Normans arrived at Baginbud Head, Co. Wexford in 1167.)

Kilmakeador

Prehistoric Houses

Unlike monumental architecture—constructed from stone to defy time or to withstand attack—domestic architecture was invariably modest, constructed from wood and other organic materials to last, at the outset, three or four generations, by ancient measure little more than a hundred years. The stone footprints of their foundations and the charred outlines of their hearths are among the only surviving clues to their shape and construction. In short, none of the actual houses from prehistoric Ireland has survived, though they admit of speculative reconstruction from the remains of their post-holes, foundations, and descendant forms. So, with some confidence, we are able to suggest that, were you in real estate in prehistoric Ireland, these are some of the model homes that you would be able to show to prospective homebuyers:

✠ Ballynagilly, Co. Tyrone ca. 4000 B.C.E.
✠ 7.4m x 6.4m
✠ Support posts and oak planking

✠ Ballyglass, Co. Mayo ca. 4000 B.C.E.
✠ 16m x 13m
✠ Post and plank

✠ Lough Gur, Co. Limerick 3rd millennium B.C.E.
✠ 10m x 5m
✠ Support post, rushes, and sod

✠ Lough Gur, Co. Limerick 3rd millennium B.C.E.
✠ 6m diameter
✠ Post ring, timber uprights, and sod fill

✚ Knocknarea, Co. Sligo 4–3 millennium B.C.E.
✚ Seasonal huts
✚ 5–10m diameter
✚ Light timber covered with thatch or hides

✚ Craggaunowen Project, Co. Clare
✚ Ringfort, fortified farm
✚ 500 B.C.E. to 1000 C.E.

Holy Wells of Ireland

Water, stones, trees, and hills have been sites of veneration for thousands of years. Water in particular was a sacred substance for early civilizations and continues to be a vital element in contemporary religious rituals.

A "holy well" can be any water-source that is deemed sacred. The water can be found in a spring, a tidal basin, a stone depression, a tree stump, a pond or lake. Often there are other objects such as stones and trees that are considered sacred near the well and are part of the rituals held there. Most holy wells are associated with healing and renewal and this power is connected to a holy or sacred person or event. The cult of holy wells can still be found in India, parts of the Middle East and Africa, in Greece, and in Ireland.

Many of the Irish holy wells, *tobar* in Irish, continue to draw worshippers to the present day. While the rituals and lore surrounding the holy wells are wrapped in a covering of Christianity, elements of the rituals conducted at these wells are considered to be similar to those enacted in pre-Christian Ireland. The synthesis of ancient Celtic religion into Christianity created a unique Irish Christianity that carries within it much of its old "pagan" traditions. Christian missionaries to Ireland had a lot to confront and compete with.

There are literally thousands of holy wells throughout Ireland. Over time, some wells have fallen out of favor and new ones have become more popular. Today's pilgrimages to wells continue to follow this ebb and flow as people's needs and beliefs change. There are some wells with significant associations that have retained strong followings through recorded time. Many of these holy wells are near the ancient sites explored in this book.

Today's pilgrimages to wells typically occur on the feast days of the patron saint of the well and the parish. This "Patron's Day" and the festivities held and prayer rotations done at a particular site are collectively called a "pattern." Often these patterns included lively revelry and celebration. Wells can be part of people's private devotions too and visits to them are not reserved only to the Saint's day. While from place to place there is some variation between the different patterns, we find far more similarities among them. One can only speculate how these practices reach back into the pre-Christian age.

The pattern rituals include: walking to or around the site a prescribed number of times and in certain directions often without shoes or on one's knees while reciting fixed prayers. Drinking the water, applying it to an ailing part, collecting dirt or clay from the site along with some of the sacred water to anoint animals/homes/those not present are practices common to almost all patterns, as is the custom of leaving an offering in or near the well.

Some offerings, or *clooties*, include interesting things such as a strip of fabric tied to a sacred bush or tree near the well. It is thought that one's ailment would be healed by the time such a cloth had rotted away. Some well sites have stone cairns to which pilgrims add their own pebbles. Other holy wells have coins, simple trinkets, buttons, or religious objects left in or around them. Purification by the sacred water can include full immersion, walking through the water, drinking the water, or using the water to touch or bathe an afflicted area.

Frequently the worshipper is required to make rounds and prayers at certain stones, markers, or trees around the well. The most common trees found around holy wells include whitethorn, hazel, ash, rowan, yew, holly, and at one time oak. Some of the sacred stones bear particular markings and some have indentations thought to be the knee or footprint of the patron of that well.

Needless to say, there are many stories told about the wells: how they became holy, visions had at the wells, curses and blessings given at the wells, and the experience of miraculous cures. Observers of Irish culture continue to write on the prevalence of the holy-well cult on the island.

The *Book of Leinster* tells of the Healing Well of Slane in Co. Sligo, west of Lough Arrow, now under the Heapstone Cairn, whose waters revived the warriors of the Tuatha Dé Danann at the second Battle of Moytura (MagTuired), where they defeated the Fir Bolg. In the 12th century Geraldus Cambrensis referred to a number of holy wells in his book on Irish history and topography.

The pre-Christian fertility festival of *Im Bolc*, also known as *Oimelc* and translated as "sheep's milk," heralded the beginning of spring on February 1. The same day is now celebrated as the feast day of St. Brigid, when churches and wells dedicated to her are visited by many of the Irish. Brigid is as venerated as St. Patrick and many homes are adorned with her woven straw crosses. She is related to the great fertility goddesses. It is interesting to note that worship of Brigid has become more widespread. She has usurped the place of other patron saints in a number of parishes and hers is the pattern observed in their place. St. Brigid's well at Faughart Hill, north of Dundalk in Co. Louth, off the N1 about 2.5 miles north of Dundalk and signposted on the road to Faughart, is one of the most famous. The well is on the site of an Iron Age hill fort and is the spot where Medb unsuccessfully ambushed Cúchulainn with fourteen unlucky warriors. [En route Itinerary #2] Another St. Brigid's well is in Kildare, signposted opposite the entrance to the National Stud and Japanese Garden. [En route Itinerary #3] Brigid's feast day remains a very important day of the year followed by St. Patrick's Day on March 17.

St. Patrick's Day is not aligned with any of the pre-Christian feast days, but it does provide a welcome break in the Lenten fast period for the observant and an excuse for much merrymaking for everyone. Patrick's wells are widespread, except in the more southern counties of Waterford, Cork, Kerry, and Clare. Patrick is said to have taken over some wells from "evil druids" by means of prayers or by using the water for baptisms. Other wells are said to have sprung from his footfall or from a strike of his staff upon the ground. His miracles are legion. St. Patrick's Well in Dromard, Co. Sligo has stones to both Patrick and Brigid and can be found west of Sligo town off the N59. From Sligo, turn at the sign for the Dromard Roman Catholic Church and follow this road about two miles and follow signs for the well, which is just past the cemetery behind the field gate and surrounded by a stone wall. [En route Itineraries #1 & 2]

By Lough Gill, just east of Sligo town, the frequented Tobernalt Well, Tobar an Ailt, the Well at the Cliff, is believed to have a sacred trout living within it; and people suffering from back pain are said to find relief from the healing stone nearby. One imagines this well, not named for any saint, as a secluded place for ancient pre-Christian worshippers as Christianity spread over the country. In Penal times, this site, as many of the well sites, was used as a secret place to conduct the forbidden Catholic Mass and rituals. Christian worshippers often visit this well on Garland Sunday, related to the pre-Christian autumnal feast of Lughnasa, to recite special prayers. A sign for the well is on the left on the N4 leaving Sligo and on the right again by the lake. [En route Itineraries #1 & 2]

About 25 miles west of Dublin, in the village of Carbury, one can visit the Trinity Well in Co. Kildare. Trinity Sunday, the first Sunday in June, is the holy day associated with this well, which is also the source of the Boyne River, and a festive pattern is still held here. To reach Carbury take the N4 to Innfield where you then take R402 to Carbury. Take a left in the village; and, along that road, at the left turn for Edenderry, stop at the gate on the right. The well is on the grounds of Newberry House, surrounded by a low wall and shaded by a large tree and stone sanctuary in the field beyond the entrance gate. The Boyne River is thought to be the embodiment of the great goddess Boann, the White Cow Goddess, and legend says it was this well that bubbled over and chased the goddess to the sea, creating the river behind her. It was to this river Boann returned to live forever. Finn Mac Cumaill is said to have received his gift of second sight by eating the Salmon of Knowledge whose powers had come from feasting on the hazelnuts dropped into this sacred well. [En route Itineraries #2 & 3]

There are numerous Irish saints, all with feast days. Many too have wells associated with them. Some of the more significant saints with multiple wells include Ciaran, Columcille, and Brendan. There are also many wells dedicated to "Our Lady," Mary. One could happily adventure across Ireland from well to well, and some visitors have done just that, driven by a curious thirst for their unusual waters. At the least it is fruitful to keep an eye open for signs to local wells as you travel across the country, and visit one now and again. You never know what you might find.

Irish Words Embedded in Today's Topography

In reading about and traveling around Ireland, you will find that many Irish words and roots have survived in the names borne by many sites and towns. Here are a number of the most common such survivals, with their frequent anglicizations in parentheses:

Abhainn (owen)	river
Art	height
Áth	ford
Baile	town
Beag (beg)	small
Bó	cow
Bóthar	road
Bóthar	foot (of a hill or road)
Carraig (carrick)	rock
Cill (kill)	church(yard), (monk's or prisoner's) cell
Cloch	stone
Cluain (clon)	meadow
Cnoc (knock)	hill
Cuillen (cullen)	holly
Dearg (derg)	red

Droichead (Drogheda)	bridge
Droim (drum)	back or ridge of a hill
Dubh (doo)	black
Dún	fort
Inis (inish)	island
Leitir (letter)	hillside
Lios (lis)	henge, fort
Mágh	plain
Mór (more)	large
Mullach (mullagh)	peak
Ráth	ringfort
Sceilg (skellig)	steep rock, crag
Sliabh (slieve)	mountain
Suí (see)	seat
Teach (ti, tigh)	church, house
Teampall (temple)	church
Tobar (tober)	well
Trá	strand
Tulach	hillock, mound

A Primer of Ancient Irish Law

Ladies, did you know you could divorce your husband with full compensation if…

⚜ Your husband told terrible lies about you to your friends.

⚜ Your husband told jokes and stories about you to make others laugh at you.

⚜ Your husband struck you and made a mark on you.

⚜ Your husband left you for another woman.

⚜ Your husband denied you sex.

⚜ Your husband gave you a potion or charm to make you have sex with him.

⚜ Your husband did not provide you with the foods you desire.

⚜ Your husband could not give you children.

⚜ Your husband could not perform sexually.

⚜ Your husband married you while deceiving you.

⚜ Your husband lost his mind.

⚜ Your husband had an illness that ruined your marriage.

⚜ Your husband was away for a long, long time.

⚜ Your husband was dead.

Gentlemen, did you know you could divorce your wife for many of the same reasons and, if your wife was in the wrong, you could get back everything she and her family received from you: all those dowry payments you've made every year of your marriage? And to top it off, there would be no heart-rending child custody battles because all of the children would have been in foster care since infancy and you parents already paid for that when the children were born.

Well, this was the situation in Ireland under Brehon Law up through the time of the Norman Invasions in the 12th century. Some laws were still in effect into the 17th century!

The Brehon Laws covered many social aspects of ancient Irish life and provide us with insights into the relationships between men and women and between the individual and the community. The Brehon Laws were based on the long-held social customs and traditions of Ireland's close-knit rural society. The laws were created to help keep community life on an even keel. Ancient Ireland was a hierarchical society; and, though there were distinctions between the classes, all people had certain rights. Penalties for offenses under the law were set by the social rank of the plaintiff, and each class of person had a specific price fixed on him/her by law. There was no large governing body that made people obey the laws, but a smaller local unit—the *tuath*—made sure that the traditions and ancient laws were brought into play when needed. Lawyers consulted the legal texts and commentaries and judged the nature and consequences of each case brought to them. But the enforcing of their judgment was the business of the kin of the injured party. In many respects, these laws were quite humane and realistic indeed.

There was no legal penalty that allowed for physical injury or capital punishment. In fact, the highest honor-price that one could pay was the worth of seven women. Now, that works out like this: one woman is worth three milking cows or six summer-heifers (non-milk producing): so the highest penalty a felon could pay is worth seven women: 21 milking cows or 42 summer-heifers, which is enough to ruin many a rural felon, as cows and women were the gold standard.

The law recognized ten different types of marriage or sexual relationships and had guidelines to address the rights of the involved parties:

1. A match of equal rank and property
2. A woman sustained by a man's property
3. A man sustained by a woman's property
4. A concubine or mistress with a man
5. A couple who periodically live together and neither supports the other wholly
6. An abducted woman and her abductor
7. A soldier and his woman
8. A union of deception when sex begins under a ruse such as sleep
9. A forced union such as rape
10. A union of "levity," described as the relationship between lunatics/idiots

Marriage was a contract to protect property and children. Any sacredness was imparted by the couple themselves or grew within the relationship they created over time. By contract, a dowry was negotiated between the prospective husband and his family and the family of the bride. The husband paid the dowry to the girl's father, who then divided it with the head of the family. The dowry continued to be paid over twenty-one years and, starting in the second year of union, the bride kept a third of it for herself. Each year the amount the wife kept increased. The remaining annual balance continued to be divided between her father and the superior head of the family. This arrangement went on for the length of the contract or as long as the marriage lasted. This enabled women to amass property and goods from her husband while she was performing her duties as a wife and mother.

All children were provided for under the law, regardless of the circumstances of conception. Some single moms had to pay for fosterage on their own and there were some deadbeat dads who had to pay if they didn't stay. It is all in the small print of the laws and there is a lot of that.

One of the more curious laws addressed the penalty for the loss of a testicle. If the right testicle was removed, the penalty was considerably less than if the left was removed; for the left testicle was thought to be vital to procreation and the right was simply there to provide proper balance. Another concerned the foster-care fee for a child born from a union of "levity." This had to be paid by the person who, in jest, coordinated the union of fools. Lastly, the just severity of the law is revealed in the penalty for violation of a girl under twelve: the same as murder.

The sophistication of the Brehon Laws and their comprehensive reach into the lives of the people of ancient Ireland are impressive. Now, at long last, some of the issues that were once addressed with legal compassion in the "native" laws are being addressed in contemporary Ireland. Divorce is now legal again and children have legal rights regardless of the situations of their birth.

A Who's Who of Ancient Ireland

As you explore the ancient sites you will see and hear many names repeated: those of kings and queens, gods and goddesses, heroes and lovers whose stories and names cling to the rocks, the roads, and the imaginative landscape of Ireland. This host of legendary Irish characters, some based on historical figures, are legion and their relationships resemble in nature and complexity those of the Greek or Indian pantheon, as well as a long-running soap opera. To help you enter this rich mythic landscape we provide here a brief list and description of some of the major figures who populate, and occasionally overlap, the various story cycles: the Mythological Cycle [M], the Ulster Cycle [U], The Finn, Fenian, or Ossianic Cycle [F], and the Cycle of Kings [K].

Aed/Bodh Derg/Dagda [M]: The Lord of the Other-world of spirits and gods, changing from tale to tale in name and manifestation, at once father and son, he is the god of fire and the creator of mankind. Enemy of Finn Mac Cumhaill, Lord of the Tuatha Dé Danann, husband to the great goddesses, and father of the fertility goddess Brigid, his many battles and deaths weave through Irish mythology.

Anu/Danu [M]: The mother of the gods and the earth mother whose perfect breasts rise as the twin hills, the Paps of Anu, in Co. Kerry.

Boann [M]: The river Boyne, Brú na Bóine, and the Boyne Valley region of Meath is named after this goddess of cows. Boann took Dagda, the great lord of the magical Tuatha Dé

Paps of Anu

Danann, as one of her husbands. From their union at the ritual fertility rites of Samain, October 31, they bore the god Oengus: harper to the gods, patron of poets, and protector of lovers.

Brigid [M]: A wise mother goddess of fertility, childbirth, healing, the sun, and artistic skill, Brigid's powers have been absorbed into the Christian Saint Brigid, an abbess of Kildare, who, with her nuns, protected and kept the sacred fire lit to Brigid, until the Norman invasions of the 12th century. St. Brigid's crosses, made of woven straw, protect cattle and homes and are fashioned in the design of ancient sun symbols.

Conchobar Mac Nessa [U]: Son of Cathbad, a master druid who foretold the birth of Deirdre of the Sorrows and the coming of mightly Cúchulainn, and Ness the queen of Emain Macha, Conchobar became the King of Ulster and leader of the Craeb Ruad, the Red Branch Knights. The Ulster Cylce of tales, tells of Conchobar's exploits from his stronghold of Emain Macha, now known as Navan Fort not far from Armagh. As high king, he became husband to many including the reluctant Deirdre and the powerful Queen Medb.

Cormac Mac Airt [F&K]: A legendary king of Ireland, Cormac was in constant state of war against the kings of Ulster. His reign was punctuated by years of blissful peace in which he composed the *Tecosca Cormaic*, his instructions for maintaining a happy nation. We include part of it here from the 1909 translation by Kuno Meyer as it still seems good advice:

> "O grandson of Conn, O Cormac," said Caibre, "what is best for the good of a tribe?" "Not hard to tell," said Cormac.
>
> A meeting of nobles, frequent assemblies, an enquiring mind, questioning the wise, quelling every evil, fulfilling every good, an assembly according to rules, following ancient lore, a lawful synod, a lawful lord, righteous chieftains, not to crush wretches, keeping treaties, mercifulness with good custom, consolidating kingship, weaving together synchronisms, fulfilling the law, legality of ancient alliances.

Cúchulainn [U]: The son of Conchobar's druidess sister, Dechtire, and Sualdam Mac Roich, the king of Cooley in County Louth, Cúchulainn is one of the super heroes of the Ulster Cycle of tales. Also known as Sétanta in his youth, Cúchulainn grew to become a spectacular warrior armed with magical weapons and endless courage. The Irish epic, *The Táin Bó Cuailgne*, The Cattle Raid of Cooley, depicts his struggle with Queen Medb. Children today still read tales of the mighty Cúchulainn.

Deirdre [U]: Set aside for marriage to Conchobar since childhood, ill-fated Deirdre fell in love with Noíse, a much younger man and one of the sons of Uisnech, and fled with him and his brothers to escape the rage of the King Conchobar. Conchobar's father had predicted that Deirdre would be the end of the Ulster kings. War over Deirdre burst aflame and treachery brought death to the lovers. Their story is one of Three Sorrowful Tales of the Ulster Cycle.

Druids: Druids go way back. Herodotus, Pliny, and Caesar have referred to druids in their writings and Irish legend includes druids among the early arrivals to the island.

Individual druids have made their mark in fiction and fact. As a group they represent a body of powerful, spiritual people who interpreted omens, read the stars, followed the lunar year, predicted the future, and engaged in some types of sacrifice. The oak was sacred to them and their influence was deeply felt in Ireland. In Irish legend, druids are often magical beings with extraordinary powers. In popular folklore, dolmens are often referred to as Druid's altars.

Ériu [M]: A sun goddess, and the source of the modern Irish word Éire for Ireland. Ériu was the last Queen of the Tuatha Dé Danann when they were crushed by the invasions of the Milesians, the Sons of Míl from Spain. Ériu's last request was to have the country she loved be named for her.

Finn Mac Cumaill [F]: The adventures of Finn and his followers, the *fianna*, make up some of the greatest hero lore of the Gaelic world. Some scholars contest that Finn was an historical figure and others deny it, but all agree, Finn had quite a time. Many of the Fenian tales concern the feud between Finn and the Clann Mac Morna whose members killed his father. Finn's name is associated with place names across Ireland and tales of Finn are enjoyed to this day.

Gráinne [M&F]: The daughter of Cormac Mac Airt and courted by a war-weary Finn Mac Cumaill, Gráinne drugged the wine of Finn at a feast at her home in Tara. As Finn lay sleeping, Gráinne made off with the dashing Diarmuid. The lovers' flight across Ireland from the pursuing Finn is immortalized in the story of "The Pursuit of Diarmuid and Gráinne," and remains one of the great Irish love stories. The countryside is scattered with caves and mountains said to be the beds of the passionate pair.

Lug [M]: A sun god of fire and mental prowess, Lug is the Zeus-like champion of the Tuatha Dé Danann. Lug was a fearsome warrior and the battle-partner of Dagda. The magical weapons of Lug were forged by his fellow deities and included a spear of lightning. Lug used cunning and the gifts of his divine fellowship to ensure many stunning victories for the Tuatha Dé Danann. He was husband of goddesses and father to warriors and met his end on the hill of Uisneach. In the *Táin* he is the divine progenitor of the peerless Cúchulainn.

Medb [U]: The ultimate power queen, Medb had her pregnant sister killed so she could take the throne of Connacht at Cruachain Connacht, the royal site near Tulsk, Co. Roscommon. And that was just the beginning. Whatever Medb wanted, Medb got. Her identity as a goddess of dawn, dusk, and war fit her nature of light and darkness. Medb appears in many of the tales and is alternately hilarious, awful, beguiling, and always politically savvy in warfare and power-building, but not sharing. The massive cairn at Knocknarea, in Co. Sligo is popularly thought to be her burial place.

Tuatha Dé Danann [M]: A race of gods and goddesses who ruled the Otherworld and played out their passions across the land of Ireland. They are thought to have arrived in Ireland as legendary/prehistoric invaders from Greece or Denmark who brought with them the druid lore of magic and prophesy. After their eventual defeat by the Mílesians, the immortal Tuatha Dé Danann became invisible and went underground to rule their domain from the *síd*, or mounds, that mark the countryside. The folklore of fairies is the echo of the Tuatha Dé Danann today and many places are associated with the various gods and goddesses of their pantheon.

The Literature of Ancient Ireland

Even the most dramatic field monuments of ancient Ireland—passage tombs, stone circles, royal enclosures, promontory forts, sea-girt monastic retreats—stand as hollow, silent stage sets without the dramas of the past to inhabit and enliven them; and we have nowhere else to turn for those dramas but the oldest surviving tales of Irish imagination, aspiration, and faith, which modern scholars have grouped into four cycles we mentioned before the biographies, and additionally, the early Irish Lives of the Saints. There is no better preparation for an on-the-ground "in-country" exploration of ancient Ireland than an on-the-page exploration of early Irish literature. The voices of the past live, after all, in books, not in stones. Stones only resonate to them.

Here are some readily available paperback suggestions:
Over Nine Waves: A Book of Irish Legends, Marie Heaney
The Tain, tr. Thomas Kinsella (Oxford University Press)
Early Irish Myths and Sagas, tr. Jeffrey Gantz (Penguin)
Patrick in His Own Words, Joseph Duffy (Veritas)
The Voyage of St. Brendan, tr. John J. O'Meara (Dufour Editions)
Giraldus Cambrensis, The History and Topography of Ireland, tr. John J. O'Meara, (Penguin)
Tales of the Elders of Ireland, tr. Ann Dooley and Harry Roe (Oxford University Press)
Life of St. Columba, Adomnán of Iona, tr. Richard Sharpe (Penguin)
The Life and Death of Saint Malachy the Irishman, Bernard of Clairvaux, tr. Robert T. Meyer (Cisterican Publications)

And for children:
Irish Tales and Sagas, Ulick O'Connor (Town House)
The Names Upon the Harp: Irish Myths and Legend, Marie Heaney (Scholastic Press)
101 Read-Aloud Celtic Myths and Legends, Joan C. Veriero (Black Dog & Leventhal)
Fin M'Coul, The Giant of Knockmany Hill, Tomie dePaola (Holiday House)
Finn MacCoul and His Fearless Wife, Robert Byrd (Dutton)
Favorite Irish Fairy Tales, Soinbhe Lally (Poolbeg Press)
Tales of Irish Myths, Benedict Flynn (Naxos Audio Books)

On-line text sources:
Irish Script On Screen www.isos.dcu.ie/
This is a vast, ongoing project sponsored by the School of Celtic Studies, a division of the Dublin Institute for Advanced Studies, to provide digital facsimiles of the oldest Irish manuscripts in their entirety. Included manuscripts are from the collections of the Royal Irish Academy, Trinity College Dublin, the National Library of Ireland, etc.

Corpus of Electronic Texts (CELT) www.ucc.ie/celt/transpage
This site, created by the Department of Archaeology of University College Cork provides a host of ancient texts—

Irish, Latin, French, and Hiberno-English—either to be read on-line or downloaded for printing. English translations are available for many of the manuscripts.

The British Library
http://www.bl.uk/onlinegallery/sacredtexts/lindisfarne.html
The Department of Manuscripts of the British Museum offers on-line access to partial digital facsimiles of many of their most rare holdings, including the Lindisfarne Gospels.

Irish Text Society www.litriocht.com
Located in Tralee, Co. Kerry, the Irish Text Society keeps in print many old and difficult-to-find Irish texts, some of which are accompanied by an English translation. These texts are not available, however, in digital form on the web.

Academy for Ancient Texts www.ancienttexts.org
A website dedicated to providing the largest on-line library of ancient texts in the world. Their list focuses on religious, metaphysical, philosophical, historical texts.

ITINERARY ONE

Pre-Celtic • Neolithic and Bronze Ages
4000 B.C.E.–700 B.C.E.

PRINCIPAL SITES

National Museum of Ireland
Brú na Bóinne....*Newgrange & Knowth passage tombs*
Loughcrew....*hilltop passage tomb complex*
Carrowkeel....*mountaintop Neolithic cemetery*
Carrowmore....*Neolithic cemetery complex*
Knocknarea....*mountaintop cairn*
Creevykeel.....*court cairn*
Céide Fields....*Neolithic farm settlement*
Burren National Park....*Pulnabrone portal tomb, wedge tombs*
Lough Gur....*Neolithic settlement site, Grange Stone
Circle, wedge tomb*
Fourknocks....*passage tomb*
Pipers Stones.....*stone circle*

TRAVERSED

Provinces of Leinster, Connacht, and Munster
County Dublin, County Meath, County Westmeath,
County Longford, County Leitrim, County
Roscommon, County Sligo, County Mayo, County
Galway, County Clare, County Limerick, County
Tipperary, County Laoise, County Kilkenny, County
Kildare, County Wicklow

Day One
Arrival in Dublin

D ublin Airport is a dream compared to most
international airports, even after its dramatic
expansion in recent years—definitely easy-in and
easy-out, regardless of what form of public transportation

73

you choose. Until the new tunnel is completed, creating a direct rapid transit link to and from the city, your best options into the city center are taxi (€30) or bus or one of the convenient shuttle-bus services to Dublin city center: Airlink Express (€6) or Aircoach (€7). You shouldn't have to wait more than fifteen minutes for a suitable option. We recommend that you begin your auto rental on Day Two and return then to the airport to pick up your car. You will pay for one less day, avoid parking fees, and spare yourself the nightmare of navigating Dublin traffic. Dublin streets and roads rank among the most desperately congested byways in Europe. As a jetlagged novice, this is not the place or the time to try out your left-lane driving skills. Better to get a night's sleep and to drive directly from the airport to County Meath, avoiding all city and rush-hour traffic.

PRINCIPAL SITE
National Museum of Archaeology and History

Ireland's National Museum is located on four distinct campuses: the Museum of Natural History on Merrion Street, the Museum of Archaeology and History on Kildare Street, and the Museum of Decorative Arts and History at the Collins Barracks, all in central Dublin. The fourth and latest addition, opened in 2001, is the Museum of Country Life at Turlough Park, just outside of Castlebar, Co. Mayo.

Regardless of which prehistoric or historical period occupies the focus of one's interests, the exploration of ancient Ireland best begins at the National Musuem of Archaeology and History, amidst an assemblage of treasures—dating from the earliest human habitation to the medieval period—amassed over several hundred years by individual collectors, the British Crown, and the Irish State. Before examining any of the holdings, be sure to admire the museum that holds them. For a start, the entrance lobby, top to bottom, from its 62-ft domed ceiling to its striking mosaic floor deserves a gaze.

Despite the splendor of its holdings, the National Museum, like any case museum, can be taxing. It is easy, even without the additional gravity of jet-lag, to grow weary of reading labels and placards and to teeter towards burnout. Consequently, we recommend that you try to take advantage of one of the frequent daily tours by a member of the museum staff. Once given your bearings across the wide sweep of holdings and the periods they represent, you can find your own way back to those items with which you want to linger.

For the first itinerary, the items of focal interest revolve around the earliest peoples' essential activities of gathering and producing food, burying their dead, and enacting in ritual their most fundamental aspirations and fears. This itinerary should be followed counter-clockwise along the outer wall as soon as you enter the center court. Here you will see many of the most important finds uncovered at sites that you will visit during the next week, including a mysterious carved phallic stone found at Knowth, a ceremonial macehead also found at Knowth, and an assortment of stone beads and pendants from the passage tombs at Carrowkeel. As for the rest, admittedly, crafted flints, stone axes, and hand-worked pottery are not in themselves electrifying, but they will take on enhanced familiarity and significance as you place them in context and imagine the lives in which they were in daily use. Ten thousand years from now, even today's cell phones and palm pilots may generate indifferent yawns, accompanied by disbelief that life could ever have been so primitive.

Of lesser importance to the itineraries in this volume, though of signal importance to the history of Ireland, are the artifacts recovered from the Early–Late Bronze Age (2500–700 B.C.E.). As the Bronze Age inhabitants of Ireland left fewer and less significant field monuments than did their predecessors, the Irish Bronze Age is best studied indoors, here in the National Museum; and this is your chance to do just that. You will note how, in the Early Bronze Age, single inhumation or cremation burials, often in unmarked, mostly below-ground cists or stone boxes, became more popular and more exclusively male. You will also trace the emergence and growth of metallurgy in Ireland, as copper and bronze tools replace their stone prototypes and as weapons of increasing lethality proliferate throughout the island. Pottery—domestic and funereal—reaches a new standard in this period, and great bronze cauldrons are in evidence. Swords with sharper edges and longer blades also make their appearance during the later Bronze Age as do more and more impressive hill forts, pointing to a greater concentration of wealth and power and, presumably a greater accumulation of wealth, exemplified in the exquisite gold ornaments that first emerge around 1200 B.C.E. and reach their peak around 700 B.C.E.

Of course you will not restrain your curiosity to the confines of the first itinerary; so be sure to explore the full scope of the museum's collections and to revive yourself, as needed, in the museum coffee shop. Just a few off-focus not-to-miss highlights are: *Ór—Ireland's Gold,* Europe's premier exhibition of prehistoric gold and *The Treasury,* an exquisite assemblage of early Celtic and Christian treasures. Upstairs, you'll find an eye-opening introduction to Viking Dublin that will deepen your appreciation of Dublin's past and give new resonance to the word "berserk."

Located at the intersection of Kildare and Molesworth Streets. (01-677-7444) Open Tues–Sat 10am–5pm, Sun 2–5pm. Closed Mondays. Free admission.

Side Sites

Dublin ranks among the top five tourist cities in Europe and not without reason. There is no question of our listing, much less discussing, its myriad attractions here. Instead, given that this is a guide to ancient Ireland and that only hours remain in your one allotted day in Ireland's capitol city, we will make a couple of modest suggestions relevant to the exploration of ancient Ireland.

Trinity College Dublin

Although not a prehistoric site, a meandering stroll in the 400-year old campus of Trinity College makes for a most tranquil and fascinating walk through the past. There is no admission fee to the college grounds, and entrance is through the main gate in College Green opposite the central branch of the Bank of Ireland, the former seat of the Irish Parliament. We recommend that that you take a college tour, especially of the Old Library and the *Book of Kells,* one of Ireland's greatest treasures. Open Mon–Sat

9:30am–5pm; Sundays, Oct–May noon–4:30pm and June–Sept 9:30am–4:30pm. Admission €€€.

Garden Strolls

To finish off your afternoon and put that final edge on your appetite for an early dinner, we recommend a walk through St. Stephen's Green, only five minutes on foot down Dawson Street from the side (Arts Block) gate of Trinity College. An idyllic alternative or supplement to St. Stephen's Green is one of Dublin's best-kept secrets, Iveagh Gardens, located behind the National Concert Hall. Both gardens are open, free admission, until dark.

St. Stephen's Green

Kid Sites

Viking Splash

Kids will surely not object if you jump the rails of the first itinerary and take them back to Viking Ireland with a "Viking Splash Tour" (www.vikingsplash.ie) aboard a reconditioned "Duck," a vintage amphibious vehicle unknown to the Vikings them-selves. Taking advantage not only of Dublin's thoroughfares but also of its canals, these tours offer an informative and entertaining introduction to Dublin's sites and stories. More to the point, kids love it, even while some humorless parents cringe. Tours every 30 min. in peak season and every 90 min. off peak. Call 01-707-6000 for more details and reservations. Fee €€€. Tours depart from Stephen's Green North, close to Grafton Street, just behind the taxi rank and water fountain.

Dublinia

Another family-oriented historical attraction in Dublin is known as "Dublinia," (www.dublinia.ie), offering a vivid walk through Medieval Dublin, 1170-1540, recreated in a series of exhibits, spectacles, and interactive experiences. There's also a gift shop and café. Located opposite Christ Church Cathedral on St. Michael's Hill. Open Apr-Sept daily 10am-5pm, and Oct-Mar Mon-Sat 10am-4:30pm. Call 01-679-4611 for details or bookings. Admission €€.

Bed and Board

You will want first to check into your lodging. If you arrive before your room is ready, you can leave your bags anyway and return later to bring them to your room. Dublin boasts hundreds of fine hotels and guest houses; most are very costly. We specially recommend several options. Dublin's three Jurys Inns (www.jurysinns.com) are affordable, convenient, and offer their own pubs and restaurants. And, in the vein of motels or motor inns, they charge by the room and not per person. Breakfast is extra. These are: the Jurys Inn Christchurch (01-454-0000) €€ CC, across from Christ-church Cathedral; and the Jurys Inn Customs House (01-854-1500) €€ CC, facing the quays in the new financial services district, and Jurys Inn Parnell Street (01-878-4900) € CC, just off the top of O'Connell Street. On a more cozy scale and with enhanced character, there is the Harding Hotel (01-679-6500 www.hardinghotel.ie), € CC, Copper Alley, Fishamble Street, once the Main Street of Viking Ireland, across from Christchurch Cathedral. If price is really no consideration, the Shelbourne (01-663-4500 www.marriott.co.uk) €€€ CC, remains the most distinguished address in Dublin, facing the northeast corner of St. Stephen's Green. Built in 1824, this is where the Irish Constitution was signed in 1921 (in room 112 to be exact). On a more contemporary note, another lodging of interest is Number 31 (01-676-5011 www.number31.ie) €€€ CC, in the heart of Georgian Dublin and a brief walk from St. Stephen's Green or the National Museum, at 31 Leeson Close overlooking Fitzwilliam Place.

The restaurant scene in Dublin is vast and ever-changing. The best advice to be given here is simply to point you towards Temple Bar, Dublin's Left Bank, and to suggest that you follow your own nose to what best suits your budget and taste. With eateries of one sort or another lined up like rungs in a fence, your only challenge will be choosing among them and securing a table without an advance reservation. Your best chance is to eat early, before 7pm. Chapter One (01-873-2266) €€€ CC, at 18–19 Parnell Square; L'Ecrivain (01-661-1919) €€€ CC, at 109 Lower Baggot St., Dublin 2; and Patrick Guilbaud (01-676-4192) €€€ CC, at 21 Upper Merrion Street, are three of Dublin's finest; and you will need to ring ahead for reservations. If you wish to plan your Dublin meal well in advance, go to www.rai.ie, Ireland's most complete online index for scouting out restaurants and to www.menupages.ie for consumer opinions and ratings. As you may have some difficulty finding a bargain—ample, wholesome, slow (as opposed to fast) food on a slim budget—we recommend these two: Wagamama Noodle Bar (01-478-2152) € CC, on South King Street opposite the Gaiety Theatre, and Chamelion (01-671-0362) € CC, at No. 1 Fownes Street Lower, Temple Bar, for exceptional Indonesian cuisine.

DAY TWO
The Question — Tour or No Tour?

You've barely arrived in Ireland and already you have a decision to make! This is your first full day in Ireland, and only you can decide whether you want to drive or be driven to the Brú na Bóinne. There are two principal sites on today's itinerary, but of them the Brú na Bóinne (comprising Newgrange and Knowth) is the most crucial. Consequently, if you are willing to miss Loughcrew, which is more of a consideration if the weather is dismal, or rise at dawn and add Loughcrew to tomorrow's sites, you have the option of spending another night in Dublin, waiting another day before fetching your rental car, and booking a one-day tour to the Boyne Valley. We recommend against the mega-coach tours and suggest something on a smaller scale, limited to under 20 persons. Two such tours currently come to mind: the Boyne Valley Tour with www.tourdublin.ie and the Newgrange tour with www.overthetoptours.com. Both €€€.

PRINCIPAL SITES
Brú na Bóinne • Newgrange and Knowth

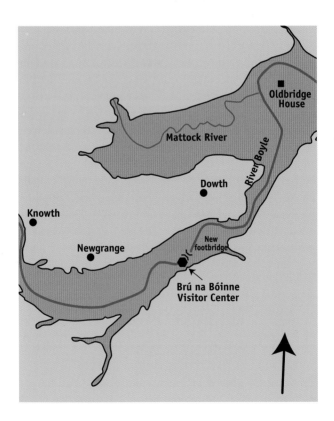

The Boyne Valley five thousand years ago was, much as it is today, given over to the growing of cereal crops and the raising of livestock. Its Neolithic settlers had already cleared extensive forests of oak, hazel, alder, elm, pine, birch, and willow to make way for tilled fields and pasturelands. They must have been skilled and successful farmers to have made space in their communal life for the massive building projects by which they are known today. Without texts or graphic images from their hands, we can know nothing precise about their social structure. On the other hand, when we calculate that it required literally millions of focused "man-hours" to construct the over forty megaliths concentrated within little more than six square miles, we must assume that they were not without leaders of some sort. "Power," explains Hannah Arendt, "corresponds to the human ability not just to act but to act in concert." By such a measure, these were a powerful people.

Rising in Kildare and meandering through Meath towards the sea just beyond Drogheda, the River Boyne—Ptolemy's Bouvinda—seems to pause here, crooking her arm to embrace the Brú na Bóinne on three sides. This is, after all, her legendary home, the Brú or "dwelling" of Bóinne or Boand, the goddess Boyne. Here she had her notorious affair with the sun-god Dagda, the all-providing king of the Tuatha Dé Danann; and in the course of a single day, from sunrise to sunset, both conceived and gave birth to Aengus Óg, the god of youth and beauty, the Irish Adonis. In the course of events, this son of the sun dispossessed his father and claimed the Brú na Bóinne for himself. Many of the legends and sagas of early Ireland are either set or visit here, where Aengus held court. The great passage tomb known today as Newgrange—a name given it in the 12th century when it was added as a "new grange" to the holdings of the Cistercian abbey at Mellifont—was first imagined, then, as a royal dwelling or palace; and only much later was it construed as a place of burial for the kings of Tara. There is, however, one ancient Fenian tale in which the mound-house of Aengus Óg is presented as a place to lay the dead, in this case Diarmuid, the tragically deceased lover of Grainne. Aengus himself brings the body of Diarmuid home to Brú na Bóinne where their conversations may somehow continue.

There was over Ériu a famous king from the Túatha Dé Danand, and Echu Ollathir was his name. Another name for him was the Dagdae, for it was he who performed miracles and saw to the weather and the harvest, and that is why he was called the Good God. Elcmar of Bruig na Boinde had a wife whose name was Eithne, though she was also called Boand. The Dagdae wanted to sleep with Boand, and she would have allowed him, but she feared Elcmar and the extent of his power. The Dagdae sent Elcmar away, then, on a journey to Bress, son of Elatha at Mag nInis; and as Elcmar was leaving, the Dagdae cast great spells upon him, so that he would not return quickly, so that he would not perceive the darkness of night, so that he would feel neither hunger nor thirst. The Dagdae charged Elcmar with great commissions, so that nine months passed like a single day, for Elcmar had said that he would return before nightfall. The Dagdae slept with Elcmar's wife, then, and she bore him a son, who was named Óengus; and by the time of Elcmar's return, she had so recovered that he had no inkling of her having slept with the Dagdae.

The Dagdae took his son to be fostered in the house of Mider at Brí Léith in Tethbae, and Óengus was reared there for nine years. Mider had a playing field at Brí Léith, and three fifties of the young boys of Ériu were there together with three fifties of the young girls. And Óengus was their leader, because of Mider's love for him and because of his handsomeness and the nobility of his people. He was also called the Macc Óc, for his mother had said "Young the son who is conceived at dawn and born before dusk."

— *"The Wooing of Etain"*, Early Irish Myths and Sagas tr. Jeffrey Gantz (Penguin, 1981), pp. 39–40.

The physical evidence from these sites presents a clearer, though more limited, picture of their use. It is clear that the Boyne Valley and its mounds were residences both for the living and for the dead. For example, the archaeological record shows that people lived *on* the hill of Knowth a thousand years before they lay their dead *in* it. And long after the passage graves were built and sealed and grown over with grass, they again became choice plots for royal residences. The dead have long seemed both distant and dangerous to the living; but it was not

Aerial view of Newgrange
Photo: "Dúchas, the Heritage Service", Dublin

always so. Many ancient cultures have conceived the living and dead as if they were merely different generations, all sharing the same world, appropriately sub-divided, vertically or horizontally, into distinct and proximate zones. The mounds, then, at certain times in their history, were much like a Brooklyn townhouse, with one generation living above and another living below. This, in fact, was precisely the solution proposed and accepted for all of Ireland by the legendary Amergain, the island's first poet. It was when the Sons of Míl had defeated in battle the Tuatha Dé Danann, and, at the request of the goddess Ériu or Erin, they gave to the conquered Tuatha all of subterranean Ireland, while the Milesians claimed all that was open to the sun. The Sons of Míl and those who followed them, then, understood the mounds constructed thousands of years before their arrival as *síd* or "otherworld" dwellings; and Newgrange was the dwelling of the sun-god himself, which may shed light, as it were, on a nearly unique feature found in the Brú na Bóinne—the "roof box," which at the time of the winter solstice permits the rising sun to penetrate and illumine the tomb's central chamber. Although many passage tombs are aligned so as to capture the sun's rising or setting at a specific point in the solar year, only one other known passage tomb—Cairn G at Carrowkeel—permits that light to enter its passageway after its entrance has been sealed.

Today, of the over forty visible prehistoric sites in the Boyne complex, including over twenty passage tombs, only two are open to the public—Newgrange and Knowth. The third focal site, Dowth—half the size of Newgrange and possibly aligned to capture the winter solstice sunset—survives in rather mutilated condition. It is interesting but inaccessible. As all visitors are led through the sites of Newgrange and Knowth by skilled and entertaining national guides, who give detailed accounts of what there is to see within and around the tombs, it would be redundant to rehearse that tour here. What is essential to say is that no one even remotely interested in ancient Ireland should think about missing this experience, no matter how long the required wait. If your time here is restricted, limit your tour to Newgrange. The thirty-some steps you will take to its core could be among the most revealing of your life. Consider that you will be travelling at a rate of 150 years per step. Consider too that the builders of these tombs, regardless of personal status, chose to live out their lives in terribly modest dwellings, none of which has survived and, like the human body, none of which was meant to outlive its occupant. Then consider that not only has Newgrange survived for 5,000 years; its roof hasn't even leaked in all that time! It is well worth trying to imagine—and imagine is all we can do—what the builders of Newgrange were thinking as they labored on a house that would endure as long as the sun but would only know its light and warmth for minutes out of every year. For all of the information with which visitors to the Brú na Bóinne are infused, what most take away are questions like these, and wonder.

Access to the Boyne sites is by guided tour only. All visitors to Newgrange and Knowth must report to the Brú na Bóinne Visitor Centre and schedule a tour of one or both sites. A fee is charged for entry to the exhibits in the center, which visitors explore on their own, usually while they are waiting for their tour to begin. The often long wait is also ameliorated by the center's pleasant dining area and substantial bookstore. These sites are in great demand, especially during the summer months, and there are times when tickets sell out early for the entire day. The safest ways to assure timely entry in high season are either to schedule an inclusive bus tour to the Boyne Valley, or, if you're driving, to rise early and arrive when the center first opens.

[M6] Near Slane, Co. Meath. (041/988-0300). Open daily Feb–Apr 9:30am–5:30pm; daily May 9am–6:30pm; daily June to mid-Sept 9am–7pm; daily mid-to-end Sept 9am–6:30pm; daily Oct 9:30am–5:30pm; daily Nov–Jan 9am–5pm. Knowth is closed to visitors Nov–Easter. OPW Heritage Card site. Approximately 18 miles from the Dublin Airport. Ask directions to the M50 south. Take the M50 south to the N2 north towards Slane. Newgrange is sign-posted off the N2.

Loughcrew • Sliabh Na Cailli

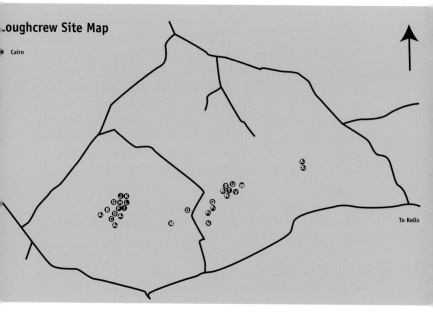

On a brilliant day, or for that matter an average one with a sunny patch now and again, the Louchcrew Hills are glorious. Even without its tomb complex, the limestone ridge rising above the valley below to form *Sliabh Na Cailli,* the "Hills of the Witch," would be well worth a climb, just to revel in the spectacular views it affords of the northern midlands below. It is no wonder that the local farmers of over 5,000 years ago turned to these hills to focus their ritual and communal lives.

The passage tombs of Sliabh Na Caillí provoke the same questions and conjectures as their contemporary mounds in the Boyne Valley. From the outside they are artificial mountains, and from the inside they are artificial caves. After all, the oldest sacred sites known to humankind seem to have been caves and mountains, the most dramatic contours and secrets of the earth's body, the mother's body. We can never know what these mounds meant to their builders, but to their discoverers they are a lasting mystery and wonder.

There are roughly thirty Neolithic tombs strewn across these several hills, the majority of which are to be found on two summits—Carnbane West and Carnbane East. The latter is the highest, rising to just over 900 feet. The modern names of these two hills are from the Irish and mean "white mound," suggesting that at least the more prominent of the Loughcrew cairns, like Newgrange, were once faced with white quartz, for which supporting evidence has in fact been found. Their other name, Sliabh Na Caillí, has a story behind it, the story of a witch or hag who—when promised majesty over all of Ireland if she completed the feat—leapt mightily from one mound to another, spilling giant stones from her apron with each bound, until she fell and broke her neck on the last peak, Patrickstown Hill, whose recent forestation mostly conceals its Neolithic remains. The witch was, as legend goes, buried on the slope of Patrickstown Hill where she took her ill-fated and final spill. These hills are also associated—it will come as no surprise—with Queen Maeve (Medb).

> Determined now her tomb to build,
> Her ample skirt with stones she filled,
> And dropped a heap on Carnmore;
> Then stepped one thousand yards, to Loar,
> And dropped another goodly heap;
> And then with one prodigious leap
> Gained Carnbeg; and on its height
> Displayed the wonders of her might.

> —*Jonathan Swift, early 18c*

From the parking area to which you are directed from R163, you can walk to one or both of the two hills on which the principal mounds are located—Carnbane East and Carnbane West. We strongly urge that you make time for both; but, if you must choose, then climb Carnbane East, for whose principal cairn you will have secured the key. The steps marking the ascent begin at the far corner of the parking lot. If you bear left and look always to the highest point, you will soon see and reach the cairns. The central monument on Carnbane East is known as Cairn T, apparently the central monument of the entire Loughcrew complex, as most of the other tombs face it, while it in turn is oriented towards the rising sun on the fall and spring equinoxes. Like the other tombs here, Cairn T is constructed from local limestone, but its curbstones and decorated stones tend to be of more durable sandstone that arrived here in the form of glacial erratics. As you enter the mound and proceed down its 16-foot passage to its deepest recess, you will see (if you remembered to bring a light) many extraordinary carvings. The Loughcrew mounds contain some of the finest Neolithic art in Ireland, or in Europe for that matter. Passages, lintels, sills, roof stones, corbel edges, orthostats are all to be examined for

Loughcrew art

decorations. In all, 120 carved stones have been discovered at Loughcrew, some of which were carved in situ, while others were clearly carved first and then set into place. Be sure to find the "Witch's Chair," Cairn T's third largest curbstone, located along the northern ring of the mound. This is alternately assigned to Queen Tailtiú, the foster mother of the sun-god Lug, Queen Maeve, of course, and the legendary lawgiver of ancient Ireland, Ollamh Fodhla. More to the present point, local lore considers it a wishing chair; so why not have a seat and dream on? You will also want to explore the five satellite tombs clustered around Cairn T and scan the horizon for some of the other local monuments, including eleven ringforts, three *cashels*, and an array of stone circles, standing stones, cooking sites, holy wells, stone crosses, and ruined castles, all bearing witness to the rich and varied history of this area across thousands of years. And, if you face west, you will see your next destination, Carnbane West.

After descending Carnbane East, and returning to the parking area, walk back down the road as if you were walking to R163. Stop at the third field gate and there, in the field to your right, you will see a standing stone. Climb the gate and cross the field. Over the rise ahead, you will see a high stone wall to your left. Keep it on your left as you climb over the next field gate and proceed up the next hill. You will soon see the mounds of Carnbane West. If this sounds too complicated, just bear left once you enter the field with the standing stone and head for the highest point.

Carnbane West boasts two major cairns. Cairn L is over 130 feet in diameter, with a rather unique pillar stone standing in its center chamber. Only one other tomb, at Carrowkeel, has been found with such a feature. Regrettably, entry to Cairn L is currently prohibited by the farmer in whose field it sits. Cairn L is curious in other ways as well. It has seven recesses off its passage and has four smaller satellite tombs of its own. The roof of Cairn L, you will notice, is concrete, and is not an original feature. Cairn L faces Cairn M to the east, both of which are aligned with the rising sun on the Celtic festivals of Samhain and Imbolc, marking the beginning and ending of winter, respectively. The other major tomb on Carnbane West is Cairn D, the largest of the Loughcrew tombs, with a diameter of 180 feet and eight mounds grouped around it. Cairn D poses a puzzle, however, as it seems to contain no inner passage. Perhaps it was a cenotaph, or else a monument of another sort altogether.

It is interesting to note, while at this height, that there appears to be an interrelationship between the siting and orientation of many of Ireland's passage tombs, mostly concentrated in the north of the island. Some face the rising sun, others the setting sun, at crucial times of the year, while still others face each other, either within a local tomb complex or across many miles, far further than the naked eye can see. Theories, of course, abound regarding the situation and alignment of Ireland's passage tombs and stone circles, but no one truly knows the answer to their riddle.

[K6] Near Oldcastle, Co. Meath. Open site. From Newgrange proceed to Slane where you pick up R163 and take it roughly 30 miles through Kells towards Oldcastle.

Loughcrew is signposted on your right from R163. Since you will need a key to enter the principal tomb, however, proceed past Loughcrew to Loughcrew Gardens on your left, open daily noon–6pm Mar 17–Sept, and weekends 1–4pm the remainder of the year. You will be required to leave a refundable deposit and your passport or driver's license for the use of the key. After fetching the key, retrace your path to the signposted turnoff for the Loughcrew passage tombs. Note that in recent years OPW guides have been on hand at the site during the summer months, offering tours of Cairn T for which no key or admission fee is required.

Side Sites

The Hill of Tara

Tara is a site wrapped in mystique, and yet its present wonder lies largely in the eye of the beholder. The more you've read about Tara and the more vivid your imagination, the more you will see and appreciate here. Lug, greatest of the old gods; Maeve without equal; Tea, queen-goddess of the Milesians; Conaire Mór and Cormac mac Airt, two of the most revered of ancient kings—all these and more called Tara theirs. The more is learned of Tara—archaeologists continue to probe its secrets—the more vivid is its legacy. The hill itself is an open site. Tours, interpretive center, and video available May 26–Sept 14 daily 9am–6pm. OPW Heritage Card site. (046-902-5903) [M7]. Signposted off the N3 10 miles south of Navan, Co. Meath.

Battle of the Boyne

Practically a stone's throw—provided Cúchulainn is throwing the stone—from Newgrange is the site of perhaps the most decisive battle in Irish history, fought on July 1, 1690, in which King William III ("King Billy") defeated his father-in-law King James II, securing British Protestant sovereignty over Ireland for another 231 years. Today you can tour the battlefield and envision its unfolding. Free admission. Access by guided tour only, upon request. Wear weather protective clothing and suitable shoes. Open Mar–Apr daily 9:30am–5:30pm; May–Sept daily 10am–6pm; Oct–Feb daily 9am–5pm. (041-980-9950). [M6] West of Drogheda off the M1 Motorway and L21, on the South Bank of the River Boyne two miles north of Donore Village, Co. Meath.

Kid Sites

Trim Castle

Also called King John's castle, this is easily the most prominent and massive Anglo-Norman castle in Ireland. Today it is more widely known as the set of the film Braveheart. Kids love castles, but for that matter so does nearly everyone else. The sheer scale of this symbol of Norman clout brings a dark thrill to the heart, even the not-so-brave heart. Recently restored as a "preserved ruin," throughout its history Trim was besieged only once and never taken. Instead, it collapsed from neglect and its own weight over 400 years after its erection. There's a lesson there somewhere. Open Easter–Sept daily 10am–6pm; Oct daily 9:30am–5:30pm; Nov–Jan weekends 9am–5pm; Feb–Easter weekends 9:30am–5:30pm. OPW Heritage Card site. (046-943-8619). [L7] In the town of Trim on the River Boyne, 9 miles southwest of Navan on R161.

Newgrange Farm

Literally surrounding the land preserved for the Newgrange passage tomb, this 333-acre farm has its own avid following and, on a good day, rivals Newgrange in numbers of visitors. A few of the many touted denizens whom guests are invited to visit and/or feed here are: sheep, goats, horse and pony, pheasants, rabbits, dogs, cats, and ants! The enthusiasm and love of animals and children of the extended family farm are contagious. Less than captivated, though captive, parents will enjoy the very pleasant coffee shop. Open Easter Saturday through August daily 10am–5pm. Admission €€ (041-982-4119) www.newgrange farm.com. [M6] Near Slane, Co. Meath. Signposted off the N51 3 miles southeast from Slane.

Bed and Board

We specially recommend four accommodations in Co. Meath, all relatively close to one or other featured site: The Glebe House, Dowth, Co. Meath (041-983-6101) €€ CC, situated on seven acres, is immediately adjacent to the Dowth passage tomb. This gracious country house, with its several lovely rose and lavender gardens, provides comfort and a touch of elegance. Guests may bring their own wine to enjoy in the lounge/drawing room. Afternoon tea is available on request. From the N51 east of Slane follow signs to Newgrange Farm until you come to a sign for Dowth, at which point you bear left towards Dowth, while the road to Newgrange Farm continues right. The Glebe House will be on the right off the Dowth Road. In the same vicinity, this time immediately overlooking Newgrange, there's Rough-grange Farmhouse, Donore, Co. Meath (041-982-3147) €. The views of Newgrange and the River Boyne from here are breathtaking. In fact, if you come equipped, a room here comes with free salmon and trout fishing on the Boyne. This is a working 250-acre farm, and the oldest part of the farmhouse dates from the mid-18th century. On the L21 (the local road to Newgrange off of the N2), you'll see the sign to Roughgrange Farmhouse, Donore, Co. Meath (041-982-3147, see www.irishfarmholidays.com) € on your right just before you come to the entrance to Brú na Bóinne on your left. Next, just outside of nearby Navan, in Ballymagarvey Village, there's the welcome calm and hospitality of Daly's B&B, Kentstown Road, Moonetown, Navan, Co. Meath (046-902 3219 www.dalysbandb.com) € CC. The guest rooms are warm and comfortable, and enjoy panoramic views of the surrounding countryside. Located on the R153 2mi south of Navan on your right. Finally, we recommend Highfield House, Trim, Co. Meath (046-943-6386) €€ CC. This elegant 18th-century period residence stands above Trim Castle and the River Boyne, with great views of both, and is only minutes by foot from Trim town and the Trim Castle Hotel. In the center of Trim, at the roundabout, turn right off of Castle Street onto R160 and take the first left onto Maudlins Road.

With the exception of Highfield House, the above accommodations offer no evening meals, either within their walls or within a short walk; so you will be on your own to find agreeable fare. This will not prove difficult. If you're willing to drive six miles north of Slane to Collon, the Forge Gallery Restaurant, Collon, Co. Louth (041-982-6272) €€ CC is highly touted and moderately expensive. At the other end of the spectrum, in Donore center, just down the road from Newgrange, there's pub grub locally recommended at Daly's. Otherwise, the most convenient and promising venue for suitable cuisine is Navan, where we personally recommend two eateries. Once you've parked in the center of Navan, a brief stroll will easily uncover both of them. Hudson's Bistro, 30 Railway Street (046-907-5230) €€ CC, is a finer restaurant than you would expect to find in this somewhat sleepy town and has a reputation reaching beyond the locals. The Loft, 26 Trimgate Street (046-907-1755) €€ CC is more laid back and, along with full dinners, offers a selection of lighter and less pretentious fare, such as burgers, chicken fajitas, and excellent gourmet pizzas.

Day Three
On the Road

Today is your first day of serious driving, a day that will put to a modest test your Irish highway skills and stamina. Leaving from somewhere in County Meath, let's say Navan, you have roughly 110 miles ahead before reaching Sligo, the day's general destination. We recommend that you take the N51 meeting the N52 from Navan to Mullingar and from Mullingar the N4 all the way northwest to Sligo. You will come to the first principal site of the day on the outskirts of Sligo before actually reaching the town. En route, if you need or prefer to break up the drive, we recommend two diversions. The first is the Lough Key Forest Park, 2 miles east of Boyle, Co. Roscommon, signposted off the N4. Modest admission fee €€ per car. This is a lovely place to stretch your legs and let the kids run loose. Spanning 840 acres, this is one of Ireland's premier lakeside parks and offers a number of attractions, such as Ireland's only tree canopy walk. A couple of miles further down the N4, you'll see the turn-off for the town of Boyle. If you follow signs to Boyle you'll soon come to Boyle Abbey, an OPW Heritage Card site, at the edge of the town. Founded in the 12th century, this was one of the earliest Cistercian monasteries in Ireland and even as a ruin retains a grandeur and serenity that may be just what you crave after several hours on the road.

County Sligo

County Sligo is one of Ireland's sleepers. It is off the most heavily trodden tourist routes and yet has everything to offer, especially for those under the spell of Ireland's earliest peoples, their monuments, and their stories. Sligo possesses roughly 40 percent of all of Ireland's known passage tombs and is simply strewn with ruins and remnants, from cairns to crannogs to castles. Our focus here, however, is on Neolithic sites and, at the outset, on passage tombs, which find their greatest concentration at Carrowkeel.

A detail of Boyle Abbey

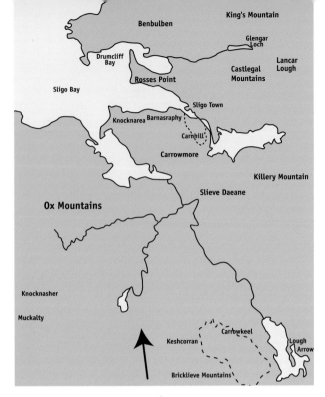

PRINCIPAL SITES
Carrowkeel • Ceathru Caol

The first impression made by Carrowkeel is the drop-dead spectacular vantage it provides on nearly the entire expanse of County Sligo. Poised atop the northern and highest extremity of the Bricklieve Mountains—in Irish, *Breac Shliabh,* "The Specked Mountains"—the Carrowkeel site affords vistas you will want to engrave in your memory for those times when the world closes in and seems almost walled. On every side are stunning summits and storied sites. Nearest at hand, to the immediate west, there is Keshcorran, perhaps an original part of the same Neolithic complex. On its peak is a massive cairn called the "Principle," and six others lie nearby. Further west is Knocknashee, with its two cairns and what is thought to have been a Neolithic village at its summit. Visible further to the southwest are the Ox Mountains and, on the clearest of days, Croagh Patrick in County Mayo. To the north and northwest rise Knocknarea with the Slieve League in Co. Donegal behind it, Ben Bulben, and Slieve Daene. To the east find Seelewey, a cairn standing on the highest point of the Plain of Moytirra, the "Plain of the Pillars," the site of the mother of all battles in Irish mythology, fought between the Tuatha Dé Danann and the Fomorians.

From a 17th century copy of a much older text describing the last day of the Battle of Moytirra:

> As they hacked at each other their fingertips and their feet almost met, and because of the slipperiness of the blood under the warriors' feet, they kept falling down, and their heads were cut off as they sat. A gory, wound-inflicting, sharp, bloody battle was upheaved, and spearshafts were reddened in the hands of foes.

> —*Gray edition, Harleian Manuscript 5280.*

North of Lough Arrow stands the Heapstown, i.e. "Heap of Stone," the largest cairn in Ireland outside of the Boyne Valley. This is said to be the burial cairn of Ailill, king of Connacht and husband of Maeve, reputed to lie or stand within the cairn atop Knocknarea. Finally, far to the east it is thought that Loughcrew may once have been visible from this spot; for if a great block of white quartz found toppled there were set upright on the northwest tip of Carnbane West, near where it was found, it would catch the setting sun and beacon it here on a brilliant day to Carrowkeel.

Although nearby Keshcorran holds its fascinations, such as the line of limestone caves said to be the birthplace of Cormac mac Cairt, and was a favorite haunt of Fionn and his band, it is today more difficult to access and lies outside our current focus.

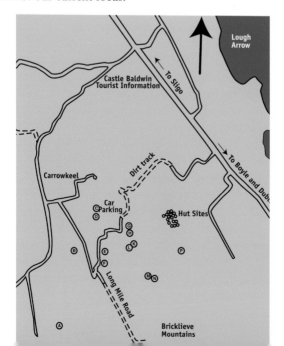

The Carrowkeel monuments date from 3800–3300 B.C.E. and so predate those of Loughcrew and the Boyne Valley. These include fourteen known passage tombs and the impressive remnants of what appears to have been the largest known Stone Age village in Ireland. The passage tombs were originally excavated in 1911 in a remarkably careless and hasty manner and some appear today as little more than massive heaps of stones. There are, however, a handful of remarkable tombs and together the entire complex has an almost haunting allure and power over those who linger here. From the votive offerings and fire circles often left here, it seems that some of its visitors linger a good while.

Using the so-called parking lot as a locator and following the map provided, you will be able to locate specific cairns. Be sure, however, to explore the full site freely, finding your own way over its slopes and exploring its treasures as you come upon them. There are probably only several cairns that need to be noted specially here. Cairn F, the largest in the complex and possibly the focal cairn, had five compartments in its chamber—two on each side and one at the end recess. It once had a rare 5-ft standing or pillar stone in its chamber as well. Only one other such stone has been found *in situ*—in Cairn L at Loughcrew, though an early antiquarian record describes there once having been a pillar stone in Newgrange's chamber. Regrettably, Cairn F's 4-ton capstone has come down through the roof of the tomb, which now lies in a heap. Of special note is the "roof box" on Cairn G, just up from the "parking lot." Newgrange is the only other tomb with such a feature, allowing the sun's rays to penetrate the passage and chamber when the portal is sealed; and the relationship between these two disparate tombs doesn't stop there. Whereas Newgrange is aligned with the winter solstice sunrise, Carrowkeel's Cairn G is aligned with its 180° opposite, the summer solstice sunset. Intriguingly, along with finds rather typical of passage tombs—beads, pendants, pottery fragments, etc.—children's bones were found within, under a roofing slab. Another cairn of special note is K, situated on the highest part of the northern extremity of the Bricklieves. It is the most intact of the Carrowkeel cairns, measuring 69 ft in diameter, with a 23-ft passage (segmented by four sills) to its cruciform chamber, over which arches a 13-ft corbelled roof. You will surely need your flashlight to explore its depths.

Finally, there is the Neolithic village, which you can view if you make your way east from Cairn K or G to the edge of the escarpment. There on a flat plateau you will see circular rings of stone, all that is left of a hundred or more huts, measuring from 23 to 49 ft in diameter. Similar Neolithic settlement sites have been found near Tobercurry, Co. Sligo and on Turlough Mountain in the Burren, Co. Clare.

As you make your way back to your car and survey the landscape once again, you may want to try to picture the land as it was when these tombs were under construction and in use. The once vast forests of elm, hazel, and oak had been diminished, partly through clearance and partly due to disease. Wheat and barley were sown in modest fields whose soil was still rich. Much more of the land was given over to grazing than to cereal production. The blanket bog was yet to form and overtake these hills. The same aquatic fossils in evidence today no doubt fascinated the farmers of the Neolithic as much as they do postmodern tourists, for they are the legacy of 340 million years ago when much of Ireland lay beneath a tropical sea. The more recent giant erratic boulders, often left in precarious and dramatic poses by the receding glaciers of the last Ice Age, break our stride and demand a gaze much as they have since first encountered nearly 10,000 years ago. Time is all a matter of perspective and one sees it differently here than one does on the evening news.

[G5] Near Ballymote, Co. Sligo. Open site. Signposted from the N4 as you approach Sligo from the east. Within a "traffic calming" area and just prior to an Esso petrol station, turn left on the Ballymote road. Follow signs marked either "Carrowkeel" or "Passage Tombs." Note that the road will become progressively more narrow, so that you will begin to suspect it is intended only for one-way traffic. No such luck. Eventually you will come to a sheep gate, which you will open and close after you. Ahead is an obvious though unmarked parking area, not the parking lot indicated on the map above, which we do not recommend your using. This is because the road up to the "car park" is narrow, rocky, uneven, and truly slippery when wet. You are not likely to put anything other than your car (tires and axles, for a start) at risk by driving further; but remember that your insurance will not cover any damage done on unpaved surfaces, and this road defines "unpaved." We advise you leave your car and make the trek on foot from here.

Carrowmore Megalithic Cemetery

The cemetery at Carrowmore, together with those at Brú na Bóinn, Loughcrew, and Carrowkeel, represents one of the major concentrations of megalithic monuments in Europe. Its extensive excavation and scrutiny over several decades by a team of Swedish archaeologists led by Göran Burenhult has raised many questions and generated new and controversial theories. The traditional theory held that the megalithic tradition in Ireland could be traced ultimately to the ancient East Mediterranean, where settled agriculturalist communities first formed and prospered. By this account, the megalithic tradition  gloriously manifested in the pyramids of Egypt and in the ziggurats of ancient Iraq spread north and west across Continental Europe to Brittany and from there to England, Wales, and eventually the east coast of Ireland. Within Ireland, the monuments of the Boyne Valley then would have represented the first and finest flowering of the Irish megalithic tradition, which diminished in skill and grandeur as it moved west from Newgrange to Loughcrew to Carrowkeel to Carrowmore. Later and more precise dating of these sites, however, has turned this earlier account on its head, more than once. For one thing, the Irish monuments have proven much older, by millennia, than those of the ancient Middle East; and some sites on the west coast of Ireland have been shown to predate those of the Boyne Valley by as much as a thousand years. What this means is that the movement of the Irish megalithic tradition quite possibly traced a path from west to east, rather than the reverse, indicating that the scale and sophistication of the builders grew rather than diminished across the 5th and 4th millennia B.C.E.

Recent excavation of a megalithic tomb atop Croaghaun in the nearby Ox Mountains has produced a probable construction date of 5600 B.C.E., more than five hundred years earlier than any of the Carrowmore monuments, which seem to range from 5000–3000 B.C.E., with the greatest activity between 4300 and 3500 B.C.E. What these very early dates question is not only the temporal primacy of the Boyne Valley sites, but more problematically the all-but-dogmatic assumption that the deepest roots of the megalithic movement can be traced no further than to the settled agricultural communities of the middle Neolithic period (3600–3100 B.C.E.) Dates from the early and mid-5th millennium, however, suggest that late Mesolithic and early Neolithic hunting and gathering communities were responsible for the earliest Irish megaliths. Unlike the bands of primitive Mesolithic hunters and gatherers of interior Ireland, who left nearly no trace across the island, this would have been a populous and complex society fishing offshore waters and local streams, gathering oysters and mussels, and hunting seals and other mammals in which the coast and coastal hills abounded. The study of nearby kitchen middens at Culleenamore, dating from the late Mesolithic, would seem to support such a theory.

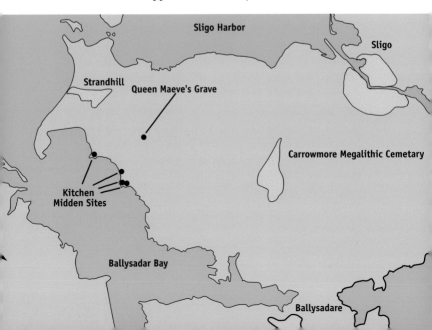

Although an 1837 survey of the Knocknarea Peninsula listed 68 megalithic sites, only 45 are to be found today, 30 at Carrowmore itself and 15 in the surrounding area. It is estimated that the original number of monuments may have numbered over 200. All of the remaining tombs and stone circles are constructed of the same crude glacial boulders dislodged from surrounding mountains and strewn across the peninsula by the receding glaciers of the last Ice Age. The Carrowmore site itself, measuring roughly 1,100 by 650 yds, is a neither random nor rigidly designed ritual landscape. The apparently focal site, Tomb 51, occupies the prime location; and the majority of the surrounding tombs more or less face it. Given that many of these tombs predate Tomb 51, the absence of uniform alignment is not surprising. The construction and design of the Carrowmore tombs is distinct from those of the other major passage tomb sites. None have the same type of passage found elsewhere, and only one shows any sign of having had a cairn.

You can either explore the Carrowmore cemetery on your own or take advantage of the free one-hour tour of the site. We strongly recommend the latter. Afterwards, then, you can do your own exploring, oriented and informed by what you've learned. Since this is a site that comes with an excellent on-site tour, we will not attempt to guide you remotely from the page, except to point you to the central tomb, #51, which occupies the high ground and the only spot in the cemetery from which Sligo Harbour to the north and Ballysadare Bay to the south are visible. Partially restored and currently undergoing further scrutiny and restoration, this is Carrowmore's "best in show," and is the only Carrowmore tomb on which decoration has been discovered. Finally, before leaving the site, be sure to cross the road directly in front of the interpretive center and explore the several striking monuments to be found in the farm fields before you. The staff in the Carrowmore center will direct you, if necessary; and it's wise to check with them regarding the possible presence of a bull in one or other of the fields.

[H5] Near Sligo, Co. Sligo (071-61534). OPW Heritage card site. Open daily Apr 21–Oct 12 10am–6pm. 2.5 miles from Sligo Town center, signposted off R292, and also signposted 5.5 miles east of Sligo Town off the N4.

> The dead are not far from us...they cling in some
> strange way to what is most still and deep within us.
>
> —*W.B. Yeats*

Side Sites

You'll be in the area for two days, and the things to see and
do in and around Sligo could easily keep you busy and
happy for much longer. We'll mention only a few.

Sligo Abbey

Once the burial place of the kings and princes of Sligo,
Sligo Abbey is a quite striking Dominican establishment
which flourished from the 13th century throughout the
Middle Ages until, after being raided, sacked, and
burned, it closed its doors in 1641. The beneficiary of
considerable restoration in recent years, the abbey is a
splendid ruin, whose most notable features are its well-
preserved cloisters, intact medieval altar, and many fine
carvings. Open Apr 21–mid-Oct daily 10am–6pm; mid-
Oct–Nov 2 weekends 9:30am–4:30pm. OPW Heritage
Card site. (071-914-6406). [G5] Abbey Street, Sligo.

Drumcliffe Churchyard

If you have a soft or devoted spot in your heart for Yeats,
then this is a magnet whose tug you will find hard to
resist—the grave of the man himself, with its famous
epitaph. Otherwise you may cast a cold eye and pass by.
[G5] Open site. Signposted on the N15, 5.5 miles north
of Sligo. The carpark and site will be on your right. Yeats
devotees may also want to visit the Yeats Memorial
Building in the center of Sligo, as well as Lissadell House,
a favorite spot for Yeats, where he occasionally dropped
anchor. Signposted off the N15 8 miles north of Sligo.

Seaweed Baths

Here's something new and different for you to try. Actually
it's an old tradition here in Sligo, dating from Victorian
times. For whatever ails you or just so you can talk
about it later, take an unforgettable soak and massage
at the Voya Seaweed Baths and Spa (071-916-8686

Kid Sites

Parkes Castle

This is a masterfully restored Plantation castle dating from the early 17th century. In our experience kids can't get enough of castles, and this is a fine one, nicely situated on the shores of Lough Gill in nearby County Leitrim. Open Mid-Mar–Oct daily 10am–6pm. OPW Heritage card site. (071-64149). [H5] On the Sligo-Dromahair Road (R286) 7 miles from Sligo Town.

Lough Gill Cruises

While you're in Yeats Country, why not take a cruise on the Lough and the Garavough River aboard the *Wild Rose*, while listening to the poetry of the master? Call 071-916-4266 for details and bookings.

Bundoran

If the kids are rebelling and need to put everything ancient behind them for a few hours, there's always Bundoran, the Irish Coney Island, 23 miles north of Sligo on the N15. There are beaches and plenty of amusements that will light up small eyes.

Parkes Castle

www.celticseaweedbaths.com), open Mon–Tues noon–8pm; Wed–Fri 11am–8pm and Sat–Sun 10am–8pm. Call ahead to book a tub. Located on the seafront at Strandhill, just outside of Sligo center. Signposted for miles from just about every possible approach.

Theater

Sligo has an active theater scene; so you may want to take in a play while you're here. The two principle local venues are the Hawk's Well Theatre, Temple Street (071-916-1518 www.hawkswell.com), and the award-winning Blue Raincoat Theatre Company (071-917-0431 www.blue raincoat.com), located at the Factory in the heart of Sligo.

Bed and Board

You simply can't go wrong with any of the accommodations we recommend in the Sligo area. At the very top of our list is Temple House, Ballymote, Co. Sligo (071-918-3329 www.templehouse.ie), €€€ CC, surely one of the most unique, memorable places to spend a night anywhere in Ireland, or anywhere else for that matter. This 1,000-acre estate and Georgian mansion overlooking the ruins of a 13th-century lakeside castle of the Knights Templar offers an exquisite blend of grandeur, elegance, and warmth that inflicts upon its guests a painful ache to move in and never leave. If you stay here, be sure to reserve a place for dinner. You'll kick yourself if you don't. Signposted from Ballymote and on the N17, 15 miles south of Sligo. Another stately lodging on the outskirts of Sligo is Markree Castle, Collooney, Co. Sligo (071-67800 www.markreecastle.ie) €€€ CC. This is County Sligo's oldest inhabited castle. If, as they say, approach is everything, the castle's mile-long driveway gives guests a sense of what they're in for. The choice between this and Temple House is a bit like the choice between a stiff polished boot and an old handcrafted shoe; and you will pay a lot more for the polish. The castle offers horseback riding, falconry, and salmon fishing. Signposted eight miles south of Sligo off the N4 at Collooney. A third luxuriant splurge is Coopershill Country House Hotel (071-916-5081 www.coopershill.com) €€€ CC, a stunning 18th-century private estate set in 500 acres of ancient woods and deer pastures. Guests and visitors may reserve a seating for dinner or afternoon tea. The board at Coopershill is as elegant as the bed, and both will take a generous bite out of your budget. Located in Riverstown, Co. Sligo, off the N4. As you approach Sligo, five miles after Castlebaldwin, at the Drumfin crossroads, turn right towards Riverstown and after 2.75 miles turn left into the Coopershill driveway. Last of the great local houses, but hardly a disappointment, is Ardtarmon House, Balinfull, Co. Sligo (071-916-3156, www.ardtarmon.com) €€€ CC. Set in a pristine and truly breathtaking landscape of sea and mountains, which you'll realize fully only when you walk behind the house to the private beach, Ardtarmon House is a working farm in the same family now since 1852. The large bedrooms are the essence of clean, simple, tasteful comfort. Located 11 miles outside Sligo Town. Take the N15 south to Drumcliffe where on the left you will pick up the road to Raghley and Lissadel House. Follow signs to Raghley. Ardtarmon House is on the left before you reach Raghley Harbour. In Sligo town center you can find affordable, spacious contemporary suites, with fully equipped kitchens, on the banks of the Garavogue River at the Riverside Suites Hotel (071-914-8080 www.riversidesuiteshotelsligo.com) €€ CC. Riverside location on JFK Parade Street.

All of the above lodgings serve dinner; so we will be sparing and select in our suggestions for additional local eateries. The most elegant restaurant in the area, along with the dining room of Markree Castle, is Cromleach Lodge, 20 miles south of Sligo Town in Ballindoon, near Castlebaldwin, Co. Sligo (071-916-5155) €€€ CC, while Glebe House, on Coolaney Road in Collooney, Co. Sligo (071-916-7787) €€ CC, offers highly acclaimed fare at a more modest cost. Another excellent choice, especially for fresh seafood, is Eithna's Seafood Restaurant in the more-than-scenic Mullaghmore Harbour (071-916-6407) €€ CC.

DAY FOUR
Staying Put

Today you'll be spending another day in the Sligo area and deciding for yourself the selection and sequence of sites to be explored. The only journey of any length would be to Céide Fields in County Mayo, about 55 miles from Sligo Town, which you may or may not wish to undertake.

PRINCIPAL SITES
Knocknarea • Maeve's Cairn (Miosgán Meadhbha)

By now you will have been staring up at this daunting sight from many vantage points for nearly a day, and the question is almost bound to arise—How do I get up there? Whether you *want* to get up there is another question. It is not a matter of what you will see up there, but rather what you will see *from* up there. The 360° views are, as you would imagine, spectacular, well worth the effort of the climb. First a word about the cairn and then a word about how best to reach it.

Carrowmore, showing Knocknarea in the distance

Approximately 35 ft high and 200 ft in diameter, Knocknarea is the largest monument in the region and is comparable in scale and age with the monuments of the Boyne Valley, dating from the final and culminating stage of the Irish megalithic tradition. What is incomparable, of course, is its location. It comes as no surprise that folklore awards this resting place to Maeve, and some say that she was interred in a standing position, more in keeping with the warrior than the love goddess in her. What is most tantalizing about *Miosgán Meadhbha*, however, is the fact that it has never been excavated nor even violated, it seems, since it was sealed over 5,000 years ago with an estimated 40,000 tons of stone, a weight that grows with each visitor. Tradition calls for each climber to the cairn to bring and add a stone to the great heap. Sharing the summit are a number of smaller monuments, including three cairns. Roughly 325 yds northeast of the great cairn you will find traces of five circular or oval hut sites, three of which have been excavated, revealing household items dating from 3300–2700 B.C.E. It is conjectured that this was a seasonal base camp for hunters and/or a hut occupied during the construction of Maeve's cairn.

Knocknarea monument

The wind has bundled up the clouds high
over Knocknarea
And thrown the thunder on the stones for all
That Maeve can say.

—*W.B. Yeats*

[G5] Open site. Begin your climb from the parking lot of the Cairn Hill Forest Park. Taking your bearings from the N4 in the direction of Sligo, take R292 Strandhill exit and proceed on R292 to a roundabout with a church ahead at 12 o'clock. Take the "12 o'clock" spoke of the roundabout and at the next crossroads take a left at the sign for "Scenic View" and "Primrose Grange House." At the first lane beyond the Grange House turn right and proceed to parking lot. The ascent will take between 45 and 60 minutes on a dry day. We would have second or third thoughts about the climb on a wet day.

Céide Fields

The trip to Céide Fields, which—if you take your time—will involve a 90-minute drive each way, affords a change of scenery and a glimpse of rural northwestern Mayo. You could even make a full day of it and drive south from Céide Fields to Achill Island.

The drama of Céide Fields does not strike you between the eyes at first sight, which is why you really must take advantage of the free and most informative guided tour on offer at regular intervals throughout the day. Otherwise, to the untrained eye, what appears before you is a stretch of blanket bog not unlike that which covers hundreds of square miles of northwestern County Mayo. And so it seemed to all until recent excavation uncovered here the oldest enclosed, that is walled, landscape in Europe. Remember, the Neolithic is all about walls, about designing, managing, claiming, taming. The Neolithic farmers who settled here over 5,000 years ago had a vision. They looked out over forest lands and saw, instead, fields, neatly laid out and walled, divided into pastures for grazing and tillage for wheat and barley. They saw too their own future homes and walled gardens scattered across a pleasingly patchworked agricultural landscape. Realizing their vision, of course, meant toil, the staggering toil of clearing well over 4 square miles of forest with stone axes and setting into place over 250,000 tons of rock to create miles upon miles of rectangular field walls.

Then came the bog. Some say these early farmers caused it, others that they played a part in its growth, others that it was inevitable. Regardless, there was no stopping the bog growth, slower but every bit as destructive as a shower of volcanic ash. Bog, over 90 percent water, creates a closed ecosystem suitable for mosses, heathers, purple moor grass, a range of bog plants and little else. Forget forever barley and wheat. And so, well before the first stone in the first Egyptian pyramid was set into place, this enterprise was abandoned to the bog, now up to 13 ft deep in some spots, which is one reason why unguided bog-walking is not an inspired idea.

The audio visual presentation and exhibits on offer in the interpretive center will enhance your understanding and appreciation of Neolithic farm life; and be sure, while you're at it, to appreciate the remarkable building that houses all this. The interpretive center has been widely and rightly touted as an exemplary work of modern Irish environmentally sensitive architecture. Be sure too to explore the cliffs, visually explore that is, across from the center. They are composed of hundreds of stratified horizontal layers of shale, sandstone, and limestone. Then, on your right to the east you'll see Downpatrick Head and Dun Briste seastack, and as far as you're likely to see in the same direction Ben Bulben. The view was much the same for the farmers at the end of a day in Céide Fields.

[D5] Near Ballycastle, Co. Mayo (096-43325) Open daily mid-Mar–May and Oct–Nov 10am–5pm, Jun–Sept 10am–6pm. OPW Heritage Card site. Roughly 60 miles from Sligo Town center. Take the N59 from Sligo to Ballina, and R514 from Ballina through Ballycastle to Céide Fields.

Creevykeel Court Cairn

You may think this is a long way to drive for a court cairn, and it is; so measure your interest and decide for yourself. As it is in the same direction and along the same road as Drumcliffe and Bundoran, you may want to combine trips to one or more of these.

Top: Céide Fields; bottom: blanket bog

Excavated in 1935, Creevykeel is a splendid example of the court cairn, the monument type widely considered to be the earliest form of megalithic construction in Ireland. The footprint of the tomb is trapezoidal, with a U-shaped open court measuring roughly 50 by 30 ft. The central gallery is segmented by portals and sills into two distinct chambers. The wedge-shaped cairn that would have originally covered the tomb must have extended roughly 230 ft in length. [G4] Signposted on the N15, roughly 15 miles north of Sligo.

Creevykeel

Side Site

Inishmurray

Another outpost of "white martyrdom," Inishmurray is a 6th-century walled Irish monastery founded by St. Molaise. Roughly one mile long and lying four miles off the Sligo coast in the open Atlantic, Inishmurray is surely one of the most unique and exciting sites of the early Christian period. The monastic enclosure measures 175 by 135 ft and its walls at their highest reach 13 ft. The monastery's walls resemble those of an Iron Age *cashel* and may have predated the monastic settlement. Within the outer enclosure, there are four distinct inner enclosures. Today, four stone churches and a beehive hut known as the "school-house" survive, together with a number of stone slabs or altars, pillar stones, and cross-slabs. Of the four churches, the largest—Teampall na bhFear or "the Church of the Men"—stands in the center of the monastic cloister. Dedicated to the monastery's founder, Teampall na bhFear is also known as Teampall Molaise. The dramatic isolation of the site is stunning. In all of the extant annals of Ireland, there is only one mention of this island that time forgot, noting tersely that: "A.D. 802. Inish Muiredach (Inishmurray) was burned by the foreigners, when they attacked Ros Commain." (*Annals of the Four Masters*)

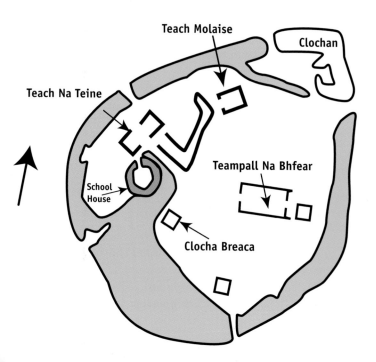

A sea-journey to Inishmurray is quite an adventure and is to be undertaken only when the seas are calm, which is the only time your boat captain will take you anyway. If you think you want to plough the waves to Inishmurray, you should be in touch with Joe McGowan (087-667-4542 www.sligoheritage.com), your captain and guide, at least several weeks in advance of your visit to reserve a spot and then get back in touch with him as the scheduled day of your expedition approaches to check on the prognosis for good weather. Like Skellig Michael, Inishmurray is not "open for business" every day at 9am. Like a pilgrim, you must await calm seas on your knees and hope for the best. The cost of the trip varies according to the number of passengers.

Kid Sites
Same as Day Three.

Bed and Board
Same as Day Three.

DAY FIVE
On the Road Again

After a day's respite from the road, or at least the long road, it's time to press the pedal again. The drive from Sligo to Ballyvaughahn, Co. Clare [E8], the northern gateway to the Burren, is roughly 110 miles. To avoid central Galway Town, you would take the N17 south and west from Sligo to the N18 south to bypass Galway. Continue on the N18 until you come to the N67 to Ballyvaughan. Allowing for traffic and short breaks, you should be able to make the journey in three hours or less.

PRINCIPAL SITE
Burren National Park

The precise extent of the Burren is a matter of opinion. A line drawn from Galway Bay to the north to Kilnaboy in the south and then northwest through Kilfenora and Lisdoonvarna to the Atlantic coast would serve as a rough, generally acceptable border. Some, however, would argue that it reaches from Gort in the east clear out to the Aran Islands in the west; for, after all, they were once connected to the mainland at this point. The Burren National Park, still in development, encompasses something like two-thirds of the about 150 square miles comprising the Burren. Its aim is to balance access to this national treasure with its preservation. The achievement of such a balance has proven a steep and some would say unattainable, challenge.

The Burren—from the Irish *bhoireann*, meaning "a stony place"—is indeed both spectacular and fragile. Once, 340 million years ago, this entire plateau was the floor of a vast carboniferous sea; and, in fact, the sea now reclaims it at a rate of one centimeter every two hundred years. This is obviously not its greatest threat. Instead, it is the fact that visitors tread underfoot, in increasing numbers, the very wonder they've come to see. The barren, fissured, limestone pavement, that covers the Burren and gives it its uniquely beautiful and bizarre lunar surface is host to a dazzling array of wildflowers whose origins reach from the Mediterranean Sea to the Arctic Circle, as well as to a fascinating list of local denizens, including pine martens, kestrels, slow worms (a snake-like lizard), otters, woodmice, and many more. Just as fragile as the ecosystem, however, are the practically innumerable and unprotected archaeological treasures strewn across this haunting and haunted landscape, silent fossils of continuous human habitation in this "stony place" for the past 6,000 years. In short, geologists, botanists, archaeologists, historians, spelunkers, hikers, and unspecialized sightseers all converge on this sparsely populated area with diverse agenda yet equal enthusiasm.

The Burren would have looked quite different to its first inhabitants than it appears to us today or, for that matter, to its medieval population. Six to eight thousand years ago the Burren was lightly forested with pine, hazel, elm, and some oak, with some open scrub and grasslands. When the Burren first felt the weight of the human foot is, however, uncertain. It is estimated that in the Irish Mesolithic, this entire area would not have been able to support more than one or two small communities of hunters and gatherers, numbering in all no more than two dozen persons. It was the Neolithic farmers who found a permanent and fruitful home here sometime in the late 5th millennium B.C.E. and placed on the limestone palate of the Burren its first stone monuments to profound human wonder, loss, and hope. These were the wedge and portal tombs, followed across the centuries and millennia by field walls, cairns, hill forts, ancient churches, round towers, high crosses, monasteries, and holy wells. Prehistory and history written in stone.

> Stony seaboard, far and foreign,
> Stony hills poured over space,
> Stony outcrop of the Burren,
> Stones in every fertile place,
> Little fields with boulders dotted,
> Grey-stone shoulders saffron-spotted
> Stone-walled cabins thatched with reeds,
> Where a Stone-Age people breeds
> The last of Europe's stone age race.
>
> —*John Betjeman*, "Ireland with Emily"
> *The Golden Treasury*

The Burren is a place to linger and roam, even when your time is short. It would be a mistake to find yourself driven to tick off one site after another. In fact, if your holiday has some stretch in it, you may want to spend an extra day here and walk part of "The Burren Way," a 26-mi signposted trail between Ballyvaughan and Liscannor. Or you could purchase Tim Robinson's hand-drawn map of the Burren, available in most any local shop, and do some serious exploring on your own. A more organized option would be to contact in advance John Connolly (087-877-9565 www.burrenwalks.com) to arrange a guided walking tour tailored to your interests and pace.

For everyone, however, we recommend an initiatory visit either to The Burren Centre (065-708-8030) in Kilfenora or The Burren Exposure (065-707-7277) a quarter of a mile outside of Ballyvaughan on the N67. Both offer, for a modest fee €€ CC, excellent audio-visual introductions to the Burren, together with exhibits that will inform and help orient your own explorations;

and both have cafés where you can have a lunch or snack after your long morning drive from Sligo. Then, at last, it will be time to explore the Burren in whatever time you can give to it.

From the Neolithic period, the greatest assembly of surviving monuments are the wedge tombs. There is no definitive count, but Tim Robinson's suggestion of 74 is the most widely accepted tally, as is his count of 450 ring forts. Ring forts are notoriously difficult to assign to one period as opposed to another. Many hilltop or promontory defensive sites, of which there are a sizeable number in the Burren, could belong to any epoch from the Neolithic to the late Medieval, though there is a long-leaning inclination to assign such forts to the Iron Age. It is mostly to these monuments, then, that we will limit our numbered suggestions.

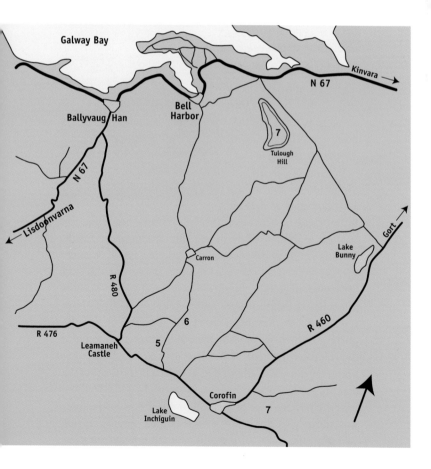

Along R480 south of Ballyvaughan there are a number of important early monuments. Just prior to the turn for Aillwee Cave you'll find on your right a rather overgrown circular earth embankment simply called An Rath (1), which is readily accessible and interesting to explore briefly. The next monument easily found on this road is the Glenisheen Wedge Tomb (below, 2), which is not marked

from the road but is readily identified on your left, shortly before coming to the Poulna-brone Portal Tomb (right, 3), dating from between 3800 and 3200 B.C.E., the most widely visited and photographed dolmen in Ireland. It is often overrun with tourists, but when the last bus tours fade away in the later afternoon and early evening you may have it to yourself. Like a house of cards, the upright walls of the tomb—sitting directly on limestone bedrock—are held in place by the massive capstone. The sillstone, no longer intact, would likely have reached up to the underside of the capstone to seal the portal. When excavated in 1986, the fragmentary, disarticulated remains of between 16 and 22 adults were found here, most of whom had never reached the age of 30 and only one of whom had lived past 40. In addition there were 6 children. One of them, however, a newborn infant, was added later sometime in the Bronze Age. Next, just under a mile south of the Poulnabrone dolmen on your left, you will see on your right a relatively well-preserved stone fort or *cashel*, Cathair Chonaill (4).

Several other Burren monuments—out of hundreds—are of particular note here. To find them, driving east and south on R476, take the first road on your left after Leamaneh Castle. The road will wind and climb until you come to the Parknabinna Wedge Tomb (below, 5), signposted on your left. This is a splendid example of a wedge tomb, which would have been covered by a mound of earth. Further along the same road you will come to a

sign indicating, on your right, the path to Cathair Chomáin (6), a remarkably impressive trivallate *cashel* perched on the edge of a ravine. The fortification walls of Cathair Chomáin at their thickest measure 28 feet, and are, in one spot, still 14 feet high. It is well worth the walk and slight climb required to reach it. The path will take you through cow fields up to a rocky plateau where you will continue across further pastures. Watch for the possible presence of bulls. We have not seen bulls here, but we did once come across a fiercely protective cow only minutes after she had given birth. We took a wide detour. Lastly, if you still have the will and the stamina, you may wish to climb nearby Turlough Hill (7), an enigmatic peak site over 900 feet above sea level, whose monuments include the remains of over 80 circular stone huts, a massive stone fort, and a great circular cairn. To reach the hill, drive north from Cathair Chomáin to the village of Carron. Continue north past Carron until you see the Burren Outdoor Education Centre on your right. The possibly still-unmarked path to the summit of Turloch Hill will be found, or not, almost exactly one-half mile beyond the center on your right.

Cathair Chomáin

Side Site

Cliffs of Moher

You've probably already seen the Cliffs of Moher several times in travel brochures, documentaries, and friends' holiday snapshots. They're a bit like the Eiffel Tower or Niagara Falls—everyone's idea of a postcard. All the same, you may not be able to return home with your head up unless you've seen them. Especially at dusk and sunset— rising over 700 feet above the crashing sea below and extending for roughly five miles—they are admittedly splendid. Open site. [D9] Located 7 miles northwest of Lahinch, Co. Clare off of R478.

Cliffs of Moher

Kid Sites

Aillwee Cave

The Burren is one big block of limestone, riddled with caves. Aillwee Cave is Ireland's "showcave," fully illumined for maximum effect. Aillwee Cave has no special ancient significance except that it's old, and kids of the non-claustrophobic variety love it. Open daily Jan–June and Sept–Oct 10am–5:30pm; daily July–Aug 10am–6:30pm. (065-707-7036 www.aillweecave.ie). [E8] Ballyvaughan, Co. Clare. Signposted off the N67. New features here include the Bird of Prey Centre and the Hawk Walk. Reduced pricing online.

Bunratty Castle and Folk Park

Bunratty Castle, celebrated as Ireland's most complete medieval castle, is the jewel in the crown of this 20-acre folk theme park. It's a tourist trap except that everyone has come willingly. We avoided it for years, then succumbed and truly enjoyed ourselves. A great family outing. Open daily Sept–May 9am–5:30pm, June–Aug Mon–Fri 9am–5:30pm and Sat 9am–6pm. (061-360788). [F9] Bunratty, Co. Clare. Signposted off the N18.

Bed and Board

The Burren's prime address, if you're up for a splurge, is in our opinion Gregans Castle Hotel, Ballyvaughan, Co. Clare (065-707-7005 www.gregans.ie) €€€ CC. The hotel, located on the estate of Burren princes is not itself a castle, but rather a 19th-century country house with all the gracious luxury lesser royalty could rightfully expect. Located 3 miles SW of Ballyvaughan off the N67. For a fraction of the price, there are two excellent B&B's in the Burren we highly recommend. First among them is Rusheen Lodge, Knocknagrough, Co. Clare (065-77092 www.rusheenlodge.com) €€ CC, very near the Aillwee Caves, which were in fact discovered by the father of your host here. Located just south of Ballyvaughan village on the N67. Another Burren favorite is Fergus View, Kilnaboy, Co. Clare (065-683-7606 www.fergusview.com) €€ CC, which in summer actually doesn't enjoy views of the Fergus but is well deserving of a night's stay all the same. Note that some of the rooms, while inviting, can be a snug fit for a full-sized visitor; so be sure to mention your preference for something spacious if that is a concern. From Ennis take the N85 west to R476, which you take through Corofin to Kilnaboy. Fergus View is on your left after you pass a ruined church on your right.

If you want to end your day at the Folk Park or take in the castle dinner, you may want to spend the night in

Bunratty, where we have a most comfy B&B to recommend, with a truly memorable breakfast. It's a short 10-minute walk down the road from the castle. Bunratty Woods, Bunratty, Co. Clare (061-369689) € CC. Follow signs off the N18 to Bunratty Folk Park. When you come to a corner with the castle on your left and across from it Durty Nelly's pub, turn left on the road running between them and Bunratty Woods will be on your left, in roughly a quarter of a mile.

Castle Dinners

If you're staying at Gregans Castle Hotel you will probably want to take advantage of their exceptionally fine dining room. Otherwise, we're going to focus our Burren dining attention on the medieval castle banquets offered by three local castles: Bunratty Castle in Bunratty, Co. Clare; Knappogue Castle, near Quin, Co. Clare; and Dunguaire Castle in nearby Kinvara, Co. Galway. Each has a different tilt to its menu and focus to its entertainment; and all are held subject to demand. It's best to ring the Shannon Heritage reservations number (061-360788) for details, availability, and bookings.

DAY SIX
Short Hop

Today is a light driving day. Whether you spent the night in the Burren or in East Clare, it is only a short drive to Craggaunowen, after which you will have to decide whether you want to explore Limerick city first and Lough Gur second, or vice versa. We would recommend that you drive from Craggaunowen directly to Lough Gur and then return to explore Limerick either in the evening or the next morning before setting out for Dublin. Traditionally, Limerick has not been a favored tourist destination, but in recent years this proud and struggling city has done its best and still has a good deal to offer.

PRINCIPAL SITE
Lough Gur

If you have the weather on your side Lough Gur is a lovely place to spend the better part of an afternoon or early evening. Young families and sweethearts, whose focus is on the future and not on the past, are nonetheless drawn to Lough Gur for picnics or strolls or to feed the swans and other waterfowl. A declared bird and wildlife sanctuary, Lough Gur is quite simply a haven. Its appeal today or, for that matter, 6,000 years ago is unmistakable; and the more you know about the place the more its aura grows. The visible traces, mostly unexcavated, of its habitation across at least six millennia are all around you. Like an old house, a very old, very beloved house, Lough Gur is full of faces, voices, memories not feeling any urge to leave. You are never alone here.

> This lake, all Munster knows, is enchanted; but the spell passes off once in every seven years. The lake then, to whoever has the luck to behold it, appears dry; and the Tree may be partly seen at the bottom of it, covered with a Green Cloth. A certain bold fellow was at the spot one day at the very instant when the spell broke, and he rode his horse towards the tree and snatched away the Brat Uaine that covered it. As he turned his horse, and fled for his life, the Woman who sat on the watch, knitting under the cloth, at the foot of the tree, cried out:
>
> *Chúghat, chúghat, a bhúaine bhalbh!*
> *Marcach ó Thir na mBan Marbh*
> *A' fúadach an bhruit úiaine dhom bhathas.*
>
> Awake, awake, thou silent tide!
> From the Dead Women's Land a horseman rides,
> From my head the green cloth snatching.
>
> At the words the waters rose; and so fiercely did they pursue him that as he gained the edge of the lake one half of his steed was swept away, and with it the Brat Uaine, which he was drawing after him. Had that been taken, the enchantment was ended for ever.
>
> —(Old woman from Askeaton, 24 April, 1879) in Fitzgerald, D. 1879–80 Irish Popular Traditions. Revue Celtique IV, 185–6.

Lough Gur—the lake itself, after some drainage in the mid-19th century—covers roughly 184 acres. Taking the shape of a C, the lake wraps its northern and southern arms around the Knockadoon peninsula; so that only the eastern portion of the peninsula is exposed, as it happens, to a marshy area. In short, the peninsula is all but an island, with the modest protection that affords. Some of its past inhabitants, we know, appreciated its defensible advantage and fortified it—Brian Boru against the Vikings in the 11th century and the Earls of Desmond, with two castles, against much later aggressors. It is on Knockadoon that evidence of very early habitation, at least by 3000 B.C.E., is evident even today to the naked eye. Two of the Knockadoon huts sites (found in the vicinity of #4 on the map below) provided the basis for the reconstructed Neolithic houses serving as Lough Gur's Interpretive Centre. Lough Gur and the surrounding area abounds with over thirty ancient sites and monuments ranging from the Neolithic to the Medieval period; and, not surprisingly, this same area has proven one of the richest sources of ancient artifacts to be found in the National Museum, as well as museums throughout Europe. For example, the conspicuous circular bronze shield in the National Museum in Dublin was found here. Many of these sites, however, have never been excavated and most lie on private property—unmarked and requiring explicit permission to visit. We will concentrate here on the easily accessible and most impressive monuments numbered on the map below.

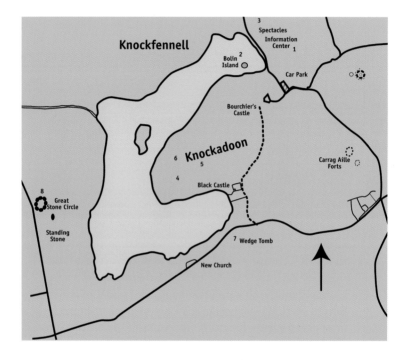

After parking in the Lough Gur parking area entering the main visitors' area on the northeastern shore of the lake, we recommend your proceeding at once to the Interpretive Centre (1) to take advantage of the audio-visual presentation, which will help prepare you for your own explorations. From the elevated vantage point of the center you will enjoy a fine view of the lake and of the crannóg now known as Bolin Island (2). Due to the current level of the lake, the so-called island, 98 feet across, appears to be attached to the shore. In fact it is an artificial island, formed by laying in place on the lake bottom a circle of great boulders and filling in the enclosure with brush and earth.

After leaving the Interpretive Centre, make your way to the ridge above the center to the location of the "Spectacles" (3). This is actually a misnomer. When this site was first studied there appeared to be two circular hut sites arranged in such a way as to suggest the lenses of a pair of eyeglasses or spectacles. There were, however, at this spot three hut sites, as well as an animal shelter and the outline of ancient fields, all dating from approximately 900 C.E. The most skillfully constructed hut measured 15 feet in diameter, with two hearths and stone foundation walls over 3 feet thick. The considerable weight of its thatched roof was borne by a number of interior posts, whose holes were discovered. The burden of ancient hut roofs could not be borne by the walls, as a common dwelling's roof, when wet, could weigh up to several tons. In this same area there are a series of sites with the remains of ancient fields, dwellings, and animal shelters. There is even a surviving set of ancient steps leading down from the "Spectacles" to the lakeshore.

On Knockadoon, which you may not have the time or opportunity to explore on your own, there are the visible traces of over 18 sites identified without formal excavation. These break down into three principal groups, including a number of stone circles. With such circles it is often difficult to distinguish ritual from domestic sites. For example #5 or Circle J seems clearly to be a ritual site or cemetery, as a number of human remains were uncovered here, while #6 or circle K would appear to mark the location of a ringfort as foundation sites and postholes were found within. If you want to explore this area in more extensive detail, we would recommend your purchasing and following the *Illustrated Guide to Lough Gur, Co. Limerick,* by M.J. & C. O'Kelly, on sale in the Interpretive Centre.

There are two not-to-miss ancient sites in the immediate vicinity, which you should make a point of seeing before leaving the area. The first is a wedge tomb (7) dating from the mid-3rd millennium B.C.E., of a type commonly found in Munster. Its overall dimensions are approximately 29 feet by 12 feet and it has a NE–SE orientation. Note that its gallery is divided into two chambers, which when excavated in 1938 contained the bones of at least 8 adults and 4 children, as well as additional cremated human remains. In its original condition, this would have been covered by a cairn of smaller stones. To find the wedge tomb, turn left out of the parking area and bear right, turning right again at the next crossing. It will be signposted on your left.

Finally, we come to the most remarkable single monument at Lough Gur, the Great Stone Circle at Grange (8), the largest surviving stone circle in Ireland and surely one of the finest. With an estimated date from the Bronze Age of roughly 2000 B.C.E., the Grange Stone Circle, also known as the *Lios,* measures 150 feet in diameter; and at its center there is a posthole thought to have once held a post whose attached rope would have been used like a compass to measure out the great and nearly perfect circle. The circle's orientation is such that the rising sun on Lammas shines through the single, narrow, east-facing entrance and illumines the inner enclosure. Between the circle and the lake below, traces of an ancient roadway have been found, perhaps suggesting a ritual road of some sort, as the lake itself is thought to have been held sacred by the early Celts. To find the Grange Stone Circle, turn left out of the Lough Gur parking area and continue straight at the first intersection. The circle will soon appear on your right.

Lough Gur, near Holycross, Co. Limerick. Open site, except for Interpretive Centre, which is open daily May–September 10am–6pm. Video presentation shown throughout the day. €€ CC. (061-385-186). [G10] Located 7 miles southeast of Limerick, signposed off R512.

Side Sites

Craggaunowen+
The Craggaunowen living history park is focused on ancient Celtic life; and so its inclusion here in this itinerary is admittedly an anachronism. That said, it's likely to prove worthwhile and engaging for anyone interested in Irish antiquity, whatever the period. A walk through the park turns into an imaginatively provoking walk through the distant Irish past. The reconstructed crannog and ring fort, to mention two of the stations on your way, have been expertly researched and painstakingly crafted. Another highlight of the park is the actual vessel constructed and sailed by Tim Severin in his historic

The Craggaunowen living history park

1970s re-tracing of the 6th-century voyage of St. Brendan the Navigator from Ireland to America. This is a great family site, with wild (well-penned) boars and ancient breeds of sheep and cows on hand to hold the attention of hearts and minds less than fully enamored of antiquity. Open daily May–Sept 10am–6pm. €€€ CC. (061-367178). [F9] Signposted off R469 roughly 10 miles east of Ennis, near Quin, Co. Clare.

Hunt Museum

Now gloriously housed in the Old Custom House, the finest 18th century building in Limerick, the Hunt Museum is a real find. The Hunt's collection—ancient, medieval, and modern—is second only to the National Museum. The Shannonside museum cafe is a perfect place to rest your feet and enjoy either a snack or a full meal. Open Mon–Sat 10am–5pm, Sun 2–5pm. €€ CC. (061-312833 www.huntmuseum.com). At the Old Custom House, Rutland St., Limerick.

Angela's Ashes *Tours*

While Frank McCourt did everything in his power to get out of Limerick, his readers have done everything in their power to go there, which has inspired various *Angela's Ashes* walking tours of the city. It is difficult to know now the future level

Kid Site

King John's Castle

You know by now our theory about kids and castles—that the former can't get enough of the latter. If so far that seems to be true, here's another one, recently restored and gussied-up at great expense for visitors. Even so, it's surely one of Limerick's highlights. Dating from the early 13th century and sporting splendid curtain walls and rounded gate towers, this is one of Ireland's oldest and finest surviving examples of medieval architecture. Open daily 10am–5pm. €€€ CC (061-411201). You can't miss it on the Limerick riverfront off Nicholas Street, but you may want to consider a miss all the same, as the entrance cost far exceeds what the site offers.

King John's Castle

of such interest and the corresponding availability of these tours, but you can find the answers to this and all your questions on the ground at the Limerick Tourism Centre on Arthur's Quay (061-317522), open year round.

Bed and Board

We specially recommend several lodgings in the Limerick area, all of which offer meals in-house or within walking distance. If you want a comfortable, convenient, basic and a bit worn city-center hotel, you can't do better for the price than Jurys Inn Limerick, Lower Mallow Street, Limerick (061-207000 www.jurysinns.com) € CC.

The river-front rooms have special appeal, and the corner river-front rooms, for which you pay nothing extra, are a rare bargain. For more luxury and atmosphere, you can drive 6 miles east of the city, off the N7, to Castle Oaks House Hotel and Country Club, Castleconnell, Co. Limerick (061-377666 www.castleoaks.ie) €€€ CC. This lovely Georgian manor house, ensconced in 25 acres of mature oak woodlands along the River Shannon will definitely put the day behind you in style, especially after a dip in their indoor pool. Another memorable place to spend the night, south of Limerick in the post-card perfect village of Adare and not all that far from Lough Gur, is Adare Country House, Co. Limerick (061-395986 www.adarecountryhouse.com) € CC. The bright, roomy, and immaculate rooms are warm and welcoming, as are your hosts here. Located in Adare Village, 15 minutes' drive from Limerick center.

Adare is awash in fine dining choices for every budget; but if you're up for an evening meal outing, you might well consider driving 20 miles for excellent Irish modern cuisine to Capard Lodge Restaurant on the Limerick road in Charleville, Co. Cork (063-21047) €€€ CC. From Adare take the N21 north to the N20 south to Charleville.

If you happen to be in Limerick at midday, two great lunch options that won't disappoint are the Hunt Museum's café (see page 127) and Finn's Bar, serving widely touted meals at 62 William Street in the heart of Limerick.

Day Seven
The Home Stretch

It is customary in Ireland and elsewhere to rest on the seventh day, but there still remains the roughly 130-mile journey between Limerick and the Dublin airport. Assuming that this is your last full day and night in Ireland, you will likely have several aims: to make the most of the day and evening, to be settled in plenty of time to pack and prepare for tomorrow's return home, and to position yourself strategically with respect to the Dublin airport for the return of the rental car. With all this in mind, we will sketch several ways in which you might meet your goals and enjoy yourself along the way.

Option #1:

Plan

Drive to Dublin airport today, drop off your rental car, and take a taxi or an airport bus the rest of the way. If you do indeed want to spend your last night in the city center, it is far preferable to drop off your car at the airport the day before departure and not attempt to deal with ghastly Dublin traffic, unavoidable in the rush hours.

Route

For the most direct and expeditious drive, take the N7 from Limerick to the M7 to the M50 north around Dublin until you join the M1 north (signposted Belfast, Dublin Airport). Follow signs to the airport.

En Route

There is one suggestion which would not involve an extensive delay or detour—the Rock of Dunamase, just outside of Portlaoise, Co. Laoise [K8], which you would otherwise bypass on the M7. To visit the Rock of Dunamase, take the N80 for four miles in a southeasterly direction and follow signs to this extraordinary ruin. Its deep history is far from fully known, but what you see is not only an enchanting pile of a 12th century castle but glorious 360° vistas of the sensuously moulded Laoise rural landscape. This open site is a bit of a climb, the perfect antidote to car crunch. Beside, you will be well-rewarded at the summit. Either straight from lunch or after a climb up the Rock, just return to Portlaoise and the M7.

Bed and Board

Same as Day One (pages 78–79).

Option #2:

Plan

Drive north of Dublin, spending the night in a lovely seafront village, from which you can gain relatively easy access to the airport the next day. Since the airport is north of the city, staying north of the city allows you to avoid the worst of Dublin traffic.

Route

From Limerick, take the N7 to the M7 to the M50 north around Dublin until you join the M1 north in the direction of Belfast. At junction four, leave the M1 and at the roundabout take the third exit and merge onto the R132 (signposted Skerries, Rush, Donabate). Follow signs to Skerries onto the R127 and eventually the R128. For Howth, take the M50 to its endpoint where it connects with the Malahide Road, the N23, until it comes to a T-junction at the coast road, and turn right following signs to Howth.

En Route

For a spectacular view and a good stretch of the legs, you can visit the Rock of Dunamase as suggested in Option #1. And, if you crave to enter one last awe-inspiring Neolithic passage tomb before returning home, we recommend a detour to Fourknocks, Co. Meath [M/N7]. Fourknocks (from the Irish "Fuair Cnocs" meaning "The Cold Hills") has a number of features that distinguish it from other passage tombs you've seen. The passage is relatively short, only 17 feet, and faces N–NE. The main circular chamber measures a spacious 18 by 21 feet. This is very different from Newgrange, whose passage is over 60 feet long, but whose central chamber and recesses are quite compressed. The central chamber roof here was not fully corbelled and may have had a framework of wooden rafters supported by a central pole. There are three recesses off the central chamber, each with a lintelled roof, two of which are boldly decorated. When excavated in the 1950s, remains of 65 burials, adults and children, were found interred here, some cremated and some unburned. There are also some quite intriguing decorations to be pondered. Surrounding Fourknocks I is a low dry-stone wall and not curbstones. I say Fourknocks I, because there are actually four tombs in this complex. Only this one has been fully excavated and opened to the public. It is an open site, but you will still need a key to enter the tomb, which can be fetched from Mr. Fintan White (041-988-0305) in return for a refundable deposit and must be returned before 6pm. Directions to Mr. White's home are given at the Fourknocks site. To reach Fourknocks from the M50 take the M1 north to exit six where you will follow the R122 to Naul. From Naul continue on the R122 for less than a mile until you come to the first sharp-right byroad. Turn right and take this

Approach to Fourknocks

narrow road northwest for roughly a mile to the T-junction. Turn left and watch for signposts on the left to a paved track to the Fourknocks mound.

Bed and Board

In Skerries [N7], you will find both bed and board at Redbank House, a landmark of hospitality in the village center. Redbank House, 6–7 Church Street, Skerries, Co. Dublin (01-849-1005 www.redbank.ie) €€€ CC. Redbank House abuts the Redbank Restaurant, which has won just about all the awards and testimonials any one board can bear. It all started with the restaurant, an eatery of considerable renown, particularly for seafood. You will eat like a king and sleep like a baby here; not a bad combination for the last night of your explorations in Ireland. Another winning combination is to stretch out for the night at The White Cottages (01-849-2231 www.thewhitecottages.com) €€ CC, sea's edge and a 10–15 minute walk from town, and to dine at prize-winning Stoop Your Head (01-849-2085 www.stoopyourhead.ie) €€ CC. If you arrive in Skerries with time left on the day's clock, look up Skerries Mills and/or Malahide Castle, two top nearby attractions, or just stroll the harbor loop at sunset.

In Howth [N7], we also recommend a winning bed-and-board combination, right in the harbor—the King Sitric Restaurant and Guest House, East Pier, Howth, Co. Dublin (01-832-5235 www.kingsitric.com) €€€ CC. All eight guest rooms enjoy sea views. Another solid choice—less central, less costly, but with alluring extras—is the Deer Park Hotel Golf and Spa (01-832-2624 www.deerpark-hotel.ie) €€ CC, atop a low hill just outside the village of Howth and just high enough to offer what H.G. Wells reputedly described as "the finest views west of Naples." Truth is that the rooms are a bit worn, however; so the view from the inside surpasses the view of the inside. That said, the grounds are spectacular; so you won't want to be spending all your time in your room. One last option is the warmly welcoming, modern, and well touted Gleann na Smól B&B, Nashville Road, Howth, Co. Dublin (01-832-2936) €, just above the harbor, where you can't go wrong for the money. Take Thormanby Road up from the village and turn left onto Nashville Road.

As you explore Howth Harbour, as you definitely should, you will find a string of great dining options along Harbour Road at the north side of the harbor. Survey the menus and their price-tags and make your own selection. You can't really go wrong here.

Option #3:

Plan
Drive south of Dublin, spending the night in Dalkey, the most appealing and relatively unspoilt coastal villages south of Dublin, from which you can gain moderately ready access to the airport the next day (provided you avoid peak commuter hours and use the East Link toll bridge across the Liffey). Be sure to consult your host on the latest and best route to the airport to catch your flight with the least possible stress or uncertainty.

Route
From Limerick, take the N7 toward Dublin until, just past Nenagh, the N7 becomes the M7. Carry on until you reach the M50, which you will exit at junction 16, merging onto the R118 (signposted Cherrywood, Loughlinstown). At the traffic light turn right onto Wyattville Road (signposted Killiney). Continue on Wyattville Road forward onto Military Road, turning left onto Killiney Hill Road. Next, bear right onto Dalkey Avenue, and at the roundabout take the third exit onto Ulverton Road, which takes you into the center of Dalkey.

En Route
If you are game for a couple of detours and a bit of exploring along the way instead of bee-lining to Dalkey first, for a spectacular view, and a good stretch of the legs,

Piper Stones

you can visit the Rock of Dunamase as suggested above in Option #1. Next, we recommend a drive through the Wicklow Mountains where we will begin at Hollywood, Co. Wicklow. To reach Hollywood, leave the M7 at junction 12 and at the first roundabout take the N7 (signposted Dublin). Then, at the second roundabout take the R413 (signposted Kilcullen). Entering Brannockstown, turn right onto the R412 (signposted Dunlavin) and watch for a left turn onto the R413 (signposted Ballymore Eustace). Your next turn will be right onto the R411 and ahead, at a major crossroads, turn right onto the N81 until you reach the intersection with the R756, where you turn left onto the R756 (signposted Hollywood). Once in Hollywood, you will be very near our first local site of major interest, the Athgreany ("Field of the Sun") Stone Circle, aka the Pipers Stones [M8], an open site. This circle has a fanciful, almost magical, placement and posture. The legend accounting for their name has it that these were once dancers who were turned to stone for frolicking on Sunday. The guilty piper may be embodied in an outlying stone found some 40 yards down the slope northeast of the circle. Seven and a half feet in diameter, the circle is composed of 14 granite boulders (the highest of which stands six feet four inches tall and has a girth of 12 feet) and may be missing two of its original number. To find the Pipers Stones, take the N81 south from Hollywood, and they will be signposted on your left after about three-quarters of a mile. Cross the field fence and the stones are on the crest of a rise about 200 yards from the road. After leaving Hollywood, you will drive across one of the most spectacular landscapes in Ireland, nearly 50,000 acres of which form the Wicklow Mountains National Park. If you want to see more of it, you can turn off R755 and follow R759 across the Sally Gap. Also en route is a site of great early Christian importance, Glendalough [M/N8], which you will pass on R756 just before you reach the village of the same name.

Glendalough, Co. Wicklow (0404-45325) is an OPW Heritage Card site and is open daily mid-Mar to mid-Oct 9:30am–6pm and mid-Oct to mid-Mar 9:30am–5pm. This idyllic setting is where St. Kevin founded one of Ireland's earliest and most famed monasteries. Apart from the monastic complex and its monuments, there are quite scenic and serene walks to be had here, if time remains in your day to enjoy them.

Bed and Board

Dalkey deserves to be a destination in its own right and not just a place to spend the night. This charming village boasts several holy wells and two castles, one of which houses the Dalkey Heritage Centre (01-285-8366 www,dalkeycastle.ie) €€ CC, where you can learn the history of Dalkey, all you never knew to ask about. Along Castle Street and its byways you will find more than enough shops, pubs, and restaurants to meet your needs. Then, when it comes time to call it a night, the last night of your journey, we recommend a splurge at the Royal Marine Hotel (01-230-0030 www.royalmarine.ie) €€€ CC, to which Queen Victoria also treated herself when visiting Ireland. But if you find yourself without a queen's coffer with which to finance your overnight, you will find that sleep comes just as easily and sweetly at the Druid Lodge (01-285-1632 www.druidlodge.ie) € CC, a charming early-Victorian residence, once the home of the legendary political leader John Dillon, perched high above Killiney Bay with a panorama often compared to the Bay of Naples, without the traffic and the traffickers. Below, for the strolling, lies one of the east coast's most splendid and unspoilt strands.

ITINERARY TWO

Pre-Christian Celtic • Late Bronze & Iron Ages • 700 B.C.E.–400 C.E.

DAY ONE
Arrival in Dublin

Dublin Airport is a dream compared to most international airports, even after its dramatic expansion in recent years. Definitely easy-in and easy-out, regardless of what form of public transportation you choose. Until the new tunnel is completed, creating a direct rapid transit link to and from the city, your best options into the city center are taxi (€30) or bus or one of the convenient shuttle-bus services to Dublin city center:

Airlink Express (€6) or Aircoach (€7). You shouldn't have
to wait more than fifteen minutes for a suitable option. We
recommend that you begin your auto rental on Day Two
and return then to the airport to pick up your car. You will
pay for one less day, avoid parking fees, and spare yourself
the nightmare of navigating Dublin traffic. Dublin streets
and roads rank among the most desperately congested
byways in Europe. As a jetlagged novice, this is not the place
or the time to try out your left-lane driving skills. Better to
get a night's sleep and to drive directly from the airport to
County Meath, avoiding all city and rush-hour traffic.

PRINCIPAL SITE
National Museum of Archaeology and History

Ireland's National Museum is located on four distinct
campuses: the Museum of Natural History on Merrion
Street, the Museum of Archaeology and History on
Kildare Street, and the Museum of Decorative Arts and
History at the Collins Barracks, all in central Dublin. The
fourth and latest addition, opened in 2001, is the
Museum of Country Life at Turlough Park, just outside of
Castlebar, Co. Mayo.

Regardless of which prehistoric or historical period
occupies the focus of one's interests, the exploration of
ancient Ireland best begins at the National Museum of
Archaeology and History, amidst an assemblage of
treasures—dating from the earliest human of Ireland to
the medieval period—amassed over several hundred years
by individual collectors, the British Crown, and the Irish
State. Before examining any of the holdings, be sure to
admire the museum that holds them. For a start, the
entrance lobby, top to bottom, from its 62-ft domed
ceiling to its striking mosaic floor deserves a gaze.

Despite the splendor of its holdings, the National
Museum, like any, can be taxing. It is easy, even without
the additional gravity of jet-lag, to grow weary of reading
labels and placards and to teeter towards burnout.
Consequently, we recommend that you try to take
advantage of one of the frequent daily tours by a member
of the museum staff. Once given your bearings across the
wide sweep of holdings and the periods they represent,

you can find your own way back to those items with which you want to linger.

For the second itinerary, your focus will fall first on the exceptionally fine bronze work and gold ornaments produced in Ireland near the end of the Bronze Age, as well as the special exhibits on Tara and Kingship and Sacrifice, aka bog bodies. From the 8th century, metal became more available in Ireland than ever before and Irish metalwork was the beneficiary of an ever-widening circle of aesthetic influences, the two most notable being the Continental Celtic cultures of Halstatt in Austria and La Tene in Switzerland. Many of the most dazzling hordes of Irish treasures preserved in the National Museum date from this period. In fact, more late Bronze Age gold work has survived from Ireland than from any other country in northern or western Europe; so be sure to study the National Museum's famed exhibit entitled *Ór—Ireland's Gold,* Europe's premier exhibition of prehistoric gold. Another relevant highlight in the National Museum is the array of fine bronze horns from the Late Bronze and Early Iron Ages. The Loughnashade trumpet, over six feet in length, found in a lake beside Emain Macha, stands out as the most finely crafted sheet-bronze trumpet of the Celtic Iron Age.

> Are you wondering what kind of sounds and music these ancient horns make? Thanks to Simon O'Dwyer, founder of PREHISTORIC MUSIC IRELAND, you don't have to wonder any longer. In the 1980's Simon cast the first precise replicas of ancient Bronze Age Celtic horns and experimented with a variety of techniques to produce sound and music from them. These experiments were so successful that in 1994 the National Museum invited him to make recordings using eight original prehistoric horns from different parts of Ireland. The sounds from those horns had not been heard for 3,000 years and are now available on two CD's from PREHISTORIC MUSIC IRELAND. To order a CD or to listen to samples and learn more about the ancient music of Ireland, go to www.prehistoricmusic.com.

Of course you will not restrain your curiosity to the confines of the second itinerary; so be sure to explore the full scope of the museum's collections and to revive yourself, as needed, in the museum coffee shop. One off-focus yet not-to-miss highlight is *The Treasury*, an exquisite assemblage of early Celtic and Christian treasures; and upstairs, you'll find an eye-opening introduction to Viking Dublin that will deepen your appreciation of Dublin's past and give new resonance to the word "berserk."

At the intersection of Kildare and Molesworth Streets. (01-677-7444) Open Tues–Sat 10am–5pm, Sun 2–5pm. Closed Mondays. Free admission.

Side Sites

Dublin ranks among the top five tourist cities in Europe and not without reason. There is no question of our listing, much less discussing, its myriad attractions here. Instead, given that this is a guide to ancient Ireland and that only hours remain in your one allotted day in Ireland's capitol city, we will make a couple of modest suggestions relevant to the exploration of ancient Ireland.

Trinity College Dublin
Although not a prehistoric site, a meandering stroll in the 400-year old campus of Trinity College makes for a most tranquil and fascinating walk through the past. There is no admission fee to the college grounds. The entrance is through the main gate in College Green opposite the central branch of the Bank of Ireland, the former seat of the Irish Parliament. We recommend that that you take a college tour, especially of the Old Library and the *Book of Kells*, one of Ireland's greatest treasures. Open Mon–Sat 9:30am–5pm; Sundays, Oct–May noon–4:30pm and June–Sept 9:30am–4:30pm. Admission €€€.

Garden Strolls
To finish off your afternoon and put that final edge on your appetite for an early dinner, we recommend a walk through St. Stephen's Green, only five minutes on foot down Dawson Street from the side (Arts Block) gate of Trinity College. An idyllic alternative or supplement to St. Stephen's Green is one of Dublin's best-kept secrets, Iveagh Gardens, located behind the National Concert Hall. Both gardens are open, free admission, until dark.

Trinity College, Dublin

KID SITES

Viking Splash

Kid's will surely not object if you jump the rails of the second itinerary and take them back to Viking Ireland with a "Viking Splash Tour" (www.vikingsplash.ie) aboard a reconditioned "Duck," a vintage amphibious vehicle unknown to the Vikings themselves. Taking advantage not only of Dublin's thoroughfares but also of its canals, these tours offer an informative and entertaining introduction to Dublin's sites and stories. More to the point, kids love it, even while some humorless parents cringe. Tours every 30 min in peak season and every 90 min off peak. Call 01-707-6000 for more details and reservations. Fee €€€. Tours depart from Stephens Green North, close to Grafton Street, just behind the taxi rank and water fountain.

Dublinia

Another family-oriented historical attraction in Dublin is known as "Dublinia," www.dublinia.ie, offering a vivid walk through Medieval Dublin, 1170-1540, recreated in a series of exhibits, spectacles, and interactive experiences. There's also a gift shop and café. Located opposite Christ Church Cathedral on St. Michael's Hill. Open Apr–Sept daily 10am–5pm, and Oct–Mar Mon–Sat 10am–4:30pm. Call 01-679-4611 for details or bookings. Admission €€.

Bed and Board

You will want first to check into your lodging. If you arrive before your room is ready, you can leave your bags anyway and return later to bring them to your room. Dublin boasts hundreds of fine hotels and guest houses; most are very costly. We specially recommend several options. Dublin's three Jurys Inns (www.jurysinns.com) are affordable, convenient, and offer their own pubs and restaurants. And, in the vein of motels or motor inns, they charge by the room and not per person. Breakfast is extra. These are: the Jurys Inn Christchurch (01-454-0000), €€ CC, across from Christchurch Cathedral; Jurys Inn Customs House (01-854-1500), €€ CC, facing the quays in the new financial services district; and Jurys Inn Parnell Street (01-878-4900) € CC, just off the top of O'Connell Street. On a more cozy scale and with enhanced character, there is the Harding Hotel (01-679-6500 www.hardinghotel.ie), € CC, Copper Alley, Fishamble Street, once the Main Street of Viking Ireland, across from Christchurch Cathedral. If price is really no consideration, the Shelbourne (01-663-4500 www.marriott.co.uk) €€€ CC, remains the most distinguished address in Dublin, facing the northeast corner of St. Stephen's Green. Built in 1824, this is where the Irish Constitution was signed in 1921 (in room 112 to be exact). On a more contemporary note, another lodging of special interest is Number 31 (01-676-5011 www.number31.ie) €€€ CC, in the heart of Georgian Dublin and a brief walk from St. Stephen's Green or the National Museum, at 31 Leeson Close overlooking Fitzwilliam Place.

The restaurant scene in Dublin is vast and ever-changing. The best advice to be given here is simply to point you towards Temple Bar, Dublin's Left Bank, and to suggest that you follow your own nose to what best suits your budget and taste. With eateries of one sort or another lined up like rungs in a fence, your only challenge will be choosing among them and securing a table without an advance reservation. Your best chance is to eat early, before 7pm. Chapter One (01-873-2266) €€€ CC, at 18–19 Parnell Square; L'Ecrivain (01-661-1919) €€€ CC, at 109 Lower Baggot St., Dublin 2; and Patrick Guilbaud (01-676-4192) €€€ CC, at 21 Upper Merrion Street, are three of Dublin's finest; and you will need to ring ahead for reservations. If you wish to plan your Dublin meal well in advance go to www.rai.ie, Ireland's most complete online index for scouting out restaurants and to www.menupages.ie for consumer opinions and ratings. As you may have some difficulty finding a bargain—ample, wholesome, slow (as opposed to fast) food on a slim budget—we recommend these two, neither of which require reservations: Wagamama Noodle Bar (01-478-2152) € CC, on South King Street opposite the Gaiety Theatre, and Chamelion (01-671-0362) € CC, at No. 1 Fownes Street Lower, Temple Bar, for exceptional Indonesian cuisine.

Dublin Castle, the center of British rule in Ireland for centuries.

DAY TWO
The Question: Drive or Be Driven?

Already, on your first morning in Ireland, you are faced with a decision. If you are feeling heavily jet-lagged and not quite up to taking the wheel, you could stay put in your Dublin lodging for another night and sign up for a one-day tour of the Boyne Valley, which is almost certain to include the Hill of Tara. If you are going to be in Ireland during a peak tourist season, you would do best to book such a tour in advance. We recommend against the mega-coach tours and suggest something on a smaller scale, limited to under 20 persons. Two such tours currently come to mind: the Newgrange and Hill of Tara Tour with www.newgrangetours.com and the Celtic Experience tour with www.overthetoptours.com. Both €€€.

PRINCIPAL SITE
The Hill of Tara

For the average visitor, without either a third eye or archaeological expertise, the Hill of Tara is likely to be an initial disappointment. All that remains today of this hallowed site—apart from a few unimpressive standing stones and a modest passage tomb—are the complex contours of the land, which must be read like Braille, with eyes all but shut, to tell the remarkable history of this revered seat of kings. It is as if Tara must be listened to instead of seen. Surely the more inhabited we are with images and voices gleaned from early Irish literature, the more Tara comes alive and reveals its perished grandeur.

"Standing at the top or southern extremity of this remain, and bearing in mind the various prose and bardic histories of the Irish annalists, one cannot help reverting to ancient times, and again, in imagination, peopling it with its early occupants. Here sat in days of yore kings with golden crowns upon their heads; warriors with brazen swords in their hands; bards and minstrels with their harps; grey-bearded ollamhs; druids with their oak-leaf crowns..."

—*William Wilde, 19c antiquarian, father of Oscar Wilde*

The origin of Tara—or Temair, as the ancient Irish knew it—as a sacred site may, with some likelihood, be traced to the Grave Mound of the Hostages, a small passage tomb (now locked shut) dating from the late fourth or early third millennium B.C.E. Whether the siting of the tomb acknowledged the sacrality of this spot or created it, this mound—like other Neolithic grave sites—became a focus of communal ritual and, in later centuries, attracted secondary burials, ritual enclosures, and eventually royal occupation. Only the earthworks remain to the naked eye, though on-going excavations and geomagnetic surveys reveal the presence, for example, of post-holes from the numerous henges or enclosures that once shaped this vast ritual complex. Quite meticulously the mystery of Tara's long history is being unraveled, as the traditional lore of yesterday's antiquarians is brought into conversation with the raw data of today's high-tech archaeologists.

Our focus here is the summit of the Hill of Tara constituting a national heritage site. The fact is that today's fences and property lines obscure and partition what was once a far more extensive and integrated ritual complex, which included, for instance, the Rath or ring-fort of Maeve just south of the summit and Rath Lugh to the northeast. Tara, long the seat of sacred kingship, was said to be as well the dwelling-place of numerous gods and goddesses, such as Lugh and Maeve, who are both intimately associated with sovereignty. The *feis Temrach,* or the royal festival of Tara, last celebrated in 560 C.E., involved ritual intercourse between the king and Maeve, the goddess of sovereignty. In fact, the word *feis* has as it root meaning "spending the night" or "sleepover." From being one of several royal inauguration sites—such as Emain Macha and Crúachain—Tara, within the aura of the pre-eminent Uí Néill federation, eventually emerged as the symbolic seat of the would-be high kings of Ireland until it was abandoned in 1022 C.E., after 3000 years of occupation.

"There was a stone here in Tara," said Oisin, "and on it was his bed. There was a wonderful thing about his bed," said Oisin, "for the biggest man of the men of Ireland would fit in the bed of the dwarf, and the smallest infant that could be found would also just fit in it. The bed and Lía Fáil 'the Stone of Fál' that was in Tara were the two wonders of Tara."

"What wonder was on 'the Stone of Fál'?"asked Diarmait, son of Cerball. "Anyone accused by the men of Ireland," said Oisin, "was placed on that stone, and if he were truthful it would turn him white and red, and if he were untruthful there would be a black spot in an obvious place on him. When the King of Ireland came onto it the stone shrieked under him and the chief waves of Ireland answered it, the Wave of Clidna, the Wave of Tuaide [the Tuns], and the Wave of Rudraige. Whenever the king of a province came on the stone it roared under him. Whenever a barren woman came on it a dew of black blood broke through it. And whenever a fertile woman came on it a many-colored moisture came through it." "Who raised that stone or brought it from Ireland?" asked Diarmait, son of Cerball. Oisin's answer has not survived.

—*Tales of the Elders of Ireland,* tr. Ann Dooley and Harry Row (Oxford University Press, 1999), p. 223.

After the Grave Mound of the Hostages (thought to be the original site of *Lia Fáil,* the royal inauguration stone), the most visible monuments on the Hill of Tara are the circular earthworks traditionally designated as a series of ring forts or "raths." These were once the royal enclosures of regional kings, although some may represent much earlier ritual centers or burial monuments. Whatever structures once stood on them would have been made not of stone but of wood and/or wattle and daub. Whatever

Aerial view of Tara
Photo: "Dúchas, the Heritage Service", Dublin

bits remain, lie buried below your feet as you trace the footprints of these ancient henges. One of the most famous notables associated with these mounds is Cormac mac Cairt, perhaps the most famed of the early kings of Ireland and the first to have made Tara his royal seat. In the Annals his reign is said to have extended from 227 to 266 C.E. His daughter, Grainne, whose rath lies nearby, several hundred yards to the north west, was the restless wife of Finn mac Cumaill and the star-crossed lover of Diarmuit. Theirs is one of the most wrenching love stories in early Irish literature. The long rectangular earthwork lying just north of the Rath of Synods was once thought to mark the remains of a enormous banquet hall, though it is more commonly thought of now as a ritual *cursus* or entrance to the site. Curiously, the Rath of the Synods, immediately south of the cursus, fell victim between 1899 and 1902 to the fanatic "British Israelites," who, in a failed search for the Ark of the Covenant, savaged the mound and yet in the process of their pillage happened to make some interesting finds.

We recommend that your visit to Tara begin at the adjoining Interpretive Centre, where an informative and stirring audio-visual presentation will offer some initial orientation to the site as well as some kindling for your imagination. You'll need both to fully appreciate Tara. Next, by all means take advantage of the roughly 40-minute tour provided by the trained guides of the Heritage Society. Be sure to ask about the latest results of the on-going archaeological surveys and excavations of the site. Surveys in 1998, 1999, and 2002 revealed exciting, previously unknown dimensions to this site, provoking new questions and conjectures regarding the history of the hill, all of which is likely to be published and discussed in the ensuing years. When the tour disbands, the hill is yours to explore and to respect on your own.

The hill itself is an open site with uneven terrain; so come prepared with all-weather gear and sturdy walking shoes. Tours, interpretive center, and video May 26–Sept 14 daily 9am–6pm. OPW Heritage Card site. (046-902-5903) [M7] Approximately 25 miles from Dublin Airport. Ask directions to the M50 south. Take the M50 south to the N3 north towards Navan. Tara is signposted off the N3 10 miles south of Navan, Co. Meath.

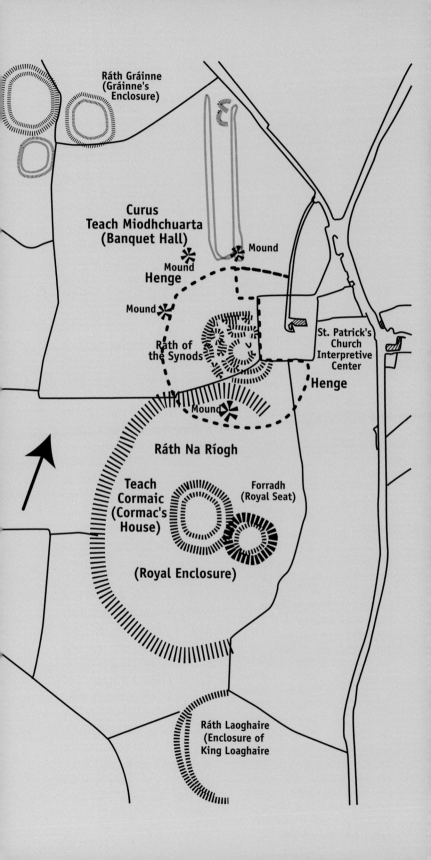

Kid Sites

Trim Castle

Also called King John's castle, this is easily the most prominent and massive Anglo-Norman castle in Ireland. Today it is more widely known as the set of the film *Braveheart*. Kids love castles, but for that matter so does nearly everyone else. The sheer scale of this symbol of Norman clout brings a dark thrill to the heart, even the not-so-brave heart. Recently restored as a "preserved ruin," throughout its history Trim was besieged only once and never taken. Instead, it collapsed from neglect and its own weight over 400 years after its erection. There's a lesson there somewhere. Open Easter–Sept daily 10am–6pm; Oct daily 9:30am–5:30pm; Nov–Jan weekends 9am–5pm; Feb–Easter weekends 9:30am–5:30pm. OPW Heritage Card site. (046-943-8619). [L7] In the town of Trim on the River Boyne, 9 miles southwest of Navan on R161.

Newgrange Farm

Literally surrounding the land preserved for the Newgrange passage tomb, this 333-acre farm has its own avid following and, on a good day, rivals Newgrange in numbers of visitors. A few of the many touted denizens whom guests are invited to visit and/or feed here are: sheep, goats, a horse and a pony, pheasants, rabbits, dogs, cats, and ants! The enthusiasm and love of animals and children of the extended family farm are contagious. Less than captivated, though captive, parents will enjoy the very pleasant coffee shop. Open Easter Saturday through August daily 10am–5pm. Admission €€ (041-982-4119) www.newgrangefarm.com. [M6] Near Slane, Co. Meath. Signposted off the N51 3 miles southeast from Slane.

Side Sites

Brú na Bóinne

Even if your primary focus is Celtic Ireland, it is all but unthinkable to be so near to the Neolithic passage tombs of Newgrange and Knowth and not to pay them a visit. These are two of Ireland's—and, for that matter, Europe's—most stunning prehistoric treasures. They are, however, accessible only by scheduled guided tours leaving from the Brú na Bóinne Visitor Centre; and for much of the year these often fill up for the day unless you are on hand in the morning to reserve a place. Consequently, you may want to make this your first stop for the day, doubling back to the Hill of Tara in the afternoon. [M6] Near Slane, Co. Meath. (041/988-0300). Open daily Feb–Apr 9:30am–5:30pm; daily May 9am–6:30pm; daily June to mid-Sept 9am–7pm; daily mid–to end Sept 9am–6:30pm; daily Oct 9:30am–5:30pm; daily Nov–Jan 9am–5pm. Knowth is closed to visitors Nov–Easter. OPW Heritage Card site. Approximately 18 miles from the Dublin Airport. Ask directions to the M50 south. Take the M50 south to the N2 north towards Slane. Newgrange is sign-posted off the N2. To reach Tara from

Newgrange, proceed back to the N2 and turn right (north), taking the N2 approximately one mile to Slane, where you will turn left onto the N51, traveling 8.5 miles southwest to Navan. In Navan, take the N3 south towards Dublin. Tara is signposted on your right off the N3 10 miles south of Navan.

Battle of the Boyne

Practically a stone's throw—provided Cúchulainn is throwing the stone—from Newgrange is the site of perhaps the most decisive battle in Irish history, fought on the 1st of July, 1690, in which King William III ("King Billy") defeated his father-in-law King James II, securing British Protestant sovereignty over Ireland for another 231 years. Today you can tour the battlefield and envision its unfolding. Free admission. Access by guided tour only, upon request. Wear weather protective clothing and suitable shoes. Open Mar–Apr daily 9:30am–5:30pm; May–Sept daily 10am–6pm; Oct–Feb daily 9am–5pm. (041-980-9950). [M6] West of Drogheda off the M1 Motorway and L21, on the South Bank of the River Boyne 2 miles north of Donore Village, Co. Meath.

Loughcrew

A more ambitious outing from Tara are the hills of Loughcrew, the "Hills of the Witch," strewn with remarkable Neolithic passage tombs and offering spectacular views of the countryside below. If you have a brilliantly clear, sunny day at your disposal, there is no better place to spend it. This is an open site and requires a steady, though not steep, climb. [K6] Near Oldcastle, Co. Meath. From Tara, proceed to the N3. Turn left and take the N3 roughly twenty miles northwest to Kells. In Kells, take R163 west approximately a dozen miles towards Millbrook. Loughcrew is signposted on your right from R163. Since you will need a key to enter the principal tomb, however, proceed past Loughcrew several minutes to Loughcrew Gardens on your left, open daily noon–6pm, Mar 17–Sept and weekends 1–4pm the remainder of the year. You will be required to leave a refundable deposit and either your passport or your driver's license for the use of the key. After fetching the key, retrace your path to the signposted turnoff for the Loughcrew passage tombs.

Bed and Board

If you can't pull yourself away from Tara and want to be able to stroll over its mounds at your leisure late into the evening, there is a modest, comfortable, and friendly B & B more or less directly across the road from the site: Seamróg, Hill of Tara, Co. Meath (046-25296) €€ CC. In addition, we specially recommend four relatively nearby accommodations in Co. Meath. The Glebe House, Dowth, Co. Meath (041-983-6101) €€ CC, situated on seven acres, immediately adjacent to the Dowth passage tomb. This gracious country house, with its several lovely rose and lavender gardens, provides comfort and a touch of elegance. Guests may bring their own wine to enjoy in the lounge/drawing room. Afternoon tea is available on request. From the N51 east of Slane follow signs to Newgrange Farm until you come to a sign for Dowth, at which point you bear left towards Dowth, while the road to Newgrange Farm continues right. The Glebe House will be on the right off of the Dowth Road. In the same vicinity, this time immediately overlooking Newgrange, there's Roughgrange Farmhouse, Donore, Co. Meath (041-982-3147 www.irishfarmholidays.com) €. The views of Newgrange and the River Boyne from here are breathtaking. In fact, if you come equipped, a room here comes with free salmon and trout fishing on the Boyne. This is a working 250-acre farm, and the oldest part of the farmhouse dates from the mid-18c. On the L21 (the local road to Newgrange off of the N2). You'll see the sign to Roughgrange Farmhouse on your right just before you come to the entrance to Brú na Bóinne on your left. Next, just outside of nearby Navan, there's the welcome calm and hospitality of Gainstown House, Trim Road, Navan, Co. Meath (046-902 3219 www.dalysbandb.com) € CC. The guest rooms are warm and comfortable, and enjoy panoramic views of the surrounding countryside. Located on the R153 2mi south of Navan on your right. Finally, we recommend Highfield House, Trim, Co. Meath (046-943-6386) €€ CC. This elegant 18th-century period residence stands above Trim Castle and the River Boyne, with great views of both, and is only minutes by foot from Trim town and the Trim Castle Hotel. In the center of Trim, at the roundabout turn right off of Castle Street onto R160 and take the first left onto Maudlins Road.

With the exception of Highfield House, the above accommodations offer no evening meals, either within their walls or within a short walk; so you will be on your own to find agreeable fare. This will not prove difficult. If you're willing to drive 6 miles north of Slane to Collon, the Forge Gallery Restaurant, Collon, Co. Louth (041-982-6272) €€ CC is highly touted and highly expensive. At the other end of the spectrum, in Donore center, just down the road from Newgrange, there's pub grub locally recommended at Daly's. Otherwise, the most convenient and promising venue for suitable cuisine is Navan, where we personally recommend two eateries. Once you've parked in the center of Navan, a brief stroll will easily uncover both of them. Hudson's Bistro, 30 Railway Street (046-907-5230) €€ CC is a finer restaurant than you would expect to find in this somewhat sleepy town and has a reputation reaching beyond the locals. The Loft, 26 Trimgate Street (046-907-1755) €€ CC is more laid back and, along with full dinners, offers a selection of lighter and less pretentious fare, such as burgers, chicken fajitas, and excellent gourmet pizzas.

DAY THREE
The Road North • Navan to Armagh

Much of today will be spent behind the wheel as you make your way from County Meath to Derry (aka Londonderry) City, via Armagh. This is a journey of roughly 150 miles in which you will cross a national border. Remember that since partition, following the Irish War of Independence, the six counties of Ulster have remained within the United Kingdom. While you're unlikely to pay much notice to crossing the border from Monaghan into Armagh, you will eventually realize that Euros don't work north of the Border, as Britain has thus far opted out of the Eurozone and has retained the pound sterling as its currency.

The first leg of your day's journey will take you from Navan, County Meath to Armagh city in County Armagh. We recommend that you take the N51 northeast to Slane, where you will pick up the N2 and take it all the way north and west to Monaghan town. From Monaghan, take the N12 northeast towards Armagh. The N12 will change names to the A3 as you cross the border. The entire trip from Navan to Armagh is just over 80 miles.

As you drive north from County Meath through Counties Louth, Monaghan, and Armagh, you will be deep in Cúchulainn country—landscape made legend in the Táin. This is where Setanta (Cúchulainn), the greatest of the Ulster heroes, held his ground for an entire Irish winter, fending off the advance of Queen Maeve, the warriors of Connacht, Leinster, and Munster as they attempted to march north with the same destination as yours, the ancient Ulster capital of Emain Macha. The modern British border fences and security checkpoints, now mostly dismantled and unmanned, dividing North from South, had their prehistoric counterparts in the series of linear earthworks— the Dorsey, the Dane's Cast, and the Black Pig's Dyke—which once stretched across portions of Counties Donegal, Monaghan, Armagh, and Down. This defensive system of banks, ditches, and timber palisades was constructed between roughly 150 B.C.E. and 500 C.E. The earliest of these, the Dorsey, built between 150 and 95 B.C.E., reached across south Armagh; and it is this line of defense which you will unwittingly cross as you make your way north today. Ulster, it seems, was "a land apart" even from ancient times—proud, defiant, and beleaguered; but it was also Irish. The Ulaid—the ancient dynasty of Ulster, with its capital at Emain Macha, defended by the Knights of the Red Branch and the *macrad* or "Boys Brigade"—were unrivalled in all of Ireland, and their heroic legends inspired the earliest Irish literature, the Ulster Cycle.

The Road North • Armagh to Derry

Derry lies just under 70 miles north and west of Armagh. You'll take the A28 north and west out of Armagh for approximately 16 miles until at Aughnacloy you pick up the A5 north to Derry. This will take you through the Sperrin Mountains of County Tyrone. The Sperrins, while they set no records for height (the highest peak, Sawel, reaches only 2,204 feet), have their own understated, unspoiled allure. They are not, however, altogether unsung, as Seamus Heaney grew up here on the edge of the Sperrins and has on occasion penned their praise.

PRINCIPAL SITE
Emain Macha

Emain Macha, or Navan Fort, lies within a far more extensive prehistoric landscape, often referred to as the Navan Complex. Over forty-six sites of prehistoric significance have been discerned, which is not to say excavated, within less than a mile of Navan Fort. Our focus here, however, is confined to the central Navan Enclosure and to a few close and closely related sites: Haughey's Fort, the King's Stables, and Loughnashade.

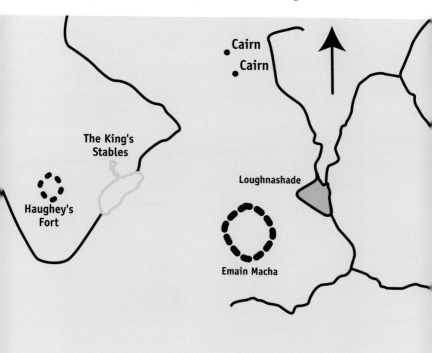

Perhaps with the one exception of the Hill of Tara, Emain Macha is unquestionably the most celebrated site in the oldest literature of Ireland. The royal seat of the kings of the Ulaid, this is the home of Fergus Mac Roech, Conchobar Mac Nessa, Cúchulainn, Deirdre of the Sorrows, and the Knights of the Red Branch, whose rivalries, wars, ecapades, and loves comprise the Ulster Cycle.

There are many explanations of how Emain Macha got its name and what it means. One of these focuses on Macha, a goddess of sovereignty and fertility with equine associations. While *emain* refers to a tumulus or otherworldly place, it has been read as well to mean "twins." This excerpt from the Ulster Cycle tells the story of Macha and her twins.

… the Ulaid held a fair, and they all went, men and women, sons and daughters. Crunniuc set out as well, with good clothes on him and a great bloom in his face. "Take care to say nothing foolish," she said to him. "Not likely that," he replied. The fair was held, and at the end of the day the king's chariot was brought on to the field, and his chariot and horses were victorious. The hosts said "Nothing is as fast as those horses are.": Crunniuc said "My wife is that fast." He was taken to the king at once, and the news was taken to his wife. "A great misfortune my having to go and free him now, when I am with child," she said. "Misfortune or no," said the messenger, "he will die if you do not come."

She went to the fair, then, and her labor pains seized her. "Help me," she said to the hosts, "for a mother bore every one of you. Wait until my children are born." She failed to move them, however. "Well then," she continued, "the evil you suffer will be greater, and it will afflict Ulaid for a long time." "What is your name?" asked the king. "My name and that of my children will mark this fairground for ever—I am Macha daughter of Sainrith son of Imbath," she said. She raced against the chariot, then, and, as the chariot reached the end of the field, she gave birth in front of it, and she bore a son and a daughter. That is why the place is called Emuin Machae (the Twins of Macha). At her delivery, she screamed that any man who heard her would suffer the pains of birth for five days and four nights. All the Ulaid who were there were so afflicted, and their descendants suffered for nine generations afterwards. Five days and four nights, or five nights and four days—that was the extent of the labor pains of the Ulaid: and, for nine generations, the Ulaid were as weak as a woman in labor.

—*Early Irish Myths and Sagas*, tr. Jeffrey Gantz (Penguin, 1981), pp. 128–129.

The heroes of the Ulster Cycle were not the first to make Emain Macha their home, but they are the ones whose names and fates have come down to us. The earliest settlement here on the Mound of Macha can be traced to the Neolithic period. The precise layers of habitation and construction since that time are complex and remain uncertain. The entire circular enclosure measures roughly 950 feet across and encompasses an area of approximately 15 acres. The placement of the ditch outside the embankment suggests that this was designed as a ritual rather than a defensive site, similar to a number of Neolithic henge monuments in Ireland and Britain; but core samples from the ditch, when dated, suggest very late Bronze Age or early Iron Age construction. Within the Navan Enclosure lie two monuments: a ring ditch, which once held three successive timber structures, and a large mound, excavated only recently, between 1963 and 1972. It is this mound that preserved Emain Macha's most profound mystery.

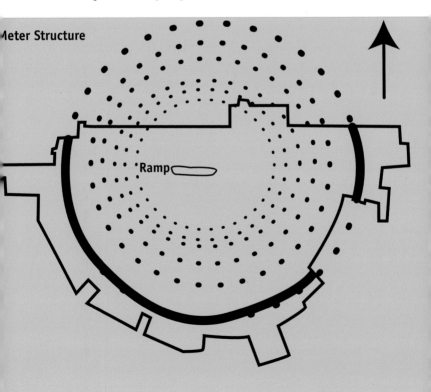

Meter Structure

Ramp

Emain Macha

In the first century B.C.E., perhaps coincident with the rise of the Ulaid and the Red Branch to preeminence, a great Celtic hall or temple was erected on the great mound within the Navan Enclosure. It consisted of six concentric rings of upright oak posts, 275 in all. In the center of this great hall stood a free-standing wooden pillar, estimated to have been as much as 40 feet in height and often interpreted as a totem pole of sorts, a "world tree" or *axis mundi,* marking the corridor between the earthly realm and the otherworld. It is wondered and debated whether this structure was roofed. The fact that the outermost circle of posts—roughly 130 feet in diameter—were doubled and erected in pairs provides support to this theory (as did the posts to the roof, if the theory be true). The deepest mystery here, however, concerns the demise of the great hall. For reasons unknown, before any of its supporting posts had even begun to rot, the interior of the hall was piled high with limestone boulders to a height of over six feet, forming an interior cairn. Then the structure was set ablaze. After the fire had consumed the massive hall, the remaining limestone cairn was covered with sod to form the grassy mound visible today. Speculations of course abound regarding the destruction of the great hall of Emain Macha. Mostly they divide into two categories: either it was a hostile act of a rival tribe or invading people; or it was an intentional, ritual act, with precedents in the Vedic sacrificial rites of ancient India, a culture clearly demonstrated to have been related to and cognate with the culture of ancient Ireland. In either case, the likely suspects are the Ulaid and the Red Branch.

The three remaining visible monuments of note in the Navan Complex lie quite nearby. To the northwest, at the base of the hill on which Navan Fort is situated, you'll find a site known as the "King's Stables," once mistakenly identified as the place where ancient kings watered and housed their horses. Instead, this was, it seems, a place of ritual sacrifice, where offerings were deposited. Only 80 feet across and 13 feet deep, this is a prehistoric artificial pool, the only such ever discovered in Ireland or Great Britain. When excavated, it was found to contain animal bones, sword molds, and a portion of a human skull. Another much larger, natural body of water also used for ritual offerings lies to the northeast, immediately downslope from Navan Enclosure. This is Loughnashade, the "Lake of the Treasure," where along with animal bones and human skulls four magnificent Bronze Age horns were found in the late 18th century, only one of which has made it into the 21st century. Known, not surprisingly, as the "Loughnashade Trumpet," you have already marveled at this particular treasure in the National Museum. Loughnashade today occupies only a little over an acre, while in prehistory it may have covered anywhere from 5 to 20 acres. Lastly, there is Haughey's Fort, three-quarters of a mile west of Navan Fort. Dating from roughly 1100 B.C.E., this was a Late Bronze Age hill fort, surrounded by three defensive ditches, an indication of its owner's high status. The outer ditch measures nearly 400 yards in diameter.

We recommend that you begin your tour of Emain Macha with a visit to the quite splendid Navan Centre. Here you'll be able to enjoy not one but three videos introducing you to the site: "The Dawning" provides an informative introduction to the world of pre-Christian Ireland and the Celts; "The Real World" presents the archaeology of Navan Fort, uncovering and tracing its ancient settlements; and, finally, "The Other World" brings to life the stories and legends of Emain Macha and its illustrious heroes. After viewing this material and exploring the interpretive center's exhibits, you would do well to take advantage of the guided tours on offer here. In recent years this site has become especially kid-friendly, with lots of opportunities to help history come alive. Would-be miniature kings, queens, and heroes can make their own shields, swords, brooches, and necklaces to take home and live the fantasy. [L4] The Navan Centre (028/3752-9644 www.armagh.co.uk) ££ CC is located at 81 Killylea Road, two miles west of Armagh city. Signposted from city center. Open Apr–Sept daily 10am–6pm, and Oct–Mar Mon–Sat 10am–4pm.

Side Sites

City of Armagh

Armagh—the ancient capital of Ulster and to this day the center of Irish Christianity—offers a number of attractions, to which The Saint Patrick's Trian Visitor Complex (028/3752-1801) in the Old Bank Building at 40 English Street will be more than glad to direct you. What will strike your eye regardless, however, will be the city's two hills, topped by two cathedrals, one Catholic and one belonging to the Church of Ireland. These are the churches of the island's two primates, Catholic and Protestant, both tracing their roots to Patrick, who is said to have had a particularly close connection with Armagh. Of particular interest to this itinerary is an Iron Age sculpture to be found against the south wall of the nave of the medieval Church of Ireland Cathedral. Known as the "Tandragee Idol," it is thought to be a carving of "Nuadha of the Silver Arm," legendary king of the Tuatha Dé Danann, who fought against the Fir Bolg and lost his arm in the first battle of Magh Tuiredh. The silver arm of note here refers to the prosthetic fashioned and fitted by Dian Cécht, the king's physician. The cathedral also houses a number of interesting later sculptures and works of art; and, buried on the north side of the cathedral, lies the famed Brian Boru, who is traditionally credited with having liberated Ireland from the Vikings.

Dáire went out to honour holy Patrick, bringing with him a marvellous bronze cauldron from overseas which held three measures. And Dáire said to the holy man: 'Look, this cauldron shall be yours!' And Patrick said: 'Grazacham!' When Dáire came home he said: 'This man is a fool, if he has nothing better to say for a marvellous bronze cauldron of three measures but only "grazacham".' And then Dáire said to his servants: 'Go, and bring us our bronze vessel back!' They went out and told Patrick: 'We are to take the bronze vessel back.' Nonetheless on that occasion also holy Patrick said 'Grazacham, take it', and they took it away. And Dáire asked his companions and said: 'What did the Christian say when you took the bronze vessel back?' And they replied: 'He said "grazacham".' And Dáire answered and said: 'Grazacham for the gift, grazacham for its withdrawal; his saying is such a good one, with these grazachams his bronze vessel shall be brought to him again!' And Dáire this time came in person and brought Patrick the bronze vessel and said to him: 'This vessel shall be yours, for you are a steadfast man whom nothing can change. Besides, I give you now that piece of land for which you once asked, so far as it is mine—dwell there.' This is the city which is now called Armagh.

—*The Patrician Texts in the Book of Armagh, Scriptores Latini Hiberniae X,* edited with introduction, translation, and commentary by Ludwig Bieler, DIAS 2000. p.111.

City of Derry

Also known as Londonderry, Derry is Northern Ireland's second largest city and perhaps its most closely kept secret. Best known for Bloody Sunday, Derry, dating from the 6th century, has often come under seige, and still does on occasion. But none of this diminishes the simple fact that Derry is one of Ireland's most appealing and intriguing cities, with more to see and do than you'll ever realize in a day or two, much less overnight. Don't be surprised or feel guilty if you find yourself sorely tempted to scrap the Iron Age and linger here for a while. You won't be the first. The Derry Visitor and Convention Bureau and Tourist Information Centre (028/7126-7284 www.derryvisitor.com), at 44 Foyle Street is your single best font of information and assistance as you plan your remaining hours or days in Derry.

Derry City   Courtesy of the Northern Ireland Tourist Board

Assuming, however, that you are holding course and have only the late afternoon and early evening to explore the city, be sure at the least to walk Derry's great 17th-century walls, roughly a mile in circumference and 18 feet thick. A stroll along these ramparts are at the same time a walk through Derry's turbulent history and provide excellent views of the city, within and beyond the walls. A menu of different guided walking tours are usually on offer through the Derry Visitor Bureau/Tourist Information Centre; and if one is available at a time convenient for you, we would strongly recommend your taking advantage of it. Cityscapes always make a lot more sense when you hear their stories. Another focal point in Derry is "the Diamond," the city's central square, just west of the River Foyle. Radiating out from the Diamond are four streets, which after several blocks come to walled gateways, each bearing the same name as the street that leads to it: Bishop's gate, Ferryquay Gate, Shipquay Gate, and Butcher's Gate. This is the heart of historic Derry. For a stirring and informative walk through Derry's history, don't miss the Tower Museum (028/7137-2411) housed in O'Doherty

Tower, a medieval-style fort, at Union Place Hall in the city center. Open Tues–Sat 10am–5pm and Sun noon–4pm, with seasonal adjustments. Admission £.

After Dark

Derry has an active, often frenetic, night scene, with something for both high and low octane visitors. Be sure to check out what is on at the Millennium Theatre Complex, Derry's grand new venue for the arts. Derry also has a number of hole-in-the-wall theater venues and, of course, is replete with pubs and night clubs. If you crave Irish traditional music, you're unlikely to be disappointed. Just walk the streets and follow your ears.

Bed and Board

In Derry, we specially recommend several accommodations. Two beautifully restored 19th-century townhouses—the Saddler's House and the Merchant's House—rank among the city's most charming places to stay. They are only a very short walk from the heart of Derry and are several blocks from each other. The Saddler's House (www.thesaddlershouse.com), a cozy Victorian, is located at 36 Great James Street; and the Merchant's House, a more elegant Georgian residence, is at 16 Queen Street. To inquire into or book either one, call 028/7126-9691 £. Just 5 minutes' drive from Derry center on the east bank of the River Foyle is Derry's newest hotel, the Waterfoot, Caw Roundabout Waterside (028/7134-5500 www.waterfoothotel.com) CC £. It's convenient, basic, and affordable, with an attractive restaurant and wine bar onsite. Finally, for a more secluded and elegant option, just outside the city center in a quiet residential area there's the Beech Hill Country House Hotel (028/7134-9279, www.beech-hill.com) CC ££ at 32 Ardmore Road, dating from 1729, boasts fine antiques and marble fireplaces in the public areas and some of its rooms have four-poster beds. The wooded hotel grounds are inviting for a short stroll; and, for a more aerobic effort, there's an in-house mini-gym. The hotel's Ardmore Restaurant is one of the top dining choices in Derry.

Kid Sites

Ulster National Folk Park
En route to Derry, this exceptional attraction is perfectly situated to break up the last leg of your day's journey to Derry and will be sure to engage the entire family. The park, an extensive outdoor living history museum, has been developed around the homestead of Thomas Mellon, father of Andrew Mellon. Thomas emigrated to Pittsburgh in the 19th century, where he and his son prospered. The museum park is also dedicated to telling the story of all the Northern Irish who emigrated to America in the 18th and 19th centuries. Among the park's diverse exhibits are a Sperrin Mountain famine cabin and a full-scale replica of an Irish emigrant ship and dockside area featuring original buildings from the old ports of Derry and Belfast. A self-guided walking tour through the park can take as little as two hours, time enough to stretch your legs and your imagination without delaying unduly your arrival in Derry, now less than 30 miles to the north. Open Oct-Feb Tues–Fri 10am-4pm; Mar-Sept Tues–Sun 10am-4pm, Sat and Sun 11am-4pm. Admission ££. (028/8224-3292). Three miles north of Omagh on Mellon Road off A5 (signposted).

The Fifth Province
A multimedia high-tech odyssey through Ireland's past, present, and envisioned future. Fantasy, history, and special effects combine for an unforgettable Celtic experience that will intrigue kids and adults. Located at the Calgach Centre, 4-22 Butcher Street (028/7137-3177). Showings year-round Mon–Fri 9.30am and 4pm. Admission £.

Dining in Derry is not much of a challenge, as there is always an array of more than acceptable options. Though you'll probably prefer to explore the laneways, scope out the menus, and follow your own nose, a few tips might prove helpful. Beech Hill's highly touted Ardmore Restaurant (CC £££) have already been noted and deserve serious consideration. For truly exceptional Italian cuisine in a congenial, relaxed setting, seek out La Sosta (028/7137-4817), nearly hidden away at 45A Carlisle Road. Easy to overlook but never disappointing. Our final suggestion is Badger's (028/7136-3306), CC £, at 16–18 Orchard Street in the heart of Derry—a low-budget, local favorite hangout for memorable pub grub and a glass of your favorite brew.

Ulster National Folk Park
Courtesy of the
Northern Ireland Tourist Board

Day Four
The Road South •
Derry to Westport

Today is another day of somewhat serious driving. It will take you through several counties: Donegal, Sligo, and Mayo. The total mileage from Derry to Westport, give or take a few miles, is identical to yesterday's bottom line of 150 miles. As both Derry and Westport are appealing towns which you are likely to leave with some reluctance, it's a toss-up whether to leave Derry late or to arrive in Westport early. I would opt for the latter, especially in the summer months, when Westport's afternoon rush hour can begin as early as 3 or 4pm and prove disheartening after a day at the wheel. Besides, there are some quite enticing stops along the way, for which you will want to create some give in your schedule.

The route we recommend takes you out of Derry on the A2, becoming the N13 at the border of the Republic. Today's principal site, the Grianan of Aileach, will be signposted on your left only a mile or so after leaving Northern Ireland. Resuming your journey, you will take the N13 west and south past Letterkenny. At Ballybofey (12 miles south of Letterkenny) the N13 merges with the N15, which you take south to Donegal town. Much of this stretch from Ballybofey to Donegal, across the Barnesmore Gap through the Blue Stack Mountains, is starkly beautiful. After the Grianan, you may want to take your first break either in Donegal town or, 40 miles further on, in Sligo town. Both have their attractions. From Donegal town, stay on the N15 south through Bundoran to Sligo town. Once in the center of Sligo, look for signs to the N4 which you will take south 9 miles to Collooney, where you will pick up the N17 south. Then, after 15 miles on N17, you will come to Charlestown, where you pick up the N5, on which you will travel the remaining 35 miles straight into Westport.

PRINCIPAL SITE
Grianan of Aileach

There are many spellings for this site, the local one being "Grianan Ailig"; so if you see any sign resembling either of these and beginning with "Grianan," chances are you have arrived.

As you climb (mostly by car) the steep ridge on which the Grianan is situated, what will likely strike you first about this fort is its privileged position, 803 feet above sea level. Its stunning and strategically commanding view of Inishowen and of the twin Loughs—Foyle to the east and Swilly to the west—is without equal here, as were its owners. In ancient times, every bit as much as in modern times, *where* you are indicates *who* you are. In other words, real estate and power go together. And the occupants of this piece of prime real estate were a local sept or branch of the Uí Néill (or O'Neills), perhaps the most powerful tribe or clan in all of ancient Ireland. To give you a sense of their reach, you will recall that for centuries the Uí Néill also claimed the kingship of Tara and ruled from Armagh. And that's only the Northern Uí Néill. The Southern Uí Néill once controlled much of the central heartland of Ireland. It would be a mistake, then, to imagine that the clout behind this daunting *cashel* reached only as far as the eye can see from its walls.

Dead Nuada rests in the Grianan of Aileach;
Ogma lies low in sídh Airceltrai;
While the Dagda, thrust into the background by his son Aengus,
Mixes little in the affairs of Érin.

—*Celtic Myth and Legend*, Charles Squire, 1901

Much of the history of this site is buried and lost beneath the massive walls of the restored fortress before your eyes. Legend has it that the Grianan was built by gods on an ancient ritual site sacred to the sun; but the only surviving evidence of earlier use seems to be several mostly obscured concentric mounds or earthworks surrounding the *cashel* and occupying roughly 5 acres. This may indeed be all that remains of a prehistoric hill fort dating from the Late Bronze or Early Iron Age. Another legend suggests that this or some earlier ring fort on this site was once called the "Weeping Place of Women," a haven where women were kept safe while their men went into battle. We are on more solid ground, however, when we date its construction to the early period of Irish Christianity. Patrick himself is said to have baptized Owen, the first Uí Néill king here—but not likely within these walls—in 450 C.E. The fort's demise—less a matter for conjecture than its origins—came in 1101, when an enraged and vengeful King of Munster, named Murtagh O'Brien, not only destroyed the *cashel* but also tried to remove it. He is said to have ordered each of his men to take one of the Grianan's stones away with him on the return south to County Clare, where O'Brien's own royal seat in Kincora, County Clare, had been demolished in 1088 by Domnall Mac Lochlainn, King of Aileach. Fortunately it is more work to recycle a *cashel* than it is to tear it down; so most of the Grianan's stonework was left behind by the invaders. The eventual reconstruction of the *cashel* in the 1870's, much as you see it today, was the work of Dr. Walter Bernard, a local historian, who made some guesses and took some liberties as he went along. For instance,

Ramparts of Grianan

the interior stairways and wall-walks are of unsure authenticity. The outer wall of the circular fortress is 17 feet high, 77 feet in diameter, and 13 feet thick. The quite long lintelled entrance is more like a passageway than a door. [J2] Access to the site is open and free of charge. Not so with the visitor's center downhill from the fort. It's your call, but we would recommend your taking a pass on the center and getting underway after you've explored the Grianan site on your own. The Grianan of Aileach is signposted off the N13 soon after you cross the border into the Republic and County Donegal.

Side Sites

Donegal Craft Village

If you decided not to make a major stop in Donegal town, you may want to pull over here for fifteen minutes or so, just to stretch your legs and window shop. This ever-changing cluster of local artisans' studios and shops is often full of surprises. Art is like that. You never know what you'll find; and it can be intriguing just to eavesdrop on the creative process. Besides, in summer months, there's a coffee shop here serving lunch and light snacks. The Donegal Craft Village (073/22015) is free and open to the public and is located on Ballyshannon Road (N15) on your left no more than a mile beyond Donegal town center.

Creevykeel Court Cairn

Creevykeel is one of the finest examples of the court cairn, the monument type widely considered to be the earliest form of megalithic construction in Ireland. The footprint of the tomb is trapezoidal, with a u-shaped open court measuring roughly 50 by 30 feet. The central gallery is segmented by portals and sills into two distinct chambers. The wedge-shaped cairn that would have originally covered the tomb must have extended roughly 230 feet in length. [G4] Open site. Signposted on the N15 roughly 7 miles south of Bundoran. Without much warning you will see the parking lot on your left.

Drumcliffe Churchyard

If you have a soft or devoted spot in your heart for Yeats, then this is a magnet whose tug you will find hard to resist—the grave of the man himself, with its famous epitaph. Otherwise you may cast a cold eye and pass by. [G5] Open site. Signposted on the N15, roughly 16 miles south of Bundoran. The parking lot and site will be on your left. Yeats devotees may also want to visit the Yeats Memorial Building in the center of Sligo, as well as Lissadell House (www.lissadellhouse.com), a favorite spot for Yeats, where he occasionally dropped anchor. Signposted off the N15 8 miles north of Sligo.

Sligo Town

Sligo comes as a surprise to many an unwitting passer-through. Though seldom touted on the tourist circuit, it is in fact a quite appealing town, the kind of place you can imagine living and not just visiting. This is due in large part to a renaissance of sorts in the 1990's when over half of the town's epicenter was refurbished. It was as if Sligo suddenly opened its windows and rediscovered its own Garavogue River, meandering across the downtown. Soon cafés and restaurants spilled outside and created a waterfront life that, while not scintillating, is at least there, when weather permits. If you haven't had lunch yet, this may be a good place to stop for a stroll and a bit of nourishment. It can take some time, however, to negotiate traffic and find parking; so, if your time is tight, you may want to heed the words of Yeats and "pass by."

Museum of Country Life at Turloch Park

This, the latest venue of the National Museum of Ireland, opened its doors in September 2001. And, as fate would have it, it is immediately off the road you are taking to Westport. If you can tolerate the delay, this is well worth an hour or two of your time. Turloch Park, with its grand gardens and artificial lake, is now home to a gem of a museum housing the nation's folklife collection and telling the story of rural life throughout Ireland. Until quite recently, Ireland was a predominantly rural and on the whole a desperately impoverished country, rich all the same in its indomitable people and folk culture. Now that vanishing world is preserved here for you to re-enter and

Kid Sites

Donegal Castle

Perched strategically above the River Eske, this magnificent 15th-century keep, beautifully restored in 1996, once belonged to the O'Donnells, a Donegal clan with considerable clout. The 20-gabled extension was added during the Plantation period in the 17th century by Sir Basil Brooke. You can breeze through on your own in fifteen minutes or take advantage of the free guided tours lasting nearly a half hour. [H4] Donegal Castle (074/972-2405) is only several minutes' walk up from the Diamond, Donegal town's triangular central market. OPW Heritage Card site. Open Easter–Oct daily 10am–6pm; Nov–Easter Thurs–Sun 9:30am–4:30pm.

Bundoran

If the kids are rebelling and need to put everything ancient behind them for a few hours, there's always Bundoran, the Irish Coney Island, 23 miles north of Sligo on the N15. There are beaches and plenty of amusements that will light up small eyes.

Westport House and Children's Animal and Bird Park

Although Westport House, the late 18th-century residence of Lord Altamount, Marquis of Sligo, is surely a quite grand historic home worthy of a peek, our focus here is on the array of children's attractions splashed over its expansive grounds. There's everything from a zoo to "pitch n' putt" experience in your imagination. There's also a most enjoyable café serving traditional hot meals, sand-wiches, and pastries through-out day. Open year-round Tues–Sat 10am–5pm and Sun 2–5pm. Admission free. (01-677-7444 www.museum.ie). [D6] Signposted on the N5 5 miles south of Castlebar.

Westport Town

Unlike Sligo, Wesport is no secret. Especially when the sun shines, it's a magnet if not a Mecca for tourists and weekenders from as far as Dublin. Situated at the edge of Clew Bay and with the tidal Carrowbeg River flowing through its central tree-lined mall, Westport ranks high among Ireland's most attractive large towns. One of the island's few planned towns, Westport was designed by Richard Castle in the 18th century, and especially of late has done its best to outgrow itself. You'll want to save some time to walk its streets, windowshop, and pay a visit to one or more of its popular pubs.

Bed and Board

With only one night in Westport, you'll probably want to be in the heart of the town; and in that case there's no better location than the Westport Plaza Hotel (98-51166 www.westportplazahotel.ie) €€ CC a stone's throw or short stroll from the center of town in a quiet setting with ample underground parking. The rooms here (miniature golf) to train rides to swan boats and amusements. So if the kids are deserving of a treat, this could be it. The hours of opening here are complicated and ever in flux, but you can count on the park and kids' stuff being open daily during the summer from early to late afternoon. For details call (098/27766) or go to: www.westporthouse.ie. Admission €€€. Located at the edge of Westport town on the road towards Westport Quay.

rise in luxury from "standard" to "presidential." If you wish for no other status than standard, you can avoid going broke here; and extras include a spa and leisure center. If

Westport

you enjoy being spoiled for choice in addition to being just plain spoiled, the Plaza's sister, the Castlecourt Hotel (98-51166 www.castlecourthotel.ie) €€ CC is just next door, with reasonably comparable luxury but without the presidential option. Then, on a more modest note, there's the cheery, bright, stylish, and ever-popular Boulevard Guest House (098/25138 www.boulevard-guesthouse.com) € CC. Located on the south side and more quiet end of the Mall. It has only five rooms, so you'll want to be sure to book well in advance. Finally, if you would prefer to be out of the town's bustle and close to the sea, there's the chic, newly refurbished Carlton Atlantic Coast Hotel (098/29000 www.atlanticcoasthotel.com) €€ CC at the Quay, offering all of the amenities of a large hotel, including a full health club. You can even ask for seaweed hydrotherapy, which more or less means sharing a hot salty tub with a large clump of fresh kelp—highly recommended for whatever ails you.

Westport is replete with restaurants, so you very likely will want to stroll and survey the options. Even without a stroll, each of the hotels would be glad to make sure you don't go to bed hungry or ill-fed. For example, the Atlantic Coast Hotel is one of Westport's prime choices for fine dining. Also at the Atlantic you'll find less expensive fare in the ground-floor pub. As it happens, there are two other excellent restaurants nearby: Quay Cottage (098/26412) €€ CC, at the gates of Westport House, specializes in seafood and has a separate non-smoking dining room; and Ardmore House (098/25994) €€€ CC, overlooking Westport Harbour. Last but far from the least is our pick of the lot, the Lemon Peel (098/26929) €€ CC, located at the Octagon and serving extraordinary modern Irish cuisine and seafood.

DAY FIVE
Galway Bound

Today's drive is likely to take your breath away. Our suggested route may seem slightly circuitous; but, so long as the skies are clear enough to provide moderate visibility, you won't regret the handful of extra miles entailed. More likely, you'll be wanting more. In

Michelin's terms, today's itinerary is solid green all the way from Westport to Galway, and much of it is bite-your-lip beautiful. In sheer numbers, we're talking roughly 85 meandering miles, in the course of which you are going to want to stop an inestimable number of times for a stroll, a climb, a swim, a photo, or perhaps just to imprint a scene on your mind for the rest of your life.

This, then, is the route we suggest south through County Mayo and Connemara, County Galway. Out of Westport you will take the coast road to Louisburgh (R335 west). This will take you past the Croagh Patrick Information Center (on your left) and the National Famine Memorial (on your right) and will, as an extra feature, provide fine vistas of Clew Bay. In Louisburgh (unless you stop in at the Granuaile Centre) you will keep going on the R335, which now aims due south to Leenane. Much of the roughly 20-mi stretch from Louisburgh to Leenane is quite spectacular. When you come to Leenane, you will take the N59 southwest towards Letterfrack with Killary Harbour (a fjord-like inlet rimmed by steep mountains) on your right for approximately 7 miles until you come to R344 in the direction of Recess. If you have decided to visit Kylemore Abbey and/or Connemara National Park, you will continue further on R344; otherwise turn left here onto R344 and proceed south through one of the most breathtaking valleys in Ireland, where you will drive along the shoreline of Lough Inagh, embraced on either side by the Maumturk and the Twelve Pin Mountains. After a little under 10 miles on R344 you'll pick up the N59 in the direction of Recess and Maam Cross, with the Lechnavrea Mountains on your left (to the north). Then, after 9 miles or so on the N59 you will reach Maam Cross, where you turn right onto R336 in the direction of Ballynahown and Galway. You'll travel pretty much due south on R336 until you reach Ballynahown and Galway Bay. At that point, since you can't go any further without a boat, R336 fortuitously bends left and east and, in less than 20 more miles, takes you along Galway Bay directly into the old city of Galway, eluding most of the urban sprawl and gridlock that plague Galway as it expands all but uncontrollably into a major city.

PRINCIPAL SITE
Croagh Patrick

Whether you reach the 2509-ft summit of Croagh Patrick—also known as "The Reek"—on foot or only with your eyes from afar, it deserves a prolonged, wondering gaze. This is Ireland's holy mountain, not only for Christians but for those who preceded them here. The annual Christian pilgrimage to its summit is but the transforming continuation of celebratory ascents and festivals dating from at least the Late Bronze and Iron Ages, and likely extending back much further to the Neolithic period. In short, people have been climbing this mountain with heightened hopes and inflamed imaginations for perhaps five thousand years. Two recent (1994–95 and 1996–98) archaeological surveys of the summit and the surrounding slopes have identified nearly 300 sites dating from the Neolithic to the early Christian periods, including hut sites, burial mounds, ring barrows, standing stones, field fences, cooking sites, ring forts, cashels, raths, enclosures, souterrains, oratories, and a crannog. All of this suggests habitation and ritual use of the summit and its slopes for the past four or five millennia. Most of these sites are of interest only to hardcore specialists and would require numerous treks with detailed topographical maps and archaeological surveys in hand. For now it is better to stand and contemplate (if you are blessed with a clear day) the glistening summit cone, whose hard Pre-Cambrian quartzite scree was so favored by prehistoric cairn-builders for its light-refractive radiance, and to decide whether you have the time, the weather, the legs, the cardio-vascular health, and the will to make the climb. Unless you are Lance Armstrong, you are unlikely to reach the summit and return in less than several hours; but you don't have to be Lance to make the journey if you take your time. Only a handful of years ago a dear friend of ours, whose cottage lies at the foot of the Reek, made the full climb with his dog on his eightieth birthday and was home in plenty of time to blow out the candles on his cake. Dress warmly in layers (one layer of which should be waterproof) no matter what the temperature below, wear sturdy supportive shoes or boots, and carry a staff. If you didn't think to pack a walking staff, don't break one off a tree. You can purchase or rent one at the foot of the mountain.

Croagh Patrick

While the more ancient route to the summit was from the southeast, today's pilgrims and trekkers mostly begin their ascent from the village of Murrisk at the Croagh Patrick Information Centre off the coast road. The medieval pilgrimage along the Tóchar Phádraig or Patrick's Way from Balintubber Abbey (founded in 1216) is still active, however. The Tóchar Phádraig, once 12 feet wide and 15 miles long, is now only a marked path, nevertheless heavily trodden once a year on the last Sunday of July, called "Reek Sunday" or *Domhnach Chrom Dubh* (Chrom Dubh's Sunday), when devout and/or avidly curious climbers, in the tens of thousands, make the ascent. It is interesting that even today the ancient pre-Christian name of this festival is preserved; for Patrick and his followers were not the first to initiate mysteries here. Chrom, a harvest god, and Lugh, a god of light, were associated with this mount long before Patrick. Until the late 19th century the hilltop festival of Chrom Dubh and of Phádraig were celebrated not on the last Sunday but on the last Friday of July, preceding only by days the festival of Lugh, Lughnasa, on the 1st of August. Even today the Casán Phádraig or "Patrick's Path" to the summit incorporates some pre-Christian mounds as "stations" around which pilgrims must walk and pray *deisal* or "sun-wise" 7 or 15 times.

For Christians, the founding legend of Croagh Patrick concerns the forty days and nights Patrick is said to have spent here in fasting and prayer. The natural indentation in the rock called the *Leaba Phádraig* or "Bed of Patrick" reputedly marks the place where he rested from his trials and rigors. Patterned after the Synoptic Gospels' accounts of Jesus' temptation in the desert, the traditional account tells how Patrick too was tempted by a demon, in this case the devil's mother, who confronted him as a great bird and a monstrous serpent. Curiously, Patrick's victory over the demonic as well as his banishing of all serpents from Ireland were accomplished by his ringing and hurling of a silver bell given him by St. Brigid. It is, of course, a fact that Ireland was without reptiles long before the time of Patrick and is more than a suspicion that Patrick never set foot on the Reek; but there seems little doubt that the summit of the mountain was the site of a very early monastic settlement and, like many other of Ireland's holy places, has long been associated with Patrick, at least since the 7th century.

> "And Patrick proceeded to the summit of the mountain, climbing Cruachán Aigli, and staying there forty days and forty nights... because to all the holy men of Ireland, past, present and future, God said 'Climb, o holy men, to the top of the mountain which towers above and is higher than all the mountains to the west of the sun, in order to bless the people of Ireland' so that Patrick might see the fruit of his labours."

> —*Tírechán (7c) quoted in Michael Herren, "Mission and Monasticism in the Confessio of Patrick," in* Sages, Saints and Storytellers: Celtic Studies in Honour of Professar James Carney, *ed, Donnchadh Ó Corráin, Liam Breathnach and Kim McCone (Maynooth, 1989), pp, 76–85.*

If you make the full climb and reach the summit, in addition to stunning views of Clew Bay and its hundreds of islands, you will encounter the subtle remains of a number of ancient monuments and sites located and identified on the plan below, based on the 1994–95 excavations here. The remains of the original drystone corbelled oratory have been radiocarbon dated between 430 and 890 C.E. Perhaps the most startling fact is that the entire summit was once encircled by a rampart wall, perhaps dating from the Late Bronze Age. C. Ottoway, visiting the summit in 1839, provided the first recorded description of this encircling wall.

"Turning in a northerly direction to where the mountain looks to the north, and presents the longest face of its summit to Clew Bay, I was surprised and gratified to find along this whole range of the platform a low wall, built of large, uncemented stones evidently of the most ancient construction—a Cyclopean monument raised ages before the Roman Patrick ascended, if ever he did ascend, built by that ancient people that have erected their solemn monuments in every land, and have left behind what proves, that however unaccountable their remains, they were created by men of intelligence and great social power. The low wall which, I believe, has never been before noticed, a wall that has borne the Atlantic tempest of thousands of years, I observed, and considered it afforded me a clue to unravel, as I think, the mystery of this mountain, and explain the traditional story of St. Patrick and the serpents… "

—*C. Ottoway,* Tour of Connaught*, p. 219.*

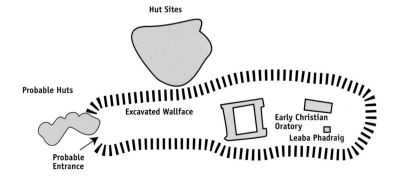

[C/D6] Croagh Patrick is best climbed from the town of Murisk at the Croagh Patrick Information Centre (098/64114), www.croagh-patrick.com, located 6 miles from Westport Quay on the coast road (R335 west) towards Louisburgh. The center, in addition to exhibits, offers a gift store and coffee shop.

Side Sites

National Famine Memorial

Directly across from the Croagh Patrick Information Centre, this remarkably poignant memorial garden and sculpture were dedicated in 1997 by President Mary Robinson "To honour the memory of all who died, suffered and emigrated due to the Great Famine of 1845–1850 and the victims of all famines." The sculpture by John Behan, entitled "Coffin Ship," conveys quite viscerally the lingering, haunting horror of all those who perished and of those who fled from starvation during those unthinkable years. Fortunately, the meditative tranquility of the memorial's garden and the seascape beyond provide a welcome balance to the nightmarish despair of the sculpture. To grasp the scale of the suffering remembered here, we need to recall that the Great Hunger claimed over a million lives in Ireland and sent another million Irish off to sea in what were often nothing but death ships. The full toll of this shameful disaster may be seen in the fact that between 1841 to 1941 the population of Ireland was cut in half.

The Boheh Stone

It's doubtful whether you should or will pay the Boheh Stone a visit, but it's important that you know what and where it is. The Boheh Stone refers to the exceptional rock art on a natural rock outcrop averaging over 7 feet in height and five feet across. It is held to be one of the most densely decorated and wonderfully carved stones in Ireland and Britain, though today its carvings are well worn and the stone itself is largely overgrown with vegetation. The most intriguing thing about the Boheh Stone is its location along the ancient *Tóchar Phádraig*, which may represent an even more ancient Late Bronze or Iron Age trackway, and its alignment with the north face of the mountain ridge of

Croagh Patrick, where a marvellous solar event occurs twice each year. This occurrence is known as "the rolling sun spectacle." On April 18 and August 24 (which together with the Winter Solstice roughly divide the year into three equal parts) the fiery disc of the setting sun appears (only from this spot) to roll slowly down the northern slope of the pyramidal cone Croagh Patrick before disappearing from sight. These two dates—April 18 and August 24—are thought to have corresponded to the times for the planting and the harvesting of crops, respectively. If you happen to be here on one of the days at sunset, here's how to find the Boheh Stone from the Croagh Patrick Information Centre. Turn right onto the coast road towards Westport. After passing an Emo gas station on your right and as the road to town veers left, bear right towards the Cloona Health Farm. You will pass a road sign for "Cloona" on the right and then, at the first T-junction, turn right onto the N59 towards Leenane. After you pass the sign for Knappagh Village, look for the nearby Knappagh shop and take the first left after the shop. Proceed to the top of the hill, veering right at the fork. Don Gibbon's house will be the first house on the right, largely obscured by trees. The Boheh Stone lies in his garden to the right as you face Don's house from the road. This is private property; so please respect that fact by knocking at Don's door and asking permission to see the stone.

Kylemore Abbey

Nearly every tour bus coursing through Connemara stops here, which may not sound appealing, but there has to be a reason for all that attention. Kylemore Abbey, though thronged and loving every minute of it, is admittedly post-card perfect, which is why you've probably already seen it several times. The truth is it lives up to its photos. Among the sites here, the recently restored Gothic chapel is the highlight; and, if you have time and energy to spare, you will be rewarded with quite a vista if you mount the steep path to the statue standing hundreds of feet above the abbey and its picturesque lake. An extensive craft and gift shop and a tea house are all part of the Kylemore complex. [C7] Kylemore House, Abbey, and grounds(095/52000, www.kylemoreabbey.com) are located 8 miles east of Clifden and roughly 10 miles west Leenane on the N59.

Kylemore Abbey

Guided tours of the Abbey are available every day from April to the end of September and of the Victorian Walled Garden from mid-April to the end of August €€ CC.

Connemara National Park

If you want to stretch your legs and take in some splendor, the nearly 5,000 acres of mountain peaks, bogs, meadows, grasslands, and heaths comprising this stunning national park have everything you're looking for. If you have 20 minutes you can see it all on film in the exhibition center, but that may only torment you if you can't take out another hour or so to sample the park's riches on one or both of the park's short guided nature trails. [C7] The Connemara National Park exhibition center is open daily Mar–May 10am–5:30pm, June–Aug 9:30am–6:30pm, and Sept–Oct 10am–5:30pm. The park grounds are open all year round. OPW Heritage Card site. Entrance and center located in Letterfrack village on the N59.

Galway City

With a population of roughly 70,000, Galway is a proper Irish city and no longer the mere town it was only decades ago. It has enjoyed a boom without yet suffering an explosion, though it may eventually outgrow itself. Whatever the recent sprawl, the heart of Galway can still be easily strolled and has lost none of its warmth, appeal, and excitement. It is a vital commercial, educational, and cultural center and stands alone as the capital city of Ireland's west country. To orient yourself and to get further information on what there is to see and do in Galway, you may want to launch your stay in Galway with a visit to the office of Ireland West Tourism (Aras Fáilte www.irelandwest.ie), Fair Green, Forster Street. While you're there, inquire into the current theatrical listings. Galway is known for its theater, and justifiably so. The Druid Theatre (091-568-660 www.druidtheatre.com) on Chapel Lane is internationally acclaimed. Call 091/568-660 for information and bookings. In the summer months, this already vibrant town comes all the more alive with the Galway Arts Festival (www.galwaysartsfestival.ie). If for some inscrutable reason you'd prefer to hole up in your room and read a good book (who knows, maybe about ancient Ireland!), Galway is home to a bookstore that is by now a legend— Kenny's Book Shop and Galleries on High Street. If you can't find it here, you likely won't find it at all. Kenny's is also online (www.bookshop.kennys.ie) with five million books on offer, along with free international delivery.

Connemara National Park

Kid Site

Granuaile Centre

Most kids think pirates are cool, and Granuaile or Grace O'Malley (1530-1600) is one of the coolest. Known, loved, and feared as "the Pirate Queen," she ruled much of the surrounding area, land and sea, from her castle base on Clare Island. As she posed a serious threat to British shipping along Ireland's west coast, Queen Elizabeth I, whose state papers recount O'Malley's exploits, tried to win over with a title, which Grace declined. She already had the title she wanted. Explore the life and legend of the Pirate Queen here at the Granuaile Centre (098/66341), signposted from the center of Louisburgh. Open year-round Mon-Fri 10am-6pm. €.

Bed and Board

Chances are you'll want to find lodgings in the center of Galway to allow you to explore the town on foot without having to cope with what can be quite formidable traffic. Galway is replete with suitable and often swell accommodations; so you will be spoiled for choice, unless you wait until the last minute. The truth is that Galway fills up, especially in the summer; so book ahead. We'll skip over The G (www.theg.ie), Galway's only five-star hotel and reputed to be Ireland's finest, just because most readers' budgets would be blasted out to sea by staying here. Instead, we'll offer a few down-to-earth suggestions. If you want to be right in the heart of things, on Forster Street off Eyre Square, you need go no further than the Park House Hotel (091/564-924 www.parkhousehotel.ie) €€€ CC, overlooking Eyre Square. This fine four-star boutique hotel is Irish-owned-and-managed, offers secure parking, and boasts an excellent restaurant. At the other end of town in the Spanish Quarter there are two more affordable options. The House Hotel (091-538900 www.thehousehotel.ie) €€ CC is the trendier, pricier choice with chic, comfortable rooms, while the Jurys Inn Galway (091/566-444 www.jurysinns.com) €€ CC opposite the Spanish Arch offers a great location and appealing, basic rooms at an even lower rate. All three of the above offer parking, a must in Galway center. If you are willing or prefer to stay just outside the center of town, Galway has myriad attractive B&B's and guesthouses on offer. Two of the most attractive bargains are in Salthill and an easy 15-minute walk from the city. Our highest recommendation goes to St Judes (091/521619, www.st-judes.com) €€ CC at 110 Lower Salthill, where dinner is prepared and served on request by Sinéad Johnstone, a graduate of the Ballymaloe Cookery School. St Judes fills up well in advance, so book early. Another good option, convenient and comfy, is Roncalli House (091/589013 www.roncallihouse.com) € CC at 24 Whitestrand Ave., Lower Salthill, where we must add that the rooms tend to be relatively small and the bathrooms can be almost miniature; so if size matters, you may want to stay elsewhere. Lastly we have to mention a unique B&B just east of Spiddal, only nine miles from the Galway center on the coast road (R336). Nancy Hopkins Naughton at Cloch na Scith or Kellough Thatched Cottages (091/553364 www.thatchcottage.com) € CC has only three guest rooms (all with private bath) in her centuries-old thatched farmhouse, and they are worth standing in line for. Your stay here will be most memorable. Tom Naughton is a gifted artist and a prize-winning traditional *sean-nos* singer; on many evenings you'll find yourself around their fireplace in the midst of a traditional Irish session.

All three of the above hotels offer their own dining options; but Galway has no shortage of fine dining at a range of prices. You may just want to pound the pavement and scan menus on your own. But we do have some sure-fire suggestions. Firstly, since you are within striking distance, we must mention Moran's Oyster Cottage in Kilcolgan (091-796113 www.moransoystercottage.com) €€ CC. Royalty, heads of state, movie stars, and locals all go out of their way to this simple, unpretentious seafood mecca on the Dun Killen River where Willie Moran, in 1960, claims he caught 105 wild salmon in a single day. It's a small menu, and everything on it is fresh, wild, and exquisite. To find Moran's, take the N18 southbound out of Galway and Moran's will be signposted after seven or eight miles on your right. Now back to Galway. For breakfast, lunch, or dinner you can't go wrong at the Gourmet Tart Company (091-861667 www.gourmettartco.com) €€ CC in Upper Salthill across from Salthill Church. For fine dining we recommend several restaurants, all €€€ CC. Oscar's Bistro (091-587239 www.oscarbistro.ie), on Lower Dominick Street; the Park Room at the Park House Hotel (091/654-924) on Forster Street off Eyre Square, offering French, modern Irish, and traditional Irish entrées, including excellent vegetarian options; and Kirwan's Lane (091-568266), not surprisingly on Kirwan's Lane, promising "creative cuisine" and not disappointing. More affordable but not necessarily less enticing alternatives are: Couch Potatoes (091-561664) at 40 Upper Abbeygate Street raises potato soup to new heights and that's only the beginning € CC; Da Tang Noodle House (091-561443) on Middle Street, does the same for noodles; and Tulsi (091-565811 www.tulsigalway.com) at 3 Buttermilk Walk offers some of the best North Indian cuisine you'll find in Ireland, though still not superb €€ CC. Finally, there's all that pub grub out there; and at Rabbitt's (091-562215), just off Eyre Square at 23 Forster Street, you'll find Galway's oldest family-run pub, frequented more by locals than by tourists, always a good sign.

DAY SIX
Across Galway Bay

Today's destination—Inishmore (Inis Mór), the largest of the Aran islands—lies in open waters between Galway Bay and the Atlantic. The traditional way to the reach the Aran Islands would be in a currach—a hide-bound, pitch-smeared rowing boat—but today's options, air taxi and ferry boat, are faster and dryer. The flight to Inishmore takes less than 8 minutes, during which time you will enjoy (unless you blink) spectacular views of the Galway coastline and the Aran Islands. The sole carrier, Aer Arann (091/593-034), www.aerarannislands.ie, has been flying to the islands since 1970 and assuredly knows the winds as well as the way. In peak season there are up to 25 flights a day, to and from the mainland and between the islands themselves. An adult return (round-trip) fare will likely run under €50. Departures are from Connemara Regional Airport in Invernin (Indreabhán) less than 20 miles west of Galway City on the coast road (R336). You can drive to the airport yourself and receive free secure parking or else take the free shuttle bus from a designated pick-up point in Galway center. If you prefer to cross by sea, we recommend Island Ferries (091-568903 www.aranislandferries.com), offering multiple daily sailings year-round for about €25 return, all leaving from Rossaveel (Ros a'Mhil), which is signposted off the coast road (R336) just over twenty-two miles west of Galway City. Again, you can make the drive yourself and park free and secure near the dock or take advantage of the shuttle bus departing from the Galway center office of Aran Island Ferries at Victoria Place 90 minutes before sailing. The crossing to Inishmore takes roughly an hour from Rossaveel.

Whether you arrive on Inishmore by air or sea you will soon find yourself in the island's main harbor village of Kilronan (Cill Ronáin), where you will be assaulted or rather greeted energetically by drivers of taxis or vans wanting to convey you around the island either on pre-fab tours or at your beck and call. The other options are, of course, to proceed on foot, bicycle, or even horseback. This is a lot to decide all at once; so before you commit yourself, we recommend that you walk (less than 5 minutes) directly to Inishmore's relatively new and attractive heritage center, Ionad Árainn (099/61355), www.visitaranislands.com, where informative exhibits will introduce you to the extraordinary history and culture of the Aran Islands. This may also be a good time to see the 1932 classic film *Man of Aran*, shown here six times daily. Admission to the center and film €. Once you've seen what the islands, and Inishmore in particular, have to offer, you will be better able—over a cup of something hot in the center's café—to sort out your day, set out your priorities, and negotiate with the local providers of transport.

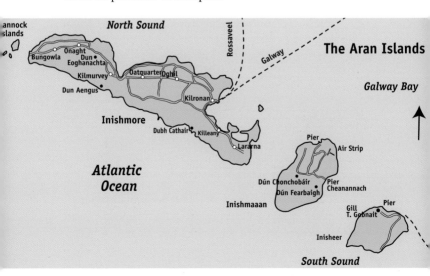

To orient yourself in the most general terms here at Kilronan, you are on the largest of the three Aran Islands. Inishmaan (Inis Meáin), at 2,252 acres, is not even a third the size of Inishmore. Inisheer (Inis Óirr), at 1,400 acres, is a mere outcrop of the nearby Burren in County Clare. Irrespective of size, each of the islands has its distinctive character; and, if time permitted, a visit to each would be richly rewarded. What primarily brings us here to Inishmore are its spectacular ancient stone forts, especially the cliff-hanging mother of all stone forts, Dún Aengus. There are seven stone forts to be found on the Aran Islands, and four of them are here on Inishmore.

Today, any visitor to Inishmore and its forts is likely to wonder what could have possessed the ancients either to attack or to defend with such monumental determination a land as remote and as barren as a desert, only wetter. The towering walls of these *cashels* are a staggering 20 feet thick in some places! Granted, stone is plentiful on Inishmore, but the sheer effort involved makes the mind go blank. It is not so much the *how* that defies description, but rather the *why*. We may perhaps assume that it was the ferocity and not the paranoia of the age that accounts for these awesome monuments, i.e. something in the blood and not in the water of the age in which they were built.

"Abundant was the stream of blood there over the white skin of young warriors mangled by the hands of eager men...the battle was a gory ghastly melee, and the river Unius rushed with corpses."

—*Cited in 'The Second Battle of Moytura,'* Revue Celtique *xii 52-130, Whitley Stokes*

In Irish mythology—a far cry from history—the Aran Islands are associated with the early Celtic invaders known as the Fir Bolg, whose Irish incursion, according to the *Lebor Gebála Erren* or "The Book of Invasions," took place many generations after the Nemedians and several decades prior to the Tuatha Dé Danann. Whether or not they originated in Greece, as the *Lebor Gebála Erren* asserts, is a matter of debate. It is more likely that they were related to the Belgae, whom Julius Caesar encountered and conquered in France and Belgium. Regardless, they are said to have ruled Ireland for 37 years before being defeated by the Tuatha Dé Danann near Lough Arrow, Co. Sligo in the First battle of Moytura (Mag Tuired). Eochaid mac Eirc, the Fir Bolg king, has been remembered as a great and gracious ruler. After their bloody defeat at Moytura, however, the Fir Bolg were driven, as the story goes, to Connacht and further still to the remote extremities of the Irish world—to the western shores of Scotland, to Rathlin Island, and to the Aran Islands. Whether the Fir Bolg were in fact the builders of any of these forts or of earlier fortresses in the same locations is a matter for speculation not knowledge.

> The Fir Bolg and Fir Gailian came, it was long ago; the Fir Domnann came, they landed on a headland in the west. Thereafter the Tuath De Danann came, in their masses of fog… The sons of Mil came from Spain, from the south, … they were strong in battle.
>
> Two hundred years, whoso relates it, after Nemed, lustrous his deeds of valour, till the Fir Bolg took the tuneful land of Ireland, from the sea-pool of ocean.
>
> The Fir Bolg gave them [the Tuatha De Danann] battle upon Mag Tuired; they were a long time fighting that battle. At last it broke against the Fir Bolg, and the slaughter pressed northward, and a hundred thousand of them were slain westward to the strand of Eochaill. There was the king Eochu overtaken, and he fell at the hands of the three sons of Nemed. Yet the Tuatha De Danann suffered great loss in the battle, and they left the king on the field, with his arm cut from him; the leeches were seven years healing him. The Fir Bolg fell in that battle all but a few, and they went out of Ireland in flight from the Tuatha De Danann, into Ara, and Ile, and Rachra and other islands besides.
>
> —*The* Lebor Gabála Erren, *1150 C.E.*
> *Irish Texts Society*

PRINCIPAL SITE
Dún Aengus (Dún Aonghasa)

The promontory fortress of Aengus, named after a Fir Bolg chieftain, consists of what appears to be the original *cashel* buttressed by three additional surrounding walls or partial walls as well as a wide ring of stone stakes, known as a *chevaux-de-frise,* driven into rock fissures at diverse angles to impede a frontal assault on the walls. Interestingly, earlier wooden *chevaux-de-frise* have been found in Germany and Belgium, which may point to a link between these forts and the ancient Belgae, whose name is thought to be the root of the Irish Fir Bolg. (*Fir* in Irish simply means "men.") An assault from the rear (from the south) is discouraged, to put it mildly, by the sheer 285-ft precipice and the pounding sea below.

Recent excavations by Ireland's Discovery Program have confirmed prehistoric settlement here long before the construction of any fortifications. As for the *cashel,* the irregular U-shaped inner fort, whose walls survive to a height of 16 feet, is likely where it all began. This fortified site was likely occupied between 1300–800 C.E.

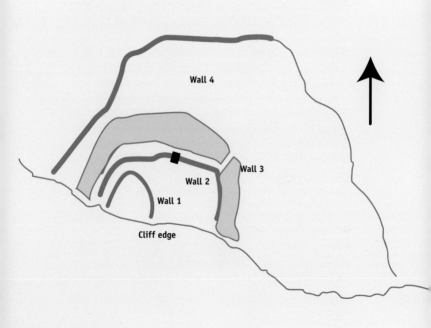

One of the best preserved hut sites uncovered in the inner, western enclosure was circular in shape and featured a paved floor and a stone hearth. The full defense-works as we see them today, however, covering 14 acres, must have been the work of centuries of addition to and renovation of a core enclosure whose form is difficult to determine with any assurance at this point.

A word of caution. Actually that should be in bold type. **A word of caution**. This is not a site where you can let either your children or your own bravado run loose. The drop-off on the southern edge of the fort is final. There are no fences or ropes to warn or restrain you from getting too close, and strong, gusting winds have in the past swept rash tourists off the edge of the cliff to their death. Unless it is your ambition in life to secure a Darwin Award, keep a healthy distance away from edge and if you must have a photo of the cliffs, purchase a postcard in the visitors center.

If you're here on a brilliant day and are feeling in need of an aerobic challenge, the village of Kilmurvey (Cill Mhuirbhigh) is roughly four miles northwest along the main road from the Kilronan pier and Dún Aengus is only another 800 yards further from there. OPW Heritage Card Site. Open daily Mar–Oct 10am–6pm and Nov–Feb 10am–4pm. There is a visitor's center with washrooms and a coffee shop. You may need both after either the walk from town or the exploration of the site.

Side Sites

At this point, especially if it's raining, you may be tempted to say that if you've seen one stone fort you've seen them all. In fact, it is possible that the modern reconstruction of so many Irish stone forts in the last two centuries may have inadvertently exaggerated their similarities. Even so, each has its own character, in large part due to its unique siting. The secret is to "hang out" in each rather than simply scan it. Think trees. They really are all different.

Inishmore has three other fine stone forts to visit, though none of these is quite so awe-inspiring as Dún Aengus, which is admittedly one of the most startling prehistoric monuments in Europe. There isn't too much point in saying a great deal about each beyond describing how to find your way to it. They do speak for themselves; and not

Kid Site

Dunguaire Castle

This is actually a rather late and curiously eclectic castle erected in the 16th century and restored early in the 20th century by Oliver St. John Gogarty as a country retreat. But all that won't matter to children who will find all they need here to ignite their imaginations. If you want to prolong the fantasy and have a memorable evening, reserve places at one of the festive medieval banquets held here each week. Call the Shannon Heritage reservations number (061-360788) for details, availability, and bookings or book online: www.shannonheritage.com/BookOnline. Dunguaire's situation on the south shore of Galway Bay is quite striking, and the views of the Burren and of Galway Bay from the castle's battlements are even better. [F8] Dunguaire Castle (061/360788), www.shannonheritagetrade.com, located just outside of Kinvara 12 miles south of Galway City on N67, is open daily May–Oct 9:30am– 5:30pm. €€.

a great deal is known about their exact age or history. All are open sites.

Dún Dúcathair (Dún Dubhchathair)

The "Black Fort," like Dún Aengus, is a restored promontory fort with a *chevaux-de-frise* contributing additional protection to its inland side. The fortress complex, whose embracing sequence of walls reach to the cliff's edge, occupies the tip of a narrow promontory undercut by the sea. The inside face of the central fort is terraced on three levels and within its embrace there are the remnants of a number of small stone huts. While the age of Dún Dúcathair is unknown, some suspect that it may be the oldest of the Inishmore forts. Note its massive cyclopean dry-stone

Dunguaire Castle

walls. Some of those stones exceed 6 feet in height! To find Dún Dúcathair from the Kilronan pier, walk inland roughly for one mile along the Inis Mór Way in the direction of Killeany (Cill Éinne) until you come to a grey building (an out-of-service power station) at the foot of a hill. Turn right here and right again at the top of the hill, following the road towards the cliffs. When you come to the end of the road, turn left and the fort will be in front of you.

Dún Eochla (Dún Eochaill)

Situated on the northeast corner of Inishmore's central plateau, this snug bivallate (double-walled) hillfort occupies the highest point on the island. If you find the height less than dizzying, it's because you are just over 400 feet above sea level. The *cashel*'s oblong inner enclosure measures roughly 90 by 75 feet, and at their highest points its walls exceed 16 feet. Its triple-layered terraced walls are roughly 13 feet thick. From its rampart walk the fort's defenders would have enjoyed a commanding view of the Kilronan Valley across to the promontory fortress of Dún Dúcathair and beyond, as visitors do today. Dún Eochla is signposted off the main road between Kilronan and Kilmurvey. You can take your bearings by the old lighthouse that stands quite close to the fort.

Dún Onaght (Dún Eoghanachta)

Located on a ridge above the village of Onaght (Eoghanachta), this is the more spectacular of Inishmore's inland hill forts, once ruled, it seems, by a branch of one of the most powerful ancient dynasties of Ireland. It may be the most recent of the lot, constructed perhaps in the early Christian centuries. It is one great ring of stone over 120 yards in circumference, most of which rises to a height of over 16 feet. The surviving walls are as thick as they are high, and there are the remains of several small stone huts within the enclosure. Dún Onaght is signposted on the left as you approach the village of Onaght from Kilmurvey.

Bed and Board

Same as Day Five.

Day Seven
The Home Stretch

Decisions, Decisions. While this itinerary assumes that today will take you back towards Dublin across the central heartland of Ireland, you do have another option at this point, which would be to jump the rail to Day Five of Itinerary #1 and explore the Burren as your Day Seven. This would mean that your departure from Ireland would be via Shannon and not Dublin; and you could spend your last night conveniently either in County Clare or County Limerick (see Bed and Board for Days Five and Six of Itinerary #1).

Otherwise, today's route will begin in Galway and end within striking distance of Dublin (or back in Dublin if you prefer.) If you decide to drop off your car at the Dublin Airport this afternoon and spend your last night car-less in the city, that is surely an option at this point. You could also follow some of the other "Home Stretch" options offered for Day 7 of Itinerary #1, adjusting for the fact that you will be approaching Dublin from the west on the N4 rather than from the southwest on the N7. Keep in mind, however, that the N4 and the N7 more or less converge at the M50 beltway around Dublin, allowing you to approach the city center from every which way but the east.

Today's recommended route begins in Galway City. Follow signs to the M6 east and take it 56 miles to Athlone. From Athlone, you may decide to detour south to Clonmacnoise. Either way, you resume today's route here in Athlone, where from the M6 you pick up the N55 north. After 17 miles you will enter Ballymahon, where you turn onto R392 north and west in the direction of Lanesboro. After about five miles you will see a sign for the Corlea Trackway Visitor Centre. Following your stay there, simply retrace your steps back towards Athlone; and, roughly three miles north of Athlone, turn left off of the N55 and pick up the R390 north and west in the direction of Mullingar (46 miles from Athlone). Before reaching Mullingar, and after roughly 20 miles, you will pass through Ballymore and then Killare. Shortly after the Killare crossroads you will see a sign on your left for

Uisneach and Aill na Míreann (the "Cat Stone," see p. 200). Once you've explored the Hill of Uisneach, you can follow our recommendation and check into a local accommodation (see Bed and Board on page 202) or continue on R390 to explore the town of Mullingar, where, if you wish, you can pick up the N4 to Dublin.

PRINCIPAL SITE
Corlea Trackway

Why would you want to focus the last day of your trip to Ireland on bogs? It's a good question to which the Corlea Trackway Visitor Centre offers an equally good answer. The story of Ireland, especially ancient Ireland, can't be told without telling the story of its bogs, a story far more fascinating and engaging than you might expect. The Corlea Trackway Centre is a neat place, with a keenly interested, informed, and welcoming staff, who go out of their way to answer all your questions and will tell you a lot of intriguing things you never would have thought to ask about.

Bogs were not only a vast and essential feature of the ancient Irish landscape, they were also a major preoccupation. Their relentless spread threatened agriculture and made tillable soil a more and more precious commodity. Bogs also impeded communication and transport, as they were impassable for much of the year. Finally, these soggy wastelands, with their vast reaches of oozing mosses, reed marshes, and stagnant pools, were in the ancient imagination inhabited by a host of demons and deities, who needed to be placated with offerings of all kinds—food and drink, tools, jewelry, weapons, and even human victims. While Ireland is not known for its bog bodies, they're most likely down there, or were before Bord na Mona, the Irish Power (Electrical) Board, possibly turned them into fuel. Finally, bogs are beautiful and constitute a unique ecosystem which you'll learn all about if you take a free bog tour here, which we urge you to do.

Corlea bog, one small bit of which you will see here, lies on the southern edge of a vast raised bog that to this day extends across a substantial share of central Ireland.

Besides posing a hazard to anyone who strayed out into it, it severed communication between the various tribes and septs of the ancient Irish population. Evidence of constructed roads or trackways across the most impassable stretches of bog has been found in numerous locations dating from as early as the Late Bronze Age. The Corlea Bog Trackway is, as it happens, the largest of its kind in Europe. After its discovery, excavation commenced here in 1985 and a spacious heritage center was built in 1994 to exhibit the nearly 60 feet of ancient road that was painstakingly restored. Its orientation (NW/SE) and its location suggest that it was part of a series of trackways facilitating direct communication between Cruachain, the royal center of Connacht roughly 16 miles to the NW and the Hill of Uisneach, a ritual site of great importance, again roughly 16 miles away, this time to the SE.

The bog road was constructed, in simplest terms, like a rail line, except that here the "rails" lay beneath the "ties." It is estimated that over 300 birches were felled to produce the road's substructure and connecting pegs, while nearly as many massive Irish oaks were cut and split to create the road's surface, a full 13 feet in width, large enough for chariot or wagon traffic. The motivation for building so monumental a roadway remains a matter of conjecture. Surely it highlighted the high status of the king who commissioned it. Ritual, military, and commercial uses all suggest themselves, as well. The mystery is that no wheel ruts have been discovered. In fact, it seems not to have been worn down at all before it sank beneath the bog. One cogent theory is that it was a mistake, an engineering miscalculation, revealing both how much its Iron Age builders knew about carpentry and how little they knew about bogs. The oak planking (one single sodden plank, when lifted from the bog, weighed over a ton) may have been simply too heavy to be supported by the bog. So, shortly after its construction (requiring countless thousands of human work-hours) it may have simply disappeared into the ooze.

Remarkably, an early Irish story known as "The Wooing of Étáin," may have preserved an account of the building of this very road. The time (148 B.C.E.) is right, the location (Cor Léith) is right. And it has about it enough of the ring of truth to have been inspired by an actual event.

Thereafter Echu's foster-father questioned him, asking how he bad obtained such riches, and Echu answered "It happened thus." "Indeed. You must take care," replied his foster-father, "for it is a man of great power who has come to you. Set him difficult tasks, my son." When Mider came to him, then, Echu imposed these famous great labours: clearing Mide of stones, laying rushes over Tethbae, laying a causeway over Móin Lámrige, foresting Bréifne. "You ask too much of me," said Mider. "Indeed, I do not," replied Echu. "I have a request, then," said Mider, "Let neither man nor woman under your rule walk outside before sunrise tomorrow." "You will have that," said Echu.

No person had ever walked out on the bog, but, after that, Echu commanded his steward to go out and see how the causeway was laid down. The steward went out into the bog, and it seemed that every man in the world was assembling there from sunrise to sunset. The men made a mound of their clothes, and that is where Mider sat. The trees of the forest, with their trunks and their roots, went into the foundation of the causeway, while Mider stood and encouraged the workers on every side. You would have thought that every man in the world was there making noise. After that, clay and gravel and stones were spread over the bog. Until that night, it had been customary for the men of Ériu to yoke oxen across the forehead, but that night it was seen that the people of the Síde placed the yoke across the shoulders. Echu thereafter did the same, and that is why he was called Echu Airem, for he was the first of the men of Ériu to place a yoke on the necks of oxen. And these are the words that the host spoke as they were building the causeway: "Place it here, place it there, excellent oxen, in the hours after sundown, very onerous is the demand, no one knows whose the gain, whose the loss in building the causeway over Móin Lámrige. If the host had not been spied upon, there would have been no better road in the entire world; but, for that reason, the causeway was not made perfect."

—*From "The Wooing of Étáin,"* Early Irish Myths and
    Sagas, *tr. Jeffrey Gantz (Penguin) pp. 53–54.*

Corlea (Cor Léith) Road is within several miles of Mider's own tumulus at Brí Léith (Near Ardagh, Co. Longford).

BOGS AND THE AULD SOD

One cannot walk in the footsteps of the ancients without traversing, or a least gazing upon, the bogs. Bogs—the color of Irish tweed—blanket hilltops and lowlands and preserve within them the very history of the island. Bogs are designated as either blanket bogs or raised bogs according to how and where they developed. Theories abound concerning the birth of bogs and the development of bog peat, but it is generally agreed that the bog stage was set about 9,000 years ago. Influences on the formation of the bogs included: climate changes, tree loss by disease and human cutting, and farming and disturbance of the land dating from the Neolithic age. Another influence is thought to be the "iron pan" phenomenon: minerals leached from the ground surface create an impermeable layer deep in the subsoil and result in waterlogged conditions at the ground surface.

While all bogs share much of the same flora and fauna, sphagnum moss is king of the bogs. Not much to look at, this extraordinary moss holds water like a sponge, thrives on scant nutrients from rainwater, and creates an acidic environment, its favorite, as it rapidly reaches out over sodden layers of dead grass and rushes. The reed Phragmites, white tufted bog cotton, sturdy heathers, and the insect-eating sundew flower are other key players in the bog landscape.

Blanket bogs, whose significant spread began in the Bronze Age, are found along the north and west coastal regions, where the nutrients flowed out of the soil and downhill with the rain. Rushes and sphagnum moss grew happily in the remaining acidic pools and puddles. The soil became waterlogged with the debris of dead plants, which, in the highly acidic environment, did not decompose, as they would have in richer soil. Time passed and the blanket bog spread as a self-generating system. Layer upon layer of compressed bog-peat was formed. This blanket of organic sponge preserved in its acid bath everything it encompassed: buried corpses, drowned trees, and deposited hoards.

Raised bogs are found in the midlands and were created from the interplay of lakes and plants beginning about 7,000 years ago. Around the fringe of numerous lakes and ponds, rushes and water plants grew. As time passed, these marshy fens extended further both into the lake and away from the lake. As the vegetation became increasingly dense and rainwater leached away the few remaining nutrients left by the plants, the mighty sphagnum moss established itself and created an enticing habitat for other congenial bog plants. As the fen and bog filled the lake, the bog plants grew to cover even the fen and create a mound where the lake had once been. Trees surrounded by the expanding bog were drowned as the bog vegetation further blocked nutrients and spread a sphagnum skirt out from the central lake mound.

[17] The Corlea Trackway Visitor Center (043-332-2386) is signposted both from the Longford-Keenagh Road (R397) and from the Lanesboro-Mullingar Road (R392). OPW Heritage Card site. Open daily late Apr–late Sept 10am–6pm. In addition to an exhibition center, an audio-visual presentation, and a bog tour, there is an inviting café serving lunches and pastries.

Side Sites

Clonmacnoise

Founded circa 548 by St. Ciaran at one of the most important intersections on the island, where the Dublin–Galway road crossed the Shannon, this was one of the most important monastic centers of learning, culture, and spirituality not only of Ireland but of Europe. While very little remains today of the monastic complex that flourished here for nearly a thousand years, the site and its ruins remain poignant and evocative. In addition to the remains of a cathedral, a castle, eight churches, two round towers, and a number of high crosses, there is an exceptional heritage center with excellent exhibits, an audio-visual presentation, and tearooms. [H/I 7/8] Clonmacnoise (090-967-4195) is open daily Nov to mid-Mar 10am–5:30pm; mid-Mar to May 10am–6pm; June–Aug 9am–7pm; and Sept–Oct 10am–6pm. OPW Heritage Card site. From the M6 just east of Athlone take the N62 less than four miles south to Ballynahown and follow signs from there. Otherwise, Clonmacnoise is also signposted further south on the N62, where you can pick up the R444 to Clonmacnoise.

Hill of Uisneach

Of all of the major sites of ancient Ireland, this may be the least explored. Here lies an archaeological adventure waiting to happen and yet surely complicated by the fact that the site is located on privately owned farmland; so be sure to contact David, the owner, (087-257-6434) before your visit. Already, very early in the Celtic period, this hill was seen to mark the center of Ireland, the point where the four cardinal points of the compass converge. As such it was from earliest times a cultic center, a place of assembly associated with druids and particular deities. Its great annual assembly was called *Mórdáil Uisnig*, and was held

on the 1st of May, the festival of Beltaine, one of the four central festivals evenly dividing the Celtic year. It was a festival of fire, when the hill must have been ablaze and is estimated to have been visible from a quarter of the island's land mass. The hill and the surrounding area are rich in ancient monuments, though you would not suspect this as you climb the southwest slope of the hill to reach the only visible marker of this extraordinary site. Slightly less than 100 feet from the summit of the hill you will come to a sizeable limestone boulder, a glacial erratic, roughly 16 feet high. This stone has many names—the Stone of the Cat, the Stone of Divisions, the *Umbilicus Hiberniae*, the Navel of Ireland.

[J7] Open site. Signposted off the Athlone-Mullingar Road (R390) between Killare and Loughanavally. Be sure to scan the fields carefully for bulls before venturing across the fields between the road and the "Cat Stone" (right).

"When these things had happened in this order, at length five chieftains who were at the same time brothers, the sons of Dela, springing from the branch of the people of Nemedus that had taken refuge in Greece, landed in Ireland. They found it uninhabited and divided it in five equal portions among themselves.

The bounds of these divisions meet at a certain stone in Meath near the castle of Kilair (Killare). This stone is said to be the navel of Ireland, as it were, placed right in the middle of the land. Consequently that part of Ireland is called Meath, as being situated in the middle of the island."

—1185 B.C.E., *Gerald of Wales,* The History and Topography of Ireland, *translated by John J. O'Meara (Penguin, 1982), p. 96.*

Above: Hill of Uisneach

Bed and Board

We have two recommendations for lodging in the Mullingar area, from which you can reach Dublin airport (roughly 50 miles away) in an hour or so, though you would do well to consult your hosts regarding traffic at various times of the day. First, for a splurge, there's Mornington House in Multyfarnham, a short drive northwest of Mullingar (044-937-2191 www.mornington.ie) €€ CC a fine 17th-century Irish country manor house, made even more in 1896, providing a tranquil and lavish retreat in an idyllic landscape. Guests stay in style here, to say the least. They can also dine like royalty, if they so choose (restaurant €€€ CC). Your host and chef here, Ann O'Hara, is a member of Eurotoque, the European Community of Chefs, and she's working with her own homegrown and local ingredients. For a more modest but still attractive night's rest we recommend a peaceful country lodge, elegantly furnished with antiques including four-poster beds, overlooking Lough Owel. Lough Owel Lodge (044-9344-8714 www.loughowellodge.com) € CC is located in Cullion, just north of Mullingar and is signposted from the N4. The Ginnells, your hosts, do not serve evening meals, but offer an outstanding breakfast buffet each morning. You will not go wanting for restaurants in nearby Mullingar, just five minutes away by car.

Mullingar is a vital, appealing midlands town, and you will enjoy strolling its main street and scanning its menus. We recommend JP's Steakhouse (044-933-3620) at 28 Dominic Street for the best steak in Mullingar (and the area is known for its fine beef) €€ CC. If you're in the mood for more of a splurge and are willing to drive 6 miles or so outside of Mullingar, then we have the place for you. Crookedwood House (044-72165, www.crookedwoodhouse.com) €€ CC, a beautifully refurbished period Rectory beside a splendid 15th-century church overlooking Lough Derravaragh, has ambience, scenery, and award-winning cuisine. This may just be the finest restaurant in the midlands. At the very least it is a contender for the crown. And, if you can't bring yourself to go anywhere after dinner, Crookedwood House is now an inn with eight spacious bedrooms, €€

CC. To find your way here take the R394 north out of Mullingar about 6 miles to Crookedwood Village. Turn right at the Wood Pub and proceed a mile and a quarter further to Crookedwood House.

ITINERARY THREE

Early Christian and Medieval • Irish Golden Age • 400 C.E.–1200 C.E.

PRINCIPAL SITES

National Museum of Ireland
Trinity College Dublin......*the Book of Kells*
Christ Church Cathedral
St. Patrick's Cathedral
Glendalough......*monastic site*
Jerpoint Abbey......*monastic site*
Kells......*medieval site*
Rock of Cashel......*ecclesiastical site*
Ardmore......*monastic site*
Skellig Michael......*monastic site*
Gallarus Oratory and Kilmakedar...... *ecclesiastical sites*
Holy Island/Lough Derg......*monastic site*
Clonmacnoise......*monastic site*

TRAVERSED

Provinces of Leinster, Munster and Connacht
County Dublin, County Wicklow, County Kildare,
County Carlow, County Kilkenny, County Tipperary,
County Waterford, County Cork, County Kerry,
County Limerick, County Clare, County Galway,
County Offaly, County Westmeath, County Meath.

Day One
Arrival in Dublin

D ublin Airport is a dream compared to most international airports, even after its dramatic expansion in recent years. Definitely easy-in and easy-out, regardless of what form of public transportation you choose. Until the new tunnel is completed, creating a direct rapid transit link to and from the city, your best options into the city center are taxi (€30), bus, or one of the convenient shuttle-bus services to Dublin city center: Airlink Express (€6) or Aircoach (€7). You shouldn't have to wait more than fifteen minutes for a suitable option. We recommend that you begin your auto rental on Day Two and return then to the airport to pick up your car. You will pay for one less day, avoid parking fees, and spare yourself the nightmare of navigating Dublin traffic. Dublin streets and roads rank among the most desperately congested byways in Europe. As a jetlagged novice, this is not the place or the time to try out your left-lane driving skills. Better to get a full night's sleep and to drive south into Wicklow in the morning, after picking up your car at the airport.

PRINCIPAL SITES
National Museum of Archaeology and History

Ireland's National Museum is located on four distinct campuses: the Museum of Natural History on Merrion Street, the Museum of Archaeology and History on Kildare Street, and the Museum of Decorative Arts and History at the Collins Barracks, all in central Dublin. The fourth and latest addition, opened in 2001, is the Museum of Country Life at Turlough Park, just outside of Castlebar, Co. Mayo.

Regardless of which prehistoric or historical period occupies the focus of one's interests, the exploration of ancient Ireland best begins at the National Museum of Archaeology and History, amidst an assemblage of treasures—dating from the earliest human habitation to the medieval period—amassed over several hundred years by individual collectors, the British Crown, and the Irish State. Before examining any of the holdings, be sure to admire the museum that holds them. For a start, the entrance lobby, top to bottom, from its 62-ft domed ceiling to its striking mosaic floor deserves a gaze.

Despite the splendor of its holdings, the National Museum, like any case museum, can be taxing. It is easy, even without the additional gravity of jet-lag, to grow weary of reading labels and placards and to teeter towards burnout. Consequently, we recommend that you try to take advantage of one of the frequent daily tours by a member of the museum staff. Once given your bearings across the wide sweep of holdings and the periods they represent, you can find your own way back to those items with which you want to linger.

For the third itinerary, the two major exhibits of greatest interest are: the Treasury on the main floor containing both pre-Christian and Christian Celtic treasures, among them the famed 8th and 9th-century Ardagh and Derrynaflan hoards and the Tara brooch; and, upstairs, equally impressive and informative exhibits focused on Viking and medieval Dublin. If you aspire to understand and imagine Dublin life, commerce, warfare and craft in its earliest period, linger here and try to forget momentarily the ever-expanding metropolis and its hordes of touristic invaders just beyond the museum's silencing walls. Especially moving, among the Viking artifacts, are the shackles and chains once used to drag off Irish monks et al. into slavery. Note too the sheer scale of the Viking weaponry, a vivid reminder of the terror once provoked by towering Norse berserkers.

If and when your legs weary, your eyes blur, and your mind overloads—all common symptoms in any museum—you may, of course, at any time pause and enjoy the museum's gift shop and café. And before making your exit, be sure to look up at the massive, colonnaded rotunda in the entrance hall, designed by Sir Thomas Newenhan Deane.

Located at the intersection of Kildare and Molesworth Streets. (01-677-7444) Open Tues–Sat 10am–5pm, Sun 2–5pm. Closed Mondays. Free admission.

Trinity College Dublin and the Book of Kells

A meandering stroll in the 400-year old campus of Trinity College makes for a most tranquil and fascinating walk through the past. There is no admission fee to the college grounds, and entrance is through the main gate in College Green opposite the central branch of the Bank of Ireland, the former seat of the Irish Parliament. We recommend that that you take a college tour, especially of the Old Library and the *Book of Kells,* one of Ireland's greatest treasures. This is only one of the magnificent ancient manuscripts housed here, manuscripts created in monastery scriptoria during Ireland's golden age and after. Open Mon–Sat 9:30am–5pm; Sundays, Oct–May noon–4:30pm and June–Sept 9:30am–4:30pm. Admission €€€.

Christ Church Cathedral

While the present structure, at least in its outward appearance, dates from the late 19th century, the cathedral site is in the oldest quarter of the city, the heart of Viking and Medieval Dublin, a heart whose modern body now sprawls across many miles in three directions. The first cathedral here on Dublin Hill, most likely of timber construction, was erected in 1038 by the then Norse King of Dublin, Sigtryggr Silkbeard. The present cathedral owes its origins to the Anglo-Norman

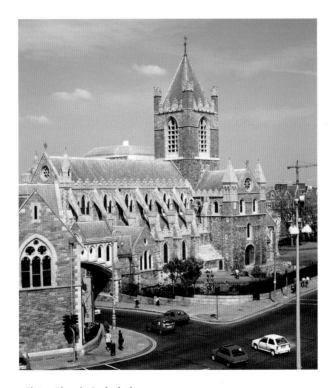

Christ Church Cathedral

conquest of Dublin and to the Norman propensity for monumental stone architecture. Strongbow—conqueror and cathedral-builder—is buried in the south aisle beside one of his sons, whom he is said to have sliced in two as punishment for cowardice in battle. There is much to explore in the cathedral, its crypt and chapter house cloister, as well as across from the cathedral in the Synod Hall, where you will find "Dublinia." Much of what remains and doesn't remain of Viking and Medieval Dublin lies nearby. If you leave the cathedral grounds, for example, and find the street that borders the cathedral grounds on the east, you will be walking in the footsteps of Dublin's oldest citizens. This is Fishamble Street, the oldest street in Dublin, once a thoroughfare through the Viking settlement of the 11th century. Christ Church (01-677-8099 www.cccdub.ie) is located at Christ Church Place west of Trinity College (following College Street to Dame Street to Lord Edward Street to Christ Church Place) and is open to the public daily except during services. Donation €€.

St. Patrick's Cathedral

The largest cathedral in Ireland, St. Patrick's, as its name suggests, is also steeped in tradition, beginning with its legendary founding by Patrick himself in the 5th century. If indeed Patrick was ever here, it was not to construct the current church which dates from the late 12th or early 13th century. The only surviving material link with Patrick may be an ancient granite slab, marked with a Celtic cross and standing on the site of one of the four oldest Celtic churches in Dublin. Here, at St. Patrick's in Insula ("St. Patrick's on the Island," so named because it stood on an island at the meeting of two branches of the River Poddle, which flows to this day beneath the cathedral) Patrick is said to have baptized several converts at a well rediscovered in 1901. The site of the well is in a small park adjacent to the cathedral; meanwhile the granite slab has been moved and placed on display in the northwest corner of the cathedral. St. Patrick's is brimming with monuments and artifacts of various sorts, including the death mask of Jonathan Swift, its one-time dean. The cathedral is located less than a mile south of

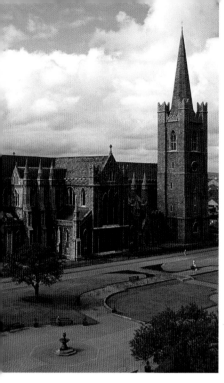

St. Patrick's Cathedral

Christ Church on Patrick Street. Open all year Mon–Fri 9am– 5pm; Sat Mar–Oct 9am–6pm and Nov–Feb 9am–5pm; Sun Mar–Oct 9–10:30am, 12:30–2:30pm, 4:30–6pm and Nov–Feb 9–10:30am, 12:30–2:30pm. Consult www.stpatrickscathedral.ie or call (01-453-9472) to confirm times of concerts and services. Admission €€.

Side Sites

Dublin ranks among the top five tourist cities in Europe and not without reason. There is no question of our listing, much less discussing, its myriad attractions here. Instead, given that this is a guide to ancient Ireland and that only hours remain in your one allotted day in Ireland's capitol city, we will make a modest suggestion relevant to the exploration of ancient Ireland and a couple more relevant to enjoying today's Dublin.

St. Audoen's

Bits of medieval Dublin survive amidst the grand pile that is Dublin, and this is surely one of the oldest and best bits. St. Audoen's (the old one that is, not the adjacent modern church of the same name) is the only surviving medieval parish church in Dublin. Its 12th-century tower (containing three of the oldest bells in Dublin) and west door remain intact and welcoming, though the church itself is mostly open only for services. There is, however, an adjoining visitor's center (01-677-0088, admission €) with exhibitions on the history of the church. St. Audoen's is located on the north side of High Street (the "Main Street" of medieval Dublin) just west of Christ Church in the Cornmarket area. St. Audoen's stands next to one of the few remaining segments of Dublin's medieval walls; and, beside Cook Street just north of the church, you'll find St. Audeon's Arch, the only surviving city gate of medieval Dublin.

"Of the goodly array of city churches which the piety of old times raised once and again on these ancient sites, and impiety and sacrilege as assiduously laboured to burn, pillage, and destroy, throughout every age of Irish history, but one remains in such a condition to tell us in any measure of fullness the tale of its former greatness, the history also of departed glories, less written on its melancholy walls than that of the indignities it has endured."

—*Sir Thomas Drew (Architect 1838–1910),*
writing about St. Audoen's.

The Brazen Head

Sitting on the site of a much earlier 12th-century tavern, the Brazen Head, dating from the 17th century, is in its own right Dublin's oldest pub. For an uplifting draught of history, visit this favorite meeting-place of Irish poets and patriots, such as James Joyce, Robert Emmet and Wolfe Tone. You'll find the Brazen Head a few minutes' walk from St. Audoen's at 20 Lower Bridge Street at the end of a cobblestone courtyard just off the south bank of the Liffey. The Brazen Head serves a full à la carte menu.

Garden Strolls

To finish off your afternoon and put that final edge on your appetite for an early dinner, we recommend a walk through St. Stephen's Green, only five minutes on foot down Dawson Street from the side (Arts Block) gate of Trinity College. An idyllic alternative or supplement to St. Stephen's Green is one of Dublin's best-kept secrets, Iveagh Gardens, located behind the National Concert Hall. Both gardens are open, free admission, until dark.

Kid Sites

Viking Splash

Kids will surely not object if you jump the rails of the first itinerary and take them back to Viking Ireland with a "Viking Splash Tour" (www.vikingsplash.ie) aboard a reconditioned "Duck," a vintage amphibious vehicle unknown to the Vikings them-selves. Taking advantage not only of Dublin's thoroughfares but also of its canals, these tours offer an informative and entertaining introduction to Dublin's sites and stories. More to the point, kids love it, even while some humorless parents cringe. Tours every 30 min. in peak season and every 90 min. off peak. Call 01-707-6000 for more details and reservations. Fee €€€. Tours depart from Stephen's Green North, close to Grafton Street, just behind the taxi rank and water fountain.

Dublinia

Another family-oriented historical attraction in Dublin is known as "Dublinia," (www.dublinia.ie), offering a vivid walk through Medieval Dublin, 1170-1540, recreated in a series of exhibits, spectacles, and interactive experiences. There's also a gift shop and café. Located opposite Christ Church Cathedral on St. Michael's Hill. Open Apr-Sept daily 10am-5pm, and Oct-Mar Mon-Sat 10am-4:30pm. Call 01-679-4611 for details or bookings. Admission €€.

Bed and Board

You will want first to check into your lodging. If you arrive before your room is ready, you can leave your bags anyway and return later to bring them to your room. Dublin boasts hundreds of fine hotels and guest houses; most are very costly. We specially recommend several options. Dublin's three Jurys Inns (www.jurysinns.com) are affordable, convenient, and offer their own pubs and restaurants. And, in the vein of motels or motor inns, they charge by the room and not per person. Breakfast is extra. These are: the Jurys Inn Christchurch (01-454-0000), www.jurys.com €€ CC, across from Christchurch Cathedral; Jurys Inn Customs House (01-854-1500), www.jurys.com €€ CC, facing the quays in the new financial services district; and Jurys Inn Parnell Street (01-878-4900) € CC just off the top of O'Connell Street. On a more cozy scale and with enhanced character, there is the Harding Hotel (01-679-6500 www.hardinghotel.ie), € CC, Copper Alley, Fishamble Street, once the Main Street of Viking Ireland, across from Christ-church Cathedral. If price is really no consideration, the

Shelbourne (01-663-4500 www.marriott.co.uk) €€€ CC, remains the most distinguished address in Dublin, facing the northeast corner of St. Stephen's Green. Built in 1824, this is where the Irish Constitution was signed in 1921 (in room 112 to be exact). On a more contemporary note, another lodging of special interest is Number 31 (01-676-5011 www.number31.ie) €€€ CC, in the heart of Georgian Dublin and a brief walk from St. Stephen's Green or the National Museum, at 31 Leeson Close overlooking Fitzwilliam Place.

The restaurant scene in Dublin is vast and ever-changing. The best advice to be given here is simply to point you towards Temple Bar, Dublin's Left Bank, and to suggest that you follow your own nose to what best suits your budget and taste. With eateries of one sort or another lined up like rungs in a fence, your only challenge will be choosing among them and securing a table without an advance reservation. Your best chance is to eat early, before 7pm. Chapter One (01-873-2266) €€€ CC, at 18–19 Parnell Square; L'Ecrivain (01-661-1919) €€€ CC, at 109 Lower Baggot St., Dublin 2; and Patrick Guilbaud (01-676-4192) €€€ CC, at 21 Upper Merrion Street, are three of Dublin's finest; and you will need to ring ahead for reservations. If you wish to plan your Dublin meal well in advancego to www.rai.ie, Ireland's most complete online index for scouting out restaurants and to www.menupages.ie for consumer opinions and ratings. As you may have some difficulty finding a bargain—ample, wholesome, slow (as opposed to fast) food on a slim budget—we recommend these two, neither of which require reservations: Wagamama Noodle Bar (01-478-2152) € CC, on South King Street opposite the Gaiety Theatre, and Chamelion (01-671-0362) € CC, at No. 1 Fownes Street Lower, Temple Bar, for exceptional Indonesian cuisine.

Day Two
The Sunny South

If Dublin has treated you to its all-too-common drizzle, there's always the hope of high pressure as you head south. That's no promise, but statistics at least are on your side.

After fetching your car—usually from the airport—take the M1 south to the M50, which you will take for approximately 14 miles around the city to the west and south to exit 12, where you will follow signs (via R113) to R115 south. Take R115 approximately 20 miles south past Glencree and through the Sally Gap to the village of Laragh. Glendalough is situated just west of the village of Laragh on R756. If you are able to complete the 20 miles from Tallaght to Laragh without pulling over, you are either encased in fog or legally blind; for the scenery here, especially in the right light, can be heart-stopping. In fact, if the sun is out, you may decide to take a detour to Powerscourt Estate (see page 219).

Today's sights and sites are so weather-dependent that it is difficult to predict or to suggest your best itinerary. The Wicklow Mountains, Powerscourt Estate, and Glendalough alone afford so many possibilities for exploring, strolling, picnicking, and even snoozing in the sun that all schedules become rapidly relative. The most basic decision that you will have to make is whether to stay here in Wicklow for the entire day and night or to make your way further south to counties Carlow or Kilkenny. Either way you will eventually follow or meet up with the route suggested here. When departing Glendalough, turn left onto R756 and drive northwest for 15 miles through the Wicklow Gap to Hollywood. From there continue on 5 miles to Dunlavin and 6 more to Crookstown, where you will pick up the M9 (signposted Waterford). Exit at junction 10 and, at the first roundabout take the first exit onto the R669 (signposted Knocktopher) which will take you to Jerpoint Abbey. In order to pass through the village of Moone and Timolin (see below), you will need to take the N9 rather than the M9 from Crookstown and join the M9 further south at Prumpelstown. Another quite luring option is to leave the N9 roughly 8 miles south of Carlow and follow R705 (the scenic Barrow Drive) south along the River Barrow (detouring to visit St. Mullin's) until you intersect R700 at Ballilogue, where you will turn right and take R700 NW to Inistiogue (pronounced Inish-teeg, one of the most charming villages you'll come across) and on to Thomastown. The lodgings recommended on pages 222–3 lie along one of these routes.

PRINCIPAL SITES
Glendalough

> "A soldier of Christ into the land of Ireland
> A high name over land and sea
> Coemgen (Kevin), the holy fair warrior
> In the valley of the two broad lakes."
> —*Feilire of Oengus*, c.800

Glendalough Round Tower

The enchanting location of Gleann Da Locha ("The Glen of the Two Lakes")—in a glaciated valley with two dark, glistening lakes—is reason enough to drop anchor here, especially if your prayers to St. Kevin, its 6th-century founder, have been rewarded with sunshine. You will have to check in first at the visitor center to receive an entrance pass and, as you wish, to watch the film and exhibits provided, all of which will surely enhance your understanding and appreciation of Glendalough. Then of course you will set out to explore the monastic complex. As the main entrance to the site has been cluttered with commerce in recent years, it is best to walk from the visitor center directly to the river, cross over, walk to the next bridge, and cross back again to the monastery proper, thus bypassing the hawkers and preserving some of the tranquility proper and precious to this site. To find your way among the monuments comprising the central monastic complex, it is probably best to follow one of the guided tours provided or to purchase a detailed guide to the site.

It is well to keep in mind, however, that with the sole possible exception of "St. Kevin's Cell"—questionably linked with the few surviving foundation stones of a beehive hut on a ledge overlooking the upper lake—none

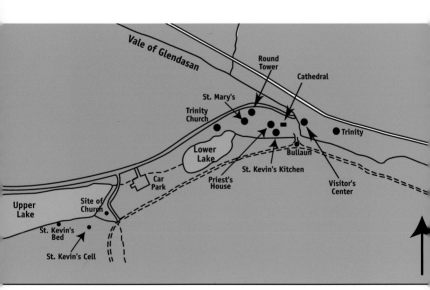

of the architecture on view today at Glendalough dates from the time of Kevin or from the ancient period. The original monastic buildings would have been of timber construction. What is original to the most ancient period is, however, the lay of the land, the landscape, the setting, which is incomparable. This is what first caught the eye and the soul of St. Kevin and daily inspired him and his brother monks to prayer. Consequently, we recommend that you not lose the power of the site by picking too long or too obsessively among the random ruins and remnants of the monastery compound—part museum, part graveyard, and part tourist trap— and that you take time instead to walk to the two lakes and to explore some of the side paths into the surrounding forests. It is here in the tranquility and relative seclusion of the upper lake's southern bank that St. Kevin likely found and founded his hermitage from which all else proceeded. Celtic Christianity, along with its profound commitment to learning, is noted for its great love of nature. The earth is, for the Irish monk, the first and consummate temple, the most perfect house of prayer.

> "Once upon a time… Saint Kevin fleeing during Lent, as was his wont, the society of men, was by himself in a small cabin which warded off from him only the sun and the rain. He was giving his attention to contemplation and was reading and praying. According to his custom he put his hand, in raising it to heaven, out through the window, when, behold, a blackbird happened to settle on it, and using it as a nest, laid its eggs there. The saint was moved with such pity and was so patient with it that he neither closed nor withdrew his hand, but held it out in a suitable position without tiring until the young were completely hatched out. In perpetual remembrance of this wonderful happening, all the representations of Saint Kevin throughout Ireland have a blackbird in the outstretched hand."
>
> —*Giraldus Cambrensis,* Topographia Hiberniae, *c.1200. Translated by John J. O'Meara, Dolmen Press, 1951.*

As an active monastery, Glendalough enjoyed and endured a long, glorious and turbulent history. It was a great center of learning and art, a famed pilgrimage center, the seedbed of saints such as St. Laurence O'Toole, the target of repeated Viking raids, and the victim of British ferocity. Nevertheless, Glendalough survived and continued to breathe as a living monastic community until the 17th century when it succumbed to British repression.

[M/N8] Glendalough Visitor Centre (0404-45325) is located on R756 just west of the village of Laragh, Co. Wicklow. Open mid-Oct–mid-Mar daily 9:30am–5pm and mid-Mar–mid-Oct daily 9:30am–6pm. OPW Heritage Card site.

Jerpoint Abbey

A daughter house of the first Irish Cistercian monastery in Mellifont, Co. Louth, Jerpoint was founded in the mid-12th century and established as the Cistercian motherhouse for Kilkenny and Kilcooly. Its placement on the banks of the Little Arrigle River, its one-time grandeur, and its current state of graceful ruination make it one of the more impressive ancient monastic sites in

Jerpoint Abbey

Ireland. Be sure to take advantage of the expert and engaging guided tour offered at regular intervals throughout the day, which will point out the architectural and artistic highlights of the monastery, relate its fascinating history, and bring alive the routine of the monks who lived, worked and prayed here from roughly 1160 to 1540. At the time of its closure under the Dissolution of Monasteries Act of 1540, the monastery lands totaled 14,500 acres. Jerpoint's extraordinary relief sculptures, especially those fashioned by the famous 15th–16th-century O'Tunney family of stone-carvers, are not to be missed. [K10] Just south of Thomastown on the R669. Open daily early Mar–Sept 9am–5:30pm; daily Oct 10am–5pm; daily Nov 9:30am–4pm; closed Dec–early Feb (056-772-4623) OPW Heritage Card site.

Side Sites

Powerscourt Estate

This 1,000-acre estate is one of the most spectacular in Ireland. Its gardens, designed and laid out by Daniel Robertson between 1745 and 1767, rank among the finest formal gardens in Europe. Regrettably, the 18th-century manor house designed by Richard Cassels was gutted by fire in 1974 and has been only partially restored. We recommend that you take a pass on the house, and revel in the gardens. If you stay on for lunch in the Terrace Cafe, you might as well dine light, as the simply stunning vista before you will make you oblivious of your meal. [N8] As a detour from R115 south, turn left (east) at Glencree following signs to Enniskerry and Powerscourt (01-204-6000), www.powerscourt.ie. Gardens and grounds, open daily 9:30am–5:30pm or dusk. Admission €€€.

Wicklow Mountains National Park

Nearly 50,000 acres of high bog and mountain forests comprise this relatively new national park. Its allure is what makes it difficult, even dangerous, to drive in Wicklow, as the road all too easily becomes an unwanted distraction. The core area of the park surrounds Glendalough. The "Wicklow Way" is a signposted walking trail beginning in the Dublin Hills and ending in

Powerscourt Estate

Clonegal. To make the full journey will take 5–7 days, but you may ingest it in small doses at will. Information and maps are available at the Wicklow National Park center in Glendalough or at any local tourist office. No admission. You can park and leave your car either at the Upper Lake, where you'll pay a minimal fee, or at the Glendalough Visitor Centre, where the parking's free. [M/N8/9]

Moone High Cross

Standing amidst the ruins of Moone Abbey, the southernmost monastic settlement attributed to St. Columba in the 6th century, the Moone Cross, recently restored in situ, is one of the most renowned high crosses in Ireland. Over 1,200 years old, the Moone High Cross is magnificent. In addition to ornate Celtic designs, its fine carvings include canonical Biblical scenes—the temptation of Adam and Eve, the sacrifice of Isaac, and Daniel in the lions' den, etc.—as well as some surprises, such as a dolphin and a curious Near Eastern fish. [L9] Open site, signposted on the N9 on the southern edge of Moone Village, Co. Kildare.

St. Mullin's

This all-but-forgotten spot, occupying no more than a handful of acres, is one of Ireland's smallest and sweetest secrets. On a sunny day, when you are able to walk about freely and enjoy its idyllic setting beside the River Barrow, St. Mullin's exudes charm. The earliest ruins here date from the 7th century when St. Moling (Mullin) founded his monastery here at Badger Wood in roughly 614. Plundered repeatedly by Viking raiders in the 9th and 10th centuries, it was later annexed to a larger Augustinian establishment. The grassy mound (often crawling with children playing "king of the hill") outside the cemetery gates, marks the remains of a 12th-century Norman motte and bailey. In the mid-14th century, during the Black Death, this was a much sought-after place of pilgrimage, where Saint Mullin's grave and the waters from his well were believed to offer solace and health. Even today, the saint's day —the 25th of July — is observed with a "pattern" or pilgrimage. In fact, the ferry service across the Barrow, established for visitors and pilgrims by St. Mullin himself in the 7th century, was only discontinued in the last century. Explore St. Mullin's on your own and you will discover much more of interest, especially if the adjoining Heritage Centre happens to be open. This is the perfect place for a driving break or, even better, a mid-day picnic. [L10] Located beside the sleepy village of St. Mullins, Co. Carlow, on the scenic Barrow Drive, 7.5 miles north of New Ross. Open site.

O Son of the living God,

ancient eternal King,
grant me a hidden hut
to be my home in the wild,

with green shallow water
running by its side
and a clear pool to wash off sin
by grace of the Holy Ghost;

a lovely wood close by
around it on every hand
to feed the birds of many voices,
to shelter them and hide...

some sensible disciples
(their number I will fix)
modest and obedient
praying to the King:

four times three—or three fours—
correct for every need;
two sixes within the church
on the north side and the south,

six pairs besides myself
gathered all about me
praying for all Eternity
to the King who lights the Sun...

From the Prayer of Manchán of Liath. 9c. Irish
Tr. Thomas Kinsella
The New Oxford Book of Irish Verse *(Oxford, 1986)*

Bed and Board

If you prove unable to break the spell of Wicklow in a single day and decide to spend the night there, we can make a few memorable recommendations. For a splurge there's Tinakilly House, a classical Victorian-Italianate getaway on R750 off the N11 in Rathnew, Co. Wicklow (0404-69274 www.tinakilly.ie). Tinakilly's Brunel Restaurant serves award-winning cuisine. €€€ CC.

A comparable splurge, with a golf course thrown in, may be found just outside Dunlavin, Co. Wicklow at Rathsallagh House (04-540-3112 www.rathsallagh.com). Rathsallagh's restaurant too has garnered its own share of awards. €€€ CC. In the likelihood, however, that you have made it past Wicklow by day's end, we have several additional suggestions. Within a stone's throw of Jerpoint Abbey (provided Cúchulainn is throwing the stone), you find Co. Kilkenny's premier lodging, Mount Juliet Estate (056-777-3000 www.mountjuliet.ie), in Thomastown. They say "approach" is almost everything, and here you'll drive for two miles along a narrow path before reaching the 18th-century manor house that will be your roof for the night. If you can afford to eat after paying for your room, it goes without saying that you can find a suitable feast here. Unfortunately, nearby Jerpoint is no longer a working monastery and thus unable to offer lodging, but the next best thing is to stay directly across from the abbey 1.5 miles south of Thomastown on the Waterford Road (N9) at Abbey House (056-772-4166). This period Georgian home is in an attractive setting beside the Little Arrigle River and offers all the warm hospitality you could look for. Mrs. Helen Blanchfield, your host, will serve dinner with advance request; and you may bring your own wine. €€ CC. Finally, if you take the more roundabout way through St. Mullins, we have a couple of attractive lodging and dining options for you. Just off R705, roughly 4 miles from Bagenalstown, Co. Carlow on the Borris Road in the serene Barrow Valley, you'll find the Lorum Old Rectory (059-977-5282 www.lorum.com), where you will discover one of the most congenial lodgings we have come across in Ireland. The Smiths are consummate hosts, and you'll want to be sure to join them and their guest for the evening meal, as Bobbi Smith is an inspired chef. Open Feb-Nov. €€€ CC. Lastly, on the same road as the Lorum Old Rectory and perhaps a half mile closer to Bagenalstown, you come upon the Kilgraney Country House (059-977-5283 www.kilgraneyhouse.com), a uniquely decorated period rectory set in secluded gardens overlooking the Barrow Valley and serving excellent meals in large part grown here in Martin Marley and Bryan Leech's gardens. €€€ CC.

DAY THREE
To the Sea

Today's drive takes you to the southern coast of Ireland where the first Christian missionaries are likely to have arrived from the Continent in the late 4th or early 5th centuries, decades before the mission of Patrick. En route you will visit a number of memorable sites and cross through the Golden Vale, one of the most breathtaking valleys on the island. We will assume that you are setting out from Thomastown, Co. Kilkenny or thereabouts. Although a direct line to day's end at Ardmore would amount to only 60 miles or so, today's route is a good deal more sinewy and circuitous than that so as to take in a day full of ruins and wonders. In giving directions, we will limit ourselves mostly to numbered roads and highways, although there are in some cases more direct routes drawn but not identified on your Michelin map. If you're feeling adventurous, by all means take the often more direct anonymous byways. They're bound to go somewhere. From Thomastown, then, take the R669 southwest towards Knocktopher and pick up the N10 north towards Kilkenny. After roughly five miles on the N10 north, at Stoneyford, you will see and follow signs to "Kells Priory" or "Medieval Kells." After exploring Kells, you can either take a side trip to Kilkenny town or continue on to Cashel. The shortest route to Cashel from Kells will take you briefly on a country road to Callan and the N76, which you will then take south towards Clonmel. On the northern edge of Clonmel you will pick up the N24 for eight miles to Cahir. From Cahir to Cashel it's another eight miles, this time on the M8 north. After visiting the Rock of Cashel, retrace your path to Cahir, whose splendid castle may prove too enticing to drive by. As you leave Cahir, head south and look for R668, which you will take roughly nine miles to Clogheen and another 14 miles through the Knockmealdown (or, more to the point, "knock-me-down") Mountains to the scenic town of Lismore on the banks of the Blackwater. Regrettably, the enchanting Lismore Castle is privately owned, and only its gardens are open to the public. And here, unless it is late in the day and darkness is approaching, we are going to urge you to throw caution to the wind and to seek out the unnumbered "green" route south in the direction of Youghal (pronounced "yawl"). The secluded beauty of this river route more than compensates for the risk of getting lost. Just follow the River Blackwater and after roughly 17 miles you'll reach the N25, which you should take northeast in the direction of Waterford and not southwest in the direction of Youghal and Cork. After a little over 4 miles you will see signs to coastal Ardmore, your last destination of the day.

PRINCIPAL SITES
Medieval Kells

Medieval Kells, as its name suggests, has no proper place in a discussion of ancient Ireland drawing to its close with the Norman Invasions beginning in 1169. The priory and town of Kells, however, were founded less than a quarter-century after the Normans arrived, so that only a slight compromise in our timeframe is required to include them here. And they are well worth it! Situated less than ten miles south of the medieval city of Kilkenny, Kells Priory is one of Ireland's best kept secrets, though the word is getting out. Long overlooked and still off the tourist map, this is one of the most intriguing historical monuments in Ireland. Embodying that curious oxymoron—the "intact ruin"—Kells both informs and summons the visitor's imagination to lift fallen stones into place and to raise the dead to life.

Medieval Kells

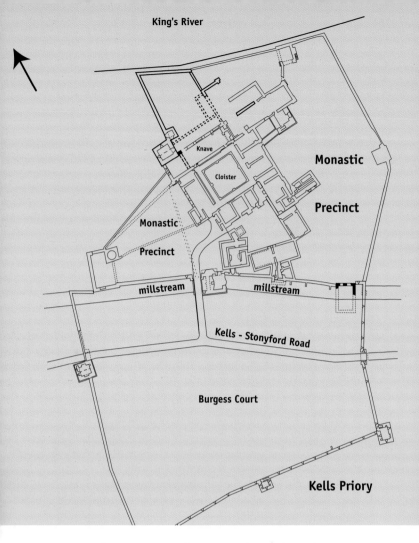

King's River

Knave

Cloister

Monastic

Precinct

Monastic

Precinct

millstream   millstream

Kells - Stonyford Road

Burgess Court

Kells Priory

Enclosing just over three acres, this 13th–15th-century Augustinian Priory, due to its imposing outer walls and towers, looks and feels more like a military fortress than a spiritual retreat. In fact, the Monastic Precinct, along the south bank of the King's River, was set apart by a millstream, walls, and towers from the fortified outer enclosure to the north, the Burgher's Court, constructed in turbulent times for the security of the local population and their cattle. Although no guided tour is available on site, you are not entirely on your own to interpret this vast complex, as an excellent visitor's guide written by Daniel Tietzsch-Tyler is on sale in the town, the perfect companion for an in-depth exploration of the site or for later reading. [K10] Open site, signposted from the N10 south of Kilkenny.

Rock of Cashel

Rock of Cashel

Few sights in Ireland can match the drama of "the Rock." The steep limestone outcrop on which this ancient site is poised rises 200 feet over the otherwise tame Tipperary countryside, which it clearly dominates. The Rock, the fortified seat of Eóganacht kings from the 4th to the 10th century, conveys an unmistakable sense of raw power—clout, not mystery. No matter whether its rulers wore crowns or miters. Eventually, indeed, bishops replaced kings on this height. It seems the royal *cashel* had ties to Christianity from very early on. A late and historically wobbly life of Patrick suggests that the saint—unlikely to have ever stepped foot on or near the Rock—once baptized a king by the name of Oengus mac Nad Froích on this spot, after having wounded him grievously.

"Patrick afterwards bade farewell to the men of Ossory at Belach Gabrain, and he left with them Martin, an elder, and a party of his people where Martharthech is at this day in Mag Raigne. Patrick passed afterwards by Belach Gabrain into the province of Munster, and preached to the territories and to the churches, so that they believed and were baptized, and he blessed them. And with them he left priests instructing (them) and practicing piety.

"When he reached Mag Femin, he was received by Oengus, son of Natfraech, King of Munster. Oengus made him great welcome and brought him to his house to Cashel. Patrick preached to him. The hinder end of the crozier went through his foot, and wounded it greatly. Patrick said, 'Why didst thou not protect thyself?' 'Methought,' saith Oengus, 'that it was a rite of religion.' Said Patrick, 'Blood shall not be shed in this place from to-day till Doom, and of all those that shall succeed thee but one king shall be slain.'

   "Oengus is baptized with great hosts along with him. Patrick blessed Oengus upon Lia Cathraige (Cathraige's stone), whereon the kings were appointed to office at Cashel."

—On the Life of St. Patrick (Leabhar Breac), translated by Whitley Stokes.

The entanglement of church and state, as it were, has a long history here at Cashel. A number of its enthroned kings were also clerics, even bishops, not without complications. Bishop-kings found themselves changing hats on short notice. Among the most distinguished of Cashel's kings was Brian Boru, who from the Rock came as close as any to ruling all of Ireland. It was King Murtagh O'Brien, a reformer and then some, who in 1101 bestowed "Cashel of the Kings" upon the Church. At the Synod of Kells, fifty years later, the ecclesiastical administration of Ireland was divided between these four seats or "sees": Armagh, Cashel, Dublin, and Tuam, thus establishing a Roman diocesan system much like that in place today. The Reformation, curiously enough, at first had little impact on Cashel, since its sitting Catholic bishop, Edmund Butler, was left in place; and Butler's successor, an appointee of the Catholic Queen Mary, was recognized by the Pope. The next archbishop of Cashel, however, was named to the post by Queen Elizabeth the first, after he had switched sides. Once a Catholic Franciscan monk and bishop he accepted royal supremacy in 1567 and was well rewarded for his move. He married twice and accrued a personal fortune. His remorseful, self-written epitaph is inscribed in the choir wall.

The ode of Miler Magrath, Archbishop of Cashe, to the passer-by:

Patrick, the glory of our Isle and Gown,
First sat a bishop in the See of Down.
I wish that I, succeeding him in place
As Bishop, had an equal share of Grace.
I served thee, England, fifty years in Jars,
And pleas'd thy Princes in the midst of Wars;
Here where I'm plac'd I'm not; and this the Case is,
I'm not in both, yet am in both Places.

He that judgeth me is the Lord. 1 Cor. 4.4. 1621
Let him who stands, take care lest he fall.

—*Latin epitaph translated by Harris.*

The colorful and conflicted history of Cashel did not, of course, end here with the notorious Miler Macgrath. It was and remained a place where blood mingled with baptismal water, a site of both Mass and massacre.

Once again we urge you to take advantage of the excellent audio-visual presentation and guided tour provided here, which will point out to you and explain the most memorable artifacts and monuments atop the Rock, the grandest of which is the 13th-century Gothic cathedral erected between 1230 and 1290. A smaller and older gem is Cormac's Chapel, one of Ireland's earliest and most striking Romanesque churches, consecrated in 1134. As you are exploring and examining the details of the Rock's many monuments, remember to look up and take in the big picture. The views of and from the Rock are among the most spectacular you will encounter.

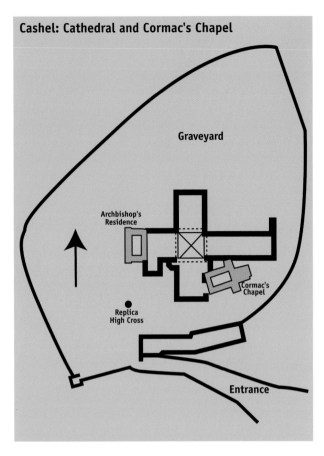

Cashel: Cathedral and Cormac's Chapel

Graveyard

Archbishop's Residence

Cormac's Chapel

Replica High Cross

Entrance

An OPW Heritage Card site. [I10] Located in the town of Cashel, Co. Tipperary (062-61437) and open mid-Sept–mid-Oct daily 9am–5:30pm; mid-Oct–mid-Mar daily 9am–4:30pm; and mid-Mar–early-June 9am-5:30; early-June–mid-Sept 9am–7:00pm

Ardmore

Even if this were not one of the most eminent early Christian sites in Ireland, it would be well worth the journey. Ardmore is a secret that has been whispered too many times for there to be any hope left of having it to yourself; but we have never seen it crowded. And the new Vikings, in their many-wheeled longboats, have not yet put it on their maps.

Ardmore's lovely beach, on which littering must be a capital offense, its impressive cliff walk, its remarkable

High Cross, its quaint Main Street, and its fine dining are all enough to draw a discerning and ever-expanding cohort of fans.

Dating from the late 4th century, Ardmore may be Ireland's earliest Christian settlement. Declan's mission here precedes by decades that of Patrick.

There were in Ireland before Patrick came thither four holy bishops with their followers who evangelized and sowed the word of God there; these are the four: Ailbe, Bishop Ibar, Declan, and Ciaran. They drew multitudes from error to the faith of Christ, although it was Patrick who sowed the faith throughout Ireland and it is he who turned chiefs and kings of Ireland to the way of baptism, faith and sacrifice and everlasting judgment.

These three—Declan, Ailbe and Bishop Ibar—made a bond of friendship and a league amongst themselves and their spiritual posterity in heaven and on earth for ever and they loved one another. SS. Ailbe and Declan, especially, loved one another as if they were brothers so that, on account of their mutual affection they did not like to be separated from one another—except when their followers threatened to separate them by force if they did not go apart for a very short time. After this Declan returned to his own country—to the Decies of Munster, where he preached and baptized, in the name of Christ, many whom he turned to the Catholic faith from the power of the devil. He built numerous churches in which he placed many of his own followers to serve and worship God and to draw people to God from the wiles of Satan.

—*The Life of St Declan of Ardmore*
Translated from the Irish by Rev. P. Power

An early life of Declan relates much more than is feasibly known of the saint, including the story of his miraculous bell, conveyed across the sea atop a massive rock that resides to this day on the southern end of the beach. Known as St. Declan's Stone, it is said to have healing powers. All you have to do is to crawl under it on July 24, St. Declan's day, raise your prayers to the saint, and believe.

Declan was beginning mass one day in a church which lay in his road, when there was sent him from heaven a little black bell, (which came) in through the window of the church and remained on the altar before Declan...

Now the bell which we have alluded to as sent from heaven to Declan, was, at that time, in the custody of Runan (son of the king of Rome) to carry as we have said, for Declan did not wish, on any account, to part with it. On this particular day as they were proceeding towards the ship Runan entrusted it to another member of the company. On reaching the shore however the latter laid the bell on a rock by the shore and forgot it till they were half way across the sea. Then they remembered it and on remembrance they were much distressed. Declan was very sorrowful that the gift sent him by the Lord from heaven should have been forgotten in a place where he never expected to find it again. Thereupon raising his eyes heavenward he prayed to God within his heart and he said to his followers: "Lay aside your sorrow for it is possible with God who sent that bell in the beginning to send it now again by some marvelous ship." Very fully and wonderfully and beautifully the creature without reason or understanding obeyed its creator, for the very heavy unwieldy rock floated buoyantly and without deviation, so that in a short time they beheld it in their rear with the bell upon it. And when his people saw this wondrous thing it filled them with love for God and reverence for their master. Declan thereupon addressed them prophetically: "Permit the bell to precede you and follow it exactly and whatsoever haven it will enter into it is there my city and my bishopric will be whence I shall go to paradise and there my resurrection will be.

—*The Life of St Declan of Ardmore*
Translated from the Irish by Rev. P. Power

Unless you are facing a formidable downpour or gale-force winds, be sure to find your way to the town's ancient monastic settlement and hilltop graveyard via the cliff walk which begins at St. Declan's Stone on the beach. The total distance from here to the early monastic site is roughly 3 miles. You can cut this down a bit and greatly reduce your climbing by driving your car to the Cliff House Hotel and following the trail from there. Then, after visiting the High Cross and other monuments, you can take a short cut back to your car.

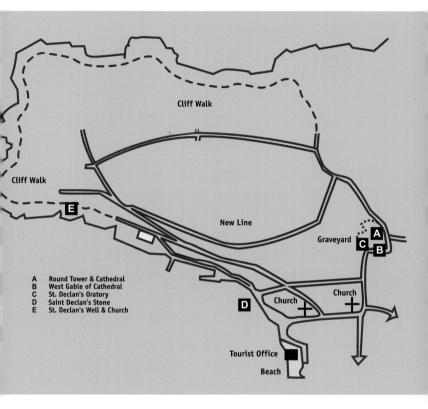

Once you've completed the cliff walk and find yourself in the Ardmore graveyard and ancient monastic site, the highlights are more or less obvious. The most striking is the perfectly intact 97-foot-high round tower, arguably the finest of all round towers in Ireland. The cone, to be fair, is a restoration. There is also, of course, the ruined cathedral, whose Irish-Romanesque nave dates from the 11th century. Be sure not to overlook the worn but still discernible bas-relief sculptures in two blind arches on the west gable of the nave, as well as two worse-for-wear ogham stones within the cathedral walls. While none of these structures date from the time of Declan, tradition has it that the small stone chapel, known as St. Declan's Oratory, marks his burial site.

Round Tower at Ardmore

This is an open site and you are free to explore the site of Declan's original monastery on your own; but you'll appreciate your visit more if you pick up a copy of "The Pilgrim's Round of Ardmore, Co. Waterford" at the local newsagent's or join the local walking tour of ancient Ardmore. It's best to ring in advance to confirm current availability and times from the Tourist Information Office (024-94444) in the harbor. [I12] Assuming that you will not find your way to Ardmore by foot along the 58-mi pilgrimage route from the Rock of Cashel known as St. Declan's Way, Ardmore is clearly signposted from the N25 roughly 40 miles southwest of Waterford.

Side Sites

Kilkenny Town

Kilkenny, a focal destination in its own right, is often touted as Ireland's most attractive town. However one casts that vote, there is no denying that Kilkenny— steeped in history and vibrantly alive—is a cultural and commercial magnet. It is also understandably congested. Both because there is so much of interest here and because there are so many people interested, it's not easy to pop in and out for a quick look. If you take a detour here, you'll want at the very least to tour the castle (expect lines and delays during the summer) and poke around in

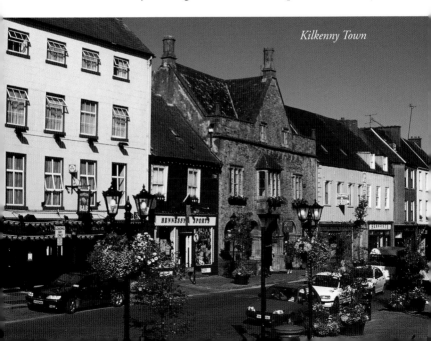

Kilkenny Town

Golden Vale

Kilkenny's many interesting galleries and shops, particularly those across from the castle in the one-time castle stables. Before you do anything, of course, you'll have to find parking; and all that adds up to hours and not minutes. [K9/10]

The Vee

Your recommended route today takes you along the 11-mi stretch of road known as "the Vee," winding through the Knockmealdown Mountains between Clogheen, Co. Tipperary, and Lismore in County Waterford. This is surely one of the most dramatically scenic drives in the southeast or, for that matter, anywhere in Ireland. You'll want to stop at the highest point of the Vee, on the Tipperary-Waterford line, and gaze northward out over the Galty Valley and Tipperary's Golden Vale far below. From this point numerous walking trails branch out to take you to nearby peaks and to the mountain lake of Petticoat Loose. Another local landmark is the rounded stone cairn that you may have noticed just off the road as you came up from Clogheen. It is in fact a tomb, wherein Samuel Grubb of Castle Grace stands—not lies—in

Kid Sites

Caher Castle

Although Kilkenny Castle is perhaps more widely known, this is more what any kid has in mind when he or she thinks "castle." Dead center in the heart of the town of Caher (often spelled "Cahir"), beside the River Suir, this is one of Ireland's grandest medieval fortresses. As early as the 3rd century there was a fortress here on the castle rock, which gave to the towns its earlier name–The City of the Fishing Fort. The current surviving Norman structure dates from the 13th and 15th centuries. With its fully restored walls, keep, courtyards and great hall (featuring 10,000-year-old antlers from an ancient Irish elk), the castle is largely intact and begs to be explored. The tour and the brief video will help you understand and appreciate the castle's history and features. The tour, however, is not inclusive; so save time for your own explorations. [I10] Caher Castle (052-744-1011) is open mid-Mar–mid-June and mid-Sept–mid-Oct daily 9:30am–5:30pm; mid-June–mid-Aug daily 9am–6:30pm; and mid-Oct–mid-Mar 9:30am–4:30pm. An OPW Heritage Card site.

death. So great was his attachment to these mountain peaks that he left explicit instructions for his burial in their midst, requesting to be entombed upright, facing north, so that he might forever gaze out over his beloved Golden Vale. [I11]

Bed and Board

Ardmore, for all its charm, is not yet noted for its accommodations. At this point we only recommend one lodging in the town proper, the Round Tower Hotel (024-94494 rth@ eircom.net), €€ CC. Nothing luxurious or exceptional, but surely clean, comfortable and convenient. For memorable accommodation and dining, you may very well want to drive east on the N25 to nearby Dungarvan where the Tannery Townhouse and (award-winning) Restaurant (058- 45814 www.tannery.ie) €€ CC will likely surpass your expectations, and at good price. Back to Ardmore, although the Round Tower has its own dining room, one of the selling points here is that it is only up the street from two very fine restaurants, White Horses and the Cliff House Hotel. You'll find the Round Tower Hotel a short drive up from the town center and beach on College Road. Only six minutes' drive from here, just outside the town, there's also the very inviting Newtown Farm Guesthouse (024-94143 www.newtownfarm.com), €€ CC. In this three-star family-run guesthouse you'll enjoy ocean views, scenic cliff walks and a full farmhouse breakfast. It's signposted from the N25. Turn left at Flemings Pub. Another option would be for you to get a slight lead on tomorrow's westward drive and stay in East Cork, in nearby Youghal or on Ballycotton Bay in Shanagarry. In this case, we have two fine suggestions. First, at 163 North Main Street in nearby Youghal, Co. Cork, you can both drop anchor and pull up a chair for dinner at Aherne's (024-92424 www.ahernes .com), €€€ CC, specializing in seafood and four-star family hospitality. Then, a bit further south and west there's the legendary Ballymaloe Country House and Restaurant (021-465-2531 www.ballymaloe.ie), €€€ CC, a mecca for chefs and connoisseurs of new Irish cuisine, known on the street as the Irish "slow food" movement. To find your way here, take the N25 west to Castlemartyr and from there follow signs and R632 to Shanagarry and Ballymaloe.

If you're spending the night in or near Ardmore, we strongly recommend that you dine at White Horses (024-94040), €€ CC. This unassuming bistro on Main Street in Ardmore outdoes itself, serving truly memorable cuisine in a friendly, informal environment. While catering to family and children's needs, they offer a wide menu, including seafood and vegetarian entrées, and quite possibly the finest fillet steak you've ever had. For a splurge at the top of the town, you'll find one of Ireland's five Michelin one-star rated restaurants and luxury spots at the Cliff House Hotel (024-87800) €€€ CC. For both of these restaurants, be sure to make an advance reservation, particularly on weekends. Finally, if you've decided to drive west to Ballymaloe House or Aherne's, you'll of course want to take advantage of their renowned in-house restaurants.

DAY FOUR
Go West!

Today will be spent largely behind the wheel; but take heart. Provided the clouds do not descend and enshroud mountains and sea, you will gaze upon some of Ireland's most spectacular land-and-seascapes, regardless of which route you select. You see, there's a fork in your road today and you must choose between two day's-end destinations. The first is the Iveragh Peninsula and the second is the

Dingle Peninsula, both in Co. Kerry. You can't go wrong with either. The principal reason for finding your way to the tip of the Iveragh Peninsula is Skellig Michael, the ancient 7th-century island monastery built over 650 feet above the sea atop a craggy pinnacle of rock. The journey to the island and the climb to this startling site is sure to be the highpoint, in every sense of the word, of your Ireland adventures. Several cautions, however, are in order. In a fog, Skellig Michael is invisible from the shore, and little or nothing can be seen from its peak. Furthermore, in choppy seas—far from the exception here—the Great Skellig cannot be approached safely by sea; so no landings are made. Finally, the ascent, while not alarmingly perilous, is not to be attempted by anyone weak of knee or nerve. In short, if you suffer from shortness of breath, weakness of limb, or vertigo, Skellig Michael is not for you. An advance telephone inquiry to the Skellig Heritage Centre (066-947-6306) or to boat captain Des Lavelle (087-237-1017 www.skelligboattrips.com) sometime today might prove informative regarding the prospects for clear skies and fair seas; but keep in mind that the weather, in Ireland of all places, is wildly unpredictable. Now, turning to the second option, there is no one site on the Dingle Peninsula to match Skellig Michael; but, setting aside that one trump card, the Dingle Peninsula has every bit as much to offer as the Iveragh and is less teeming with tourists. The Iveragh Peninusla, home to Killarney and the Ring of Kerry, is the most powerful tourist magnet in Ireland; but it's fame feeds on itself. Skellig aside, we prefer the Dingle; but ultimately it comes down to a coin toss.

The road west is the same, however, for most of the day's journey. Assuming Ardmore as your point of departure, take the N25 roughly 35 miles west into Cork where you will follow signs to Killarney, picking up the N22 west. On the N22 it is roughly 54 miles from Cork to Killarney, the point at which you will have to decide between the Iveragh and the Dingle Peninsulas.

Option #1 • Iveragh Peninusla

With the Skellig as your ultimate destination, you actually have more than one choice to make. You can stay on the

N22 from Cork all the way to Killarney, where you will pick up the N22 south to Kenmare and, from there, the N70 (aka Ring of Kerry) past Waterville to Portmagee (via R565). You can also take a more roundabout and spectacularly scenic route through the Caha Pass, by leaving the N22 just over 20 miles outside of Cork and just shy of Macroom, finding R584 southwest to Ballylickey, where you will in turn pick up the N71 in the direction of Glengariff and Kenmare. If you're taking your time and feel you can spare a couple of hours for a special diversion, you might consider a boat trip to Ilnacullin Island, also known as Garinish, in Bantry Bay, Co. Cork. Boats leave from Glengariff Harbour every half hour or so. Garinish, once a barren, nondescript sliver of offshore real estate, was nearly a century ago transformed into an exquisite Italianate garden. Almost better than Garinish with its exotic plants and flowers from many continents, however, are the colonies of seals, oftentimes replete with pups, encountered en route. Resuming your journey west, once in Kenmare, you will pick up the N70 as above, following it past Waterville to your turnoff for R565 and Portmagee. Whichever route you take, you will pass through bright and bustling Kenmare, an especially attractive town for a bit of window-shopping and a bite to eat. To complicate matters further, if you feel drawn or compelled to spend time in and even stay in Killarney, you could surely do so for one or both of your nights in Co. Kerry. It would just mean rising quite early and driving the roughly 73 miles out to Portmagee to make your sailing to Skellig.

Bed and Board

At the northwestern tip of the Iveragh Peninsula, in close proximity to the Skellig Heritage Centre and to boat launches to the Great Skelling, we have two recommendations for lodging. The Moorings (066-947-7108 www.moorings.ie), €€ CC, opposite the harbor in Portmagee, offers the charm of a small inn and all of the conveniences of a modern hotel, including fine dining. A short stroll from town and across the bridge from the Skellig Heritage Centre, on Valencia Island, there's another fine choice. Shealane Country House (066-947-6354 maryshealane@gmail.com), €€ CC, is an exceptionally

242　THE ANCIENT IRELAND GUIDE

attractive B&B with spacious, pine-paneled rooms and sea
views. In addition to the Moorings Restaurant, there's
another great local dining opportunity on Valencia Island.
The Ring Lyne Pub (066-947-6103) offers first-class bar
food € CC, with an emphasis on local seafood prepared in
the traditional manner with few frills to obscure the fact
that you're often eating today's catch. The Ring Lyne also
offers lodging. To find the Ring Lyne, cross the bridge from
Portmagee and make your first right onto R565. The Ring
Lyne is straight ahead less than two miles in Chapeltown.

Killarney is swarming with tourists and is nearly paved
with places to stay, many of them decidedly upscale. Our
select suggestions offer varying degrees of tranquility and
convenience at affordable rates. In town, on a side,
residential street, only a 5-min walk from the heart of
Killarney, there's Earl's Court Hotel—six-time winner of
the Little Gem award—an exceptionally tasteful and
comfortable lodging, furnished with Irish antiques and
serving an excellent breakfast either in the formal dining
room or in your own bedroom. Earl's Court (064-663-
4009 www.killarney-earlscourt.ie), €€ CC, located on
Woodlawn Road off Woodlawn Junction, is signposted
from the N71 (Muckross Road) just south of the town
center. Far more secluded, yet only a mile from town,
there's the Gleann Fia Country House (064-663-5035
www.gleannfia.com), €€ CC, in Deerpark, Killarney.
This modern, spacious, Victorian-style guesthouse is set
in its own 26 acres of lawns, woodlands and gardens. At
the end of a long day, this is a true haven, with its own
riverside nature walk. As you enter Killarney from the
north on the N22 you will come to a roundabout with
the Ryan Hotel on the left. Take the second exit off this
roundabout (direction Tralee) and drive one mile. Gleann
Fia Country House is signposted on your right. Finally, a
real bargain, there's Carriglea House (064-663-1116
www.carrigleahouse.com) € CC, an inviting 200-year-
old country home on your left just over a mile south of
Killarney center on the N71 (Muckross Road). Set above
the road house enjoys grand views of the Killarney Lakes
and the Mangerton Mountains.

As you would expect in a major tourist mecca, the
restaurant scene runs in high gear, with lots of offerings
and a fair degree of turnover. You will inevitably walk the

streets and scan the street-side menus; but amidst all of this choice, we can suggest two sure-fire hits. The first is Killarney's most revered destination for traditional Irish fare at its best. Here at Bricín (064-663-4902) €€ CC, the signature dish may be traditional Kerry boxty dishes, but there is much more, including seafood, pastas and Irish stew. Bricín is in the heart of Killarney at 26 High Street. The very popular Chapter Forty Restaurant found at 40 New Street (064-667-1833) €€ CC offers a menu of creative European cuisine and touted Kerry lamb in perfect morsels.

Option #2: Dingle Peninsula

The route described above, originating in Ardmore, points you towards Killarney on the N22. To reach the Dingle Peninsula, remain on the N22 for 16 miles past Killarney, where you will merge with the N21 and, in 4 more miles, come into Tralee. From Tralee take the N86 west 9 miles to Camp, where you have a decision to make. Assuming your destination is Dingle town, you can take from this point either a northern or a southern route. The northern route—via Stradbally, Kilcummin and Ballyduff—takes you through the quite spectacular and sometimes harrowing Conor Pass. If the road is wet, the sky foggy, or your nerves bare, you might want to save this spectacle for another day (but don't miss it altogether!). The southern route has two options: first, to cut immediately south from

Conor Pass

Camp on the green biway to Auglis, positioning you to stop and explore the grandly scenic Inch beach; or, second, to stay on the N86 from Camp, taking it all the way to Dingle via Lougher, Anascaul and Lispole. Whatever you do, don't torment yourself over such decisions; for you can't miss, whatever route you take. Each has its ample rewards. Besides, you will no doubt be exploring the Dingle's roads and byways quite fully for the next day or so. No matter what road you take to Dingle, expect traffic. Wee Dingle is a favored spot and its main street is easily choked with cars and pedestrians in the summer months.

Bed and Board

In a secluded spot overlooking Dingle Bay, yet only several minutes by car and 15 minutes by foot from town, Milltown House (066-915-1372 www.milltownhouse dingle.com) €€€ CC is a fine base for your two days in Dingle. Half of the spacious guest rooms in this gracious 130-year-old period home have sea views and all but a few have patios. The most sought-after room is #2, which belonged to Robert Mitchum while he was filming *Ryan's Daughter*. Milltown House is just beyond the western edge of town, at the beginning of Slea Head Drive (R559) and is signposted on your left. Then, only minutes from Dingle town center by car, there's another great choice, Greenmount House (066-915-1414 www.greenmount house.com) €€/€€€ CC. All of the rooms here have large sitting areas and sea views. Perched above the town, this beautifully landscaped haven offers a panoramic vista of Dingle Bay. To reach Greenmount House turn right at the roundabout on the eastern edge of town, then right again at the next junction. Drive to the top of the hill and Greenmount will be on your left.

Dingle is bristling with eateries. Among them we especially recommend two. Out of the Blue (066-915-0811) €€/€€€ CC boasts a number of awards, including Winner of the 2011 Best Restaurant in Kerry by the Restaurants Association of Ireland. Unpretentious and committed to fresh seafood, Out of the Blue claims, "If there's no fish, the restaurant doesn't open." That said, call ahead for a memorable meal. A cozy and more affordable choice, Doyle's Seafood Bar (066-915-2674) €€ CC is a pub with atmosphere and great seafood. The blackboard menu offers today's catch right off the decks off Dingle fishing boats. For the peninsula's finest cuisine, however, you're going to have to take a drive to Gorman's Clifftop House Hotel (066-915-5162) €€€ CC in the townland of Glashabeg (Glaise Bheag) near the small fishing village of Ballydavid, facing the open Atlantic. Not surprisingly, the specialities of the house are drawn from Irish tradition and straight from offshore waters. From Dingle town, take R559 to Murreagh and from there follow signs to Ballydavid and Gorman's. O'Gorman's also offers lodging. While a bit out of the way, the rooms here provide breathtaking views of sea and mountains. If you're interested, consult www.gormans-clifftophouse.com for more information.

DAY FIVE
Exploring

Your main task yesterday was to find your way from County Waterford to County Kerry and to select and establish your base, either on the Iveragh or on the Dingle Peninsula. Now, ensconced in your same lodging for another night, you have before you a full day for sites and adventures. Some of these will be unanticipated, as you will surely make discoveries and follow whims of your own; for the rest, we have some eager recommendations to offer below.

Option #1 • The Iveragh Peninsula

PRINCIPAL SITE
Skellig Michael

This World Heritage Site is quite simply beyond words. Among other things, it stands to define "white martyrdom," the bloodless self-immolation embraced by thousands of early Irish hermits and cenobites, inspired by the still earlier Christian ascetics of Egypt and North Africa. Ordinarily, we equate solitude and prayer with silence, but here the pounding seas, howling winds, and incessant screeching and chatter of seabirds can be all but deafening. It is men and their worldly aspirations that are silenced here, not God and his Creation. In an age when EXT or "Extreme" is the ultimate epithet, this may surely be understood as Extreme Christianity.

Skellig Michael

Courtesy of John Victor Luce

"Whoever has not stood in the graveyard on the summit of that cliff among the beehive dwellings and their beehive oratory does not know Ireland through and through."

—*George Bernard Shaw*

Skellig appears with some frequency in the oldest Irish manuscripts, beginning with the account of a 1400 B.C.E. shipwreck in which the Milesian invader-hero Irr lost his life, only to be buried on Skellig's high cliffs. It was, we are told, a place of refuge for kings and bishops in flight, attempting to save their lives or their souls. It was also a favorite target for Viking raids, laconically chronicled in the Annals of Ulster, Inisfallen, and of the Four Masters. There is even an entry in the *Annals of the Four Masters,* noting that Olav, the patron saint of Norway and son of the Viking King Olav Trygvasson was baptized by a Skellig monk.

Literally, the highpoint of any pilgrim's or visitor's journey to the Great Skellig, Skellig Michael, named for the Archangel, is the 6th-century monastic complex 8 miles from the Kerry mainland and roughly 600 feet above the sea. The surviving monuments comprising this ancient settlement include six corbelled, beehive huts, two boat-shaped oratories, the ruins of an 11–12th-century medieval church, several graves and wells, and an assortment of upright stones and crosses. It is estimated that this was home at any given time for between ten and twenty monks, living on the water, eggs, fowl and seafood provided by the island and its waters, as well as on whatever donations or trade came their way from the mainland.

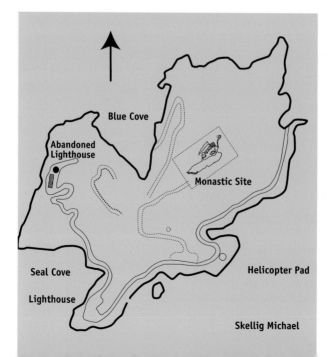

There are a number of local boat captains, working out of the Portmagee Harbour [B12], who ferry tourists to Skellig and back in spring and summer. Most leave around 10:15am and return in the mid-afternoon at 3pm, always dependent on weather and sea conditions. We most highly recommend Des Lavalle (087-237-1017 www.skelligboattrips.com), who has been taking people to Skellig for decades and has written a fine book on the island entitled *The Skellig Story*. The cost of a Skelling tour varies somewhat and will likely increase from one year to the next; but at the moment it runs roughly €45 per person.

Whether or not you are able to make the ascent to the monastic site atop Skellig Michael [A12], we recommend highly that you take in "The Skellig Experience," which is the name given to the architecturally intriguing and truly informative Skellig Heritage Centre (066-947-6306 www.skelligexperience.com), €€ CC on Valencia Island, just over the bridge from Portmagee. Rain or shine, rough or calm the sea may be, the center's exhibitions and audio-visual presentation brings you to the Skellig Rocks, introducing you to their fascinating history and wildlife (including a spring/summer puffin colony). Also, April through September, weather and sea permitting, the Skellig Heritage Centre, for an additional fee €€€ CC, offers 2-hr sea cruises circuiting the Great and Little Skellig, and pointing out the rich array of seabirds off the Kerry coast, as well as the occasional Bottlenose or Common dolphin, Minke whale, or Basking shark. Open May, June, & Sept daily 10am–6pm; July–Aug 10am–7pm; Mar, Apr, Oct, Nov 10am–5pm; we recommend that you call 066-947-6306 for exact times/days.

Side Sites

Muckross House and Gardens
This ivy-covered 19th-century Victorian mansion and its exquisite gardens is one of Killarney's stand-out attractions. Upstairs you can see how the gentry or "quality" once lived, while in the cellars, converted to craft and gift shops, you can bring back something to enhance your own estate. A stroll through the gardens and over to the Middle Lake, and lunch or a snack in the garden restaurant make this an

Muckross House and Gardens

easy place to loll away the better part of an afternoon. The gardens and surrounding park are open year-round, free of charge. [D11] Muckross House (064-667-0144 www.muckross-house.ie), €€ CC is located on the Kenmare Road (N71) just south of Killarney center, and is open Sept-June daily 9am–5:30pm, July–Aug daily 9am–7pm. Combination tickets available with Muckross Traditional Farms (see Kid Sites on next page).

Staigue Stone Fort

Strategically situated on an elevated plain, encircled by a large bank and fosse, and surrounded on three sides by mountains, Staigue Fort is one of the largest and best preserved dry stone *cashels* or ringforts in Ireland. The outer wall measures 90 feet in diameter, 18 feet at its highest point, and is 13 feet thick at its base. Stone forts are notoriously difficult to date. One likely guess would put it in the early Iron Age, though it was probably in use for many centuries, well into the Christian period. [B12] Staigue Fort is signposted from the N70 west of Sneem and is located roughly 2 miles off the main road. Open site, with a small donation expected to contribute to its upkeep. The Staigue Fort Exhibition Centre just off of the N70 is a private enterprise unrelated to the fort site and in our opinion charges a tad too much for its exhibition and video.

Kid Sites

Muckross Traditional Farms

The aim of this 70-acre park is to give its visitors a hands-on, walk-through sense of what rural Irish life looked, smelled, and sounded like in the 1930's and 40's. Private homes, artisans' shops, farm fields and animal pens are all on display and in use. Kids enjoy the exploration of this rural setting and often emerge remarkably grateful for the plumbing, electricity, and generally soft life they have taken, and probably will continue to take, for granted. [D11] Muckross Traditional Farms (064-667-0144 www.muckross-house.ie), €€ CC is located on Kenmare Road (N71) just south of Killarney center, and is open mid-Mar-Apr and Oct Sat-Sun 1-6pm; May and Sept daily 1-6pm; June-Aug daily 10am-7pm. Combination tickets available with Muckross House (see previous page).

Jaunting Cars & Boat Tours

If you are road weary and sore of foot, there are two attractive alternatives available in Killarney—jaunting cars and river boats. They abound in Killarney National Park and will eagerly take you on long or short sight-seeing trips. If you want to arrange a tour in advance, call Tagney Tour (064-663-3358 www.killarneyjauntingcars.com). There are also very pleasant and deeply scenic boat tours on the Killarney Lakes, which take just over an hour and can be arranged through Tagney Tours or through M.V. Pride of the Lakes Tours (064-662-7737 www.killarneylake tours.ie). €€€.

Cahergall and Leacanabuile Stone Forts

These two surprisingly splendid and finely restored stone forts are well worth the slight detour required to explore them. Both most likely date from the 9th or 10th century and belonged to relatively well-to-do local farmers. Thanks to their recent restoration, both are open to exploration and enable you to climb their ramparts and walk their walls. These forts are rather minimally signposted from the center of Cahersiveen. If you are on the N70 entering Cahersiveen from the south (Waterville), you will see a sign for "Stone Forts" on your left before the library. Follow subsequent signs approximately 2 miles to the forts. [B12] Open site.

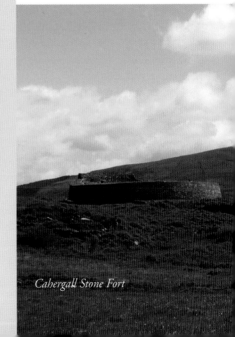

Cahergall Stone Fort

Leacanabuile Stone Fort

Bed and Board
Same as Day Four.

Option #2 • The Dingle Peninsula

PRINCIPAL SITE
Gallarus Oratory and Kilmakeador

The earliest Christian monastic complexes were of wood construction. Many centuries passed before the Cistercian monks and Norman invaders introduced monumental cut-stone architecture to Ireland. The earliest and far more modest indigenous dry-stone constructions were either of beehive design, as found on Skellig Michael and along the Dingle coast, or boat-shaped. One of the most perfect examples of the latter is the Gallarus Oratory, which is perfectly preserved and whose corbelled-roof, after 1,300 years, is yet to leak. You are bound to shake your head in astonishment at the skill of its ancient builders. This little gem is well worth a visit; and the audio-visual presentation in the Gallarus Heritage Centre (066-915-5333) €€ is instructive, but also a bit pricey for what is offered. The oratory itself is an open site. [A/B11] Driving east from Ballyferriter or north from Milltown, Gallarus Oratory is signposted from R559.

Gallarus Oratory

Once at Gallarus, the Kilmakedar Church is only minutes away. You can just about see it from Gallarus, but getting there by car can be a bit confusing. It's best to ask directions on the ground from the Gallarus site. The church, an early Irish-Romanesque structure whose roof reveals a transition from corbel to tile construction, likely dates from the 12th century, though it stands amidst the ruins of a much older monastic settlement traced to St. Maolcethair, who died in 636. In exploring the site, be sure to find (in the church) the ogham alphabet stone and (in the churchyard) the carved stone cross, the sundial stone, and an Ogham Stone bearing the inscription ANM MAILE-INBIR MACI BROCANN (the name of Mael Inbir, son of Brocán). Take note, as well, of the unusual sculptures on the tympanum over the church's Romanesque doorway. To reach Kilmakedar from Dingle: after crossing the bridge for the road west to Ventry and Dunquin, take the first right for 3 miles and bear right at the Y-junction, following signs for Kilmakedar Church. [A/B11] Open site. About 150 yards to the northeast is a medieval stone structure known as St. Brendan's House, which probably served as a priest's residence.

Side Sites
The Blasket Centre (Ionad An Bhlascaoid Mhoir)

The Blasket Centre (066-915-6444)—perched on the westerly tip of the Dingle Peninsula, facing the Atlantic and the far off Blasket Islands—stands in living commemoration of the lives and culture that once flourished on the now uninhabited Great Blasket, abandoned in 1953. The story of the Blaskets is a gripping one and it is told with compelling power here through a series of displays, exhibits, and video presentations. There may be no way to capture the power of this site in a few words; but we guarantee that you will not be disappointed. It is one of the very finest heritage centers in Ireland. The center offers a research room, a bookshop specializing in local literature, and restaurant with panoramic views of the sea and the Blaskets. Open Apr–Oct 26 daily 10am–6pm. Closed Nov–Mar. An OPW Heritage Card site. [A11] Signposted off R559 in Dunquin.

Blasket Islands

The brendan voyage

Who discovered America? This became a less pressing question once Americans looked to the east rather than to west for the answer, and realized that the first "Americans" walked into the 50th state 14,000, not 500, years ago. Nevertheless, westerners retain a sliver of curiosity over the so-called "discovery" or "re-discovery" of America. Were the intrepid explorers Phoenecians, Danes, Britains, Italians, Spaniards, or were they Irish monks? Don't even think about answering this question, much less celebrating another Columbus Day, until you read or re-read about the Navigatio Brendani, the Brendan Voyage. Here is a brief sketch of this remarkable man.

Brendan, the "Navigator Saint," is believed to have heralded from Tralee in County Kerry. Born in the century of Ireland's conversion to the Christian faith, Brendan burned with a fervor that sent off monks and nuns in all directions, fleeing their world and seeking another. These were the "white martyrs" relinquishing everything they knew for what they only believed. This was the "Age of the Saints," the new heroes, and their legends took many of the same forms as the familiar tales of the Irish Ulster Cycles, most notably *echtrai* "adventures," *immrama* "voyages," and *aislinge* "visions." The life of Brendan was replete with all three.

It is said that Brendan set off from his monastery at Clonfert, Co. Galway into the North Atlantic with seventeen monks wedged into a traditional pitch-coated fishing boat called a *curragh* to find the "Land of Promise," by which they did not mean America. After seven years at sea, rich in adventures and visions, they returned to Ireland, spewing with stories of all they had witnessed in the "Paradise of Birds" and points west. Several hundred years later the Navigatio Brendani appeared on the shelves, an ancient page-turner if there ever was one. Many efforts have been made to chart Brendan's voyage on modern maps and to identify his fantastic ports of call with actual New World destinations such as Jamaica and Newfoundland. The discovery of Irish-style stone beehive huts along the eastern seaboard of North America has only fueled speculation that Brendan had trumped Columbus by nearly a thousand years.

To silence those who said it couldn't have happened, not in a curragh, the creative archaeologist-adventurer Tim Severin built a replica of Brendan's boat and sailed from Brandon Creek on the Dingle Peninsula to the coast of Newfoundland. Severin barely made it; but so did Brendan, if we take him at his word.

For further reading:
The Voyage of St. Brendan, tr. John J. O'Meara (Dufour Editions, 1991)
The Brendan Voyage, Vol. 1, Tim Severin, Jon Krakauer, ed., (Random House, 2000)
For Children: *Brendan the Navigator: A History Mystery about the Discovery of America*, Jean Fritz, Enrico Arno (Penguin, 1999)

Mount Brandon

The Dingle Peninsula was an important center of maritime pilgrimage, and its holiest site was Mount Brandon, at 3027 feet the second highest peak in Ireland. Along Ireland's Atlantic coast, three sacred mountains were singled out as focal pilgrimage sites: Slieve League, Croagh Patrick and Mount Brandon. After establishing a monastic community at Ardfert and visiting the monastery atop Skellig Michael, Brendan is said to have climbed to the top of Mount Brandon and to have constructed there an oratory, where he prepared spiritually and strategically for his great sea journey, which is thought to have been launched at the foot of the mountain at Brandon Creek. [B11] Brandon Mountain (whose name is unrelated to Brendan) was a place of spiritual significance and power long before the Christian period; but its association with Saint Brendan crowned it as a highpoint of Christian pilgrimage. Two early pilgrimage routes led to the summit, one from Kilmakeador and one from Cloghane or Fahan. Today, the trailhead for this latter, eastern ascent is signposted just past Cloghane on the road to the town of Brandon. After 3 miles on this road you will come to a small parking lot and the Lopsided Tea House. It's a rigorous climb to the Paternoster Lakes, through a glacial valley, and finally to the summit; but, if you're up for it, it's one of Ireland's most spectacular treks. Roundtrip, it will take at least 4 or 5 hours. Allow plenty of time and equip yourself for changes in the weather.

Dunbeg Promontory Fort

This Iron Age promontory fort at the base of Mount Eagle is perched on a sheer cliff overlooking Dingle Bay at Fahan, on the Slea Head Drive (R559) west of Dingle town. You'll want to circuit the Slea Head Drive in any event for the sheer beauty of its seascapes, and a stop here is well worth the effort of applying the brakes. Although the fort is in ruins and much of its western rampart has fallen into the sea, the setting is impressive. Radiocarbon dates suggest that this site was inhabited as early as 580 B.C.E. and as late as the 10th or 11th century C.E. The *clochaun,* or beehive hut, within the rampart is like many beehive huts strung along the Slea Head drive, most of which stand on private property. You'll see signs to them; and usually a fee is

Kid Sites

Dingle Oceanworld

If you're wondering what manner of critters lie in the waters offshore Dingle, here's a chance to encounter them up close and personal, in Ireland's most impressive aquarium. Except for the sharks and the tourists, all the denizens of Dingle Oceanworld are local. In addition to being instructive, this place is full of hands-on fun, especially for kids, who can distribute the grub at the regular afternoon feeding times and touch some of the creepiest of Oceanworld's lodgers. There's also a café, gift shop, and exhibits on Brendan the Navigator and the Spanish Armada. Dingle Oceanworld (066-915-2111 www.dingle-oceanworld.ie) €€€ CC over-looks Dingle Harbour in the town center and is open all year from 10am daily. [B11]

Fungie the Dolphin Tours

Dingle's most famous citizen, Fungie is a local free-range Bottlenose dolphin with a special affection for our species. He shows up in the harbor most mornings and swims with visitors. If you go down to the [B11] Dingle Pier or call 066-915-2626 (www.dingledolphin.com) you should be able to arrange, depending on weather conditions, a dolphin tour or even an early morning swim with Dingle's #1 dolphin. If you're going for a morning swim with Fungie, you'll need to pick up your wetsuit and gear the day before. The risk-free agreement on Fungie tours is usually "no Fungie, no fee." €€€.

required for a look. It has been suggested by Peter Harbison that these huts may have been constructed as medieval pilgrim hostels and, if so, would be Ireland's first motels. Entrance to [A11] Dunbeg Fort is usually monitored and entails a small fee €.

Sciuird Archaeological Tours

These 2–3 hour tours, partly on foot and partly by mini-bus, led by a local expert, offer an engaging on-the-ground introduction to life and legend on the Dingle Peninsula from the Stone Age to the medieval period. Four or five ancient monuments are visited. Tours are small, from 6–11 people. Advance booking is essential. Call 066-915-1606/1937 or email archeo@eircom.net for further information and booking.

Bed and Board

Same as Day Four.

Dunbeg Fort

DAY SIX
Shannonside

Compared to the past five, today is a day of relative leisure. Think of it as a day off—to take advantage of the breathtaking beauty and many attractions surrounding you in Kerry and, once you arrive, on the banks of the Shannon. Today's only destination is the Lower Shannon and Lough Derg. If we arbitrarily place a pin in Killaloe as our end-point, the drive is only roughly 80 miles starting from Killarney, 120 miles from Valencia Island, and 110 miles from Dingle. If you take your time to enjoy some of the sites or attractions in Kerry that you may have reluctantly passed by on Days 4 and 5, you can still reach the Lower Shannon by early afternoon, unless you decide to apply the brakes in Limerick and explore some of its attractions (see Itinerary I, Day 6). Whether you are coming from the Iveragh or the Dingle Peninsula you will take the N21 NE from Castleisland towards Limerick until it joins up with the N20 into the city. Once you are in the city center, look for and take R463 roughly 15 miles north to Killaloe. Then, once on the Shannon, depending on the time of day and weather, you may want to explore Killaloe, continue the R463 scenic drive north along the Shannon, take a boat shuttle out to Holy Island, or rent a boat at Killaloe and cruise the Shannon on your own. In exploring the Lower Shannon region, don't be confused by the convergence of counties, as you will effortlessly pass from Clare to Galway to Tipperary and back again without any change in atmosphere or cabin pressure.

PRINCIPAL SITES
Holy Island/Lough Derg

If Holy Island or Iniscaltra (Inis Cealtra) for all its merits, exerts no particular pull on you, see it as an opportunity or excuse for venturing out on Lough Derg, the largest of the Shannon's "great lakes." The original and full Irish name for the lake is *Loch Derg Dherc*, "the Lake of the Red Eye," referring back to the story of an ancient one-eyed poet, Aitherne, who after having his second eye plucked out by

Above: St. Caimin's Church, Holy Island
Below: Holy Island Confessional

the king, reddened the lake's waters with his blood. As for
how "Holy Island" became holy, it seems to have been held
sacred by the Celts well before Christian hermits, under St.
Colum Mac Cremthainn, took it over in the 6th century.
Not surprisingly, apart from banked enclosures, hut sites,
and remnants of paths and roads, no traces of the island's
earliest monastic communities have survived. Early Irish
monks and hermits tread lightly on the earth and left few
footprints. A second and distinct monastic tradition was
established on the island in the 7th century by St. Caimin,
under whose guidance Holy Island became a place noted
for learning and piety, an island of proverbial scholars and

saints. In the 9th and 10th centuries, Norse raids were common on the Shannon, and Holy Island was a favored victim. The Annals of Clonmacnoise, for example, tell of a Viking raid on the island in 836; and the Annals of Innisfallen describe how in 922 a Norse commander named Tomrar swept down on Holy Island and "drowned its relics and its shrines and its books." Relief from such raids was, in part at least, due to the efforts of King Brian Boru, whose brother was once abbot of the island's monastery and who may have been responsible for the construction of St. Caimin's Church, which stands today on Holy Island. A good deal of the devastation found on the island today may be traced back to the 17th century and the dissolution of the monasteries, when among other things the roofs of all of the island's buildings were brought down. In recent years, the Heritage Service has restored the roof on St. Caimin's Church.

Of the island's principal remains—four churches and a truncated round tower—the only more or less intact structure is an early oratory known as St. Camin's Church. This represents the earliest effort to build a sizeable stone church on the island. The present, rather ornate west doorway was constructed by the Board of Public Works in the 1970's. The Romanesque chancel at the east end of St. Caimin's Church is a later 12th-century addition sometimes referred to separately as St. Colum's Church. The structure traditionally known as the "Confessional" is in fact the ruins of an anchorite cell, in which a devout hermit would voluntarily seal himself or herself off and endure religious "solitary confinement," not so much for sins committed but rather for the avoidance of sins not yet committed and now surely never to be committed. Another variation on the theme of "white martyrdom," the anchorite cell was understood as a living sepulcher in which, without the shedding of blood, life yielded to a kind of death. A group of curious items which you'll come across as you explore the island are the "bullaun stones," associated in the pre-Christian period with various celtic rites and later used by monks for a variety of tasks and rituals—grinding corn, pounding iron, and even baptizing.

This entire area—the island itself and all that you see around you from the island—is steeped in Irish legend and history. For example, the highest peak of the Arra

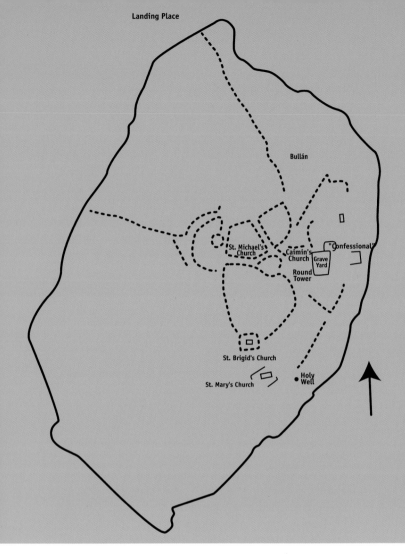

Landing Place

Bullán

St. Michael's
Church

Caimin's
Church

"Confessional"

Grave
Yard

Round
Tower

St. Brigid's Church

St. Mary's Church

Holy
Well

Mountains—known as *Tul-Tuinne* or "Hill of the Wave"—clearly visible from Holy Island (to the southeast in Co. Tipprary) is, according to the *Lebor Gabala Erren* or The Book of Invasions, the Irish Mount Ararat, on top of which the Irish Noah, Fionntan, survived the primeval flood.

For your trip to Holy Island [G9], you can either hire a boat and take yourself or schedule a guided boat tour of the island €€€. For either option, we recommend that you contact Gerard Madden at the East Clare Heritage Centre (061-921351 www.eastclareheritage.com). For boat trips, hire Holy Island tours (call 086-874-9710), or simply drive to the Mountshannon marina where you will find boats and tours available from a designated trailer in the parking lot. If you are going to guide yourself around the island and wanted fuller details about the island's monuments, we recommend that you purchase in advance (at the Killaloe tourist information office or the East Clare Heritage Centre) a copy of *Holy Island, Jewel of the Lough: A History*, by Gerard Madden. Even if you have to swim, make a point of getting out into or on the lake, if you can. It's a beautiful opportunity to enjoy Irish H_2O that is, for a change, not descending from above. And the views, from the water and island, are quite grand. Once on the island, however, we urge you to beware of bulls or overly interested cows. The island is used as pasturage and some wariness is advisble. Keep in mind that tourists are commonplace on Holy Island and we know of no mishaps. That said, we still suggest that you exercise caution and perhaps avoid wearing red, just in case. Holy Island is an open site once you get there.

Side Sites

Historic Killaloe

Killaloe, despite the summer bustle of boaters and tourists, remains a small town; but it is a small town with an ancient and distinguished history. It takes its Irish name—Cill Dalua or "Church of Lua"—from the 7th century St. Lua (or Molua), who together with his successor St. Flannan are the town's two local patrons. Although many of Killaloe's most notable monuments are named after these two, none of those structures date from the saints' time, with the exception of St. Flannan's Well which was likely there long before Flannan drank from or baptized with its waters. Killaloe was, then, in the 7th and 8th centuries a flourishing center of early Christianity and was later, for a time, a pilgrimage destination. In recent years, tourists have replaced and outnumbered the ancient pilgrims. Killaloe's other favorite son is no less than King Brian Boru, who erected his royal palace here on the summit of the hill occupied today by the Catholic Church. For twelve years (1002–1014), believe it or not, Killaloe may be said to have been the capital of Ireland. Not a trace remains, however, of Brian's palace, Ceann Coradh or Kincora. What does survive, barely, is Beal Boru, Brian's massive Shannonside fort. If you stop at the sign marking the spot just north of Killaloe on R463 and walk in towards the river, you come to the remnants of the fort's once formidable earthworks, now only an overgrown bank, ditch and enclosure.

St. Flannan's Oratory

In fact, there's a good deal to see in [G9] Killaloe town; and the best way to explore what the town has to offer is to go to the Tourist Information Office at the bridge and purchase a copy of *Historic Killaloe: A Guide to its Antiquities,* by Sean Kierse containing everything you'd ever want to know about the town and a good deal more, complete with maps and directions. Otherwise, climb the town hill and begin asking directions to the highlights— St. Flannan's Cathedral (13th century), St. Flannan's Oratory (12th century) and Well, and St. Lua's Oratory (9th or 10th century).

East Clare Heritage Centre

This local center is housed in Ireland's oldest church in continuous use, constructed around 930 C.E. In fact it is claimed that Brian Boru worshipped here. The truth is that the number of treasures and wonders claimed by this church and churchyard provoke wonder and strain belief. A few are: the tomb of a pre-Christian princess, the oldest oak in Ireland, the earliest round tower in written record. Regardless, the center and its folk museum are quite interesting and probably worth the admission fee. You can't miss the [G9] East Clare Heritage Centre (061-921351 www.eastclareheritage.com), if you look for it on your left as you come into Tuamgraney, Co. Clare on R463.

Portumna Castle and Gardens

This is the place—if you've made it all the way to [H8] Portumna, Co. Galway, and would like to stretch your legs and take in a remarkable semi-fortified Jacobean castle with its recently restored 17th-century walled kitchen garden. Due to extensive fire damage in 1826, only the ground floor has been fully restored and opened to the public. Portumna Castle (90-974-1658) is open Apr 21–Sept 28 daily 9:30am–6pm; Oct weekends 9:30am-5pm; and is an OPW Heritage Card site. Entrance to the castle, from the town of Portumna, is at the end of Castle Avenue.

Kid Sites

Crag Cave

These limestone caves, formed over a million years ago but only discovered in 1983, boast some of the largest stalactites in Europe. The guided tour travels 2.5 miles into the cave system. Don't worry, it's well lit and the guides know their way back. For children under 10 there is, for an additional fee €€ CC, an indoor soft play area called "Crazy Cave." Crag Cave (066-714-1244), www.cragcave.com, €€€ CC, is open mid-Mar–June daily 10am-6am; July–Aug daily 10am-6:30pm; Sept-Dec daily 10am-6pm; Jan-Feb Wed-Sun 10am–4pm. [D11] Signposted off the Limerick Road (N21) just north of Castleisland, Co. Kerry.

Triathalon

If the Shannon shines on you, this may the day for some riverside sports—say swimming, boating, or cycling. Lough Derg's water has a reputation for being clear and unpolluted; so you may want to take a dip. The best public swimming areas are at Dromineer, Co. Tipperary and Portumna, Co. Galway (which has changing rooms and showers). Boat rentals are also plentiful along the Shannon. Assuming you want a modest outboard, we recommend Whelan's Boat Hire (086-814-0559, whelans@killaloe.ie) at the bridge in Killaloe, Co. Clare. If you're a hardcore landlubber and want to cycle the Shannon's shores, you can phone or stop by the East Clare Heritage Centre (061-921351, www.eastclareheritage.com; for boat trips, hire, Holy Island tours: 086-874-9710). The center is housed in an ancient church on your left as you come into Tuamgraney, Co. Clare on R463. There's also windsurfing and waterskiing and lots more.

Bed and Board

We'll start with a couple of splurges. The Lakeside Hotel & Leisure Centre (061-376122 www.lakesidehotel.ie), €€€ CC, is graciously situated on the banks of the Shannon overlooking Lough Derg in Killaloe, Co. Clare. The stand-out extra here is the fine leisure center which includes a 40-meter indoor pool. Fine dining is available in the Lakeside's in-house restaurant. Another less pricey but still attractive and convenient option is Lakeland House Bed and Breakfast (061-375658 www.lakeland-killaloe.com) € CC on Boher Road within a short walk of Ballina. The setting is quiet, the rooms spacious, the breakfasts superior, and the price right. All in all, this is a fine base for your explorations of Lough Derg and the Lower Shannon. Another affordable choice is Shannon Cottage (061-377118 www.shannoncottage.com) €€ CC just beyond (east of) the center of O'Briensbridge, Co. Clare. This 200-year-old extended cottage literally on the banks of the Shannon enjoys an idyllic location and offers simple, spacious, eminently tasteful rooms (country pine, duvets, etc.), as well as a memorable breakfast in a glass conservatory with grand views. What's more, just out the door from Shannon Cottage there are miles of walking trails along the Shannon. And if you don't want to get in your car to go anywhere for dinner, just walk a few minutes to the Village Bistro.

The most touted restaurant in the Killaloe area is the Cherry Tree Restaurant (061-375688) €€€ CC, specializing in modern Irish cuisine, seafood, and creative vegetarian entrées. It has won several recent awards, including Bridgestone's "worth a detour" award. And it's only across the bridge on the Ballina (east) side of the Shannon. Once over the bridge, just follow the signs. For the same appetite but a slimmer budget, our pick is Wood Brothers Bistro on Main Street (061-376230), € CC. Here you'll get great home cooking from breakfast to dinner, made with fresh local ingredients. Open year round. Call for current hours. Another sure bet, especially if you're staying at Shannon Cottage (above), we recommend the Village Bistro € CC, on Main Street in tiny downtown O'Briensbridge, offering simple home fare and lots of daily specials. No need for a phone number, no reservations taken. Think diner.

Day Seven
Back to the Pale

Apart from one outstanding early Christian site— Clonmacnoise on the Shannon—today is primarily a day of return, positioning yourself well to enjoy a leisurely evening and, with some ease and convenience, to catch your flight home the following day. Starting from Killaloe, we suggest that you drive along the Shannon north 34 miles to Portumna. From here you will have to follow your own map closely, tracing a northeast course on the R355 and then the R356 to Banagher, Co. Galway via Ballycrossaun, Fahy, Eyrecourt (with a possible detour to Clonfert), and Rooaun. From Banagher, trace a further course northwest to Shannon-bridge, Co. Offaly via Shannon Harbour and Clonony. Finally, from Shannon-bridge, you will see signs pointing you north on the R444 Clonmacnoise. After all this, it may seem difficult to accept that, for centuries, Clonmacnoise was at the cross-roads of Ireland!

After visiting, and perhaps lunching at, Clonmacnoise, we suggest two basic options: either to spend the night in the Westmeath countryside near Mullingar, within striking distance of Dublin or to spend the night on the north coast, in Skerries or Howth, even nearer the airport. Either way you will avoid the tangle of Dublin on your last day. For the first option you will want to allow an hour to the airport and for the second perhaps half that, all depending of course on the unpredictable flow of traffic.

For either of these options, from Clonmacnoise you will want to find your way to the N6 just east of Athlone. If you have someone point you towards the N62 north you will soon intersect the N6, which you will take east in the direction of Dublin. If you decide to stay in the Mullingar area, leave the M6 at junction four in Tyrellspass and take the N52 north to Mullingar. If you are coast-bound, stay on the M6 until it joins the M4, which you will take until you meet the M50 beltway around Dublin. Take the M50 north (see Option #2 for further directions).

Clonmacnoise

PRINCIPAL SITES
Clonmacnoise

Founded circa 548 by St. Ciaran at one of the most important intersections on the island, where the Dublin–Galway road crossed the Shannon, this was for several centuries (700–1200 C.E.) one of the most important monastic centers of learning, culture and spirituality, not only of Ireland but of Europe. While very little remains today of the monastic complex that flourished here for nearly a thousand years, the site and its ruins remain poignant and evocative.

Once the saint (Columba) stayed for some months in the midland region of Ireland, and during this period by God's direction he founded the monastery of Durrow. At that time it pleased him to visit the brethren of St Ciarán in the monastery of Clonmacnoise.

Hearing of his approach, the monks who were in the fields around the monastery came from all sides, assembling with those who were inside, and all eagerly followed their abbot Ailither out past the boundary bank of the monastery and went with one mind to meet St Columba as if he were an angelic messenger of the Lord. On seeing him, they bowed their heads and each kissed him reverently, and to the accompaniment of hymns and praises they brought him with honor to the church. So that the saint should not be troubled by the pressing crowd of brethren, four men kept pace with him, holding about him a square frame of branches tied together.

Meanwhile, a boy belonging to the community approached from behind, hiding himself as much as possible. He was generally much looked down on for his outward expression and his attitude, and was not well thought of by the seniors. This boy hoped that he might secretly touch the hem of the cloak that the saint was wearing, if possible without St Columba's feeling or knowing it. But it did not escape the saint's notice, for what he could not see behind him with his bodily eyes, he saw with the eyes of the spirit. At once he stopped and reached behind him, and taking hold of the boy by the neck, he brought him forward to face him. Everyone standing nearby said: "Send him away. Send him away. Why do you hold on to this unfortunate and mischievous boy!"

continued on next page

In reply, the saint delivered from his pure heart this prophetic answer: "Hush, brethren, let be." And to the boy, who was shivering apprehensively, he said: "My son, open your mouth and put out your tongue." In terror the boy opened his mouth as he was told and put out his tongue. The saint reached forward and blessed it, speaking this prophecy: "Although this boy may seem to you now worthless and to be scorned, do not let that make you despise him. For from this hour he will cease to displease you; indeed, he will please you greatly, and grow little by little day by day in goodness of life and greatness of spirit. Wisdom and judgement will increase in him from today and he will be an outstanding figure in your community. God will endow his tongue with eloquence to teach the doctrine of salvation."

This was Ernéne mac Craséni, a man who was later famous through all the churches of Ireland and very highly regarded.

—Adomnan of Iona, Life of Saint Columba, *tr. Richard Sharpe (Penguin, 1991), pp. 115–116.*

Once a center of power, Clonmacnoise today is off-track—utterly tranquil and enchanting—much closer, we might surmise, to the site chosen by its founder Ciaran than to the bustling hub of ideas, art and commerce that it eventually became. Today a place of great beauty and serenity, the lure of Clonmacnoise at the height of its influence lay more in its lands and wealth, inspiring attack not only by Irish chieftains but eventually by the Vikings whose first of many raids on the monastery occurred in 842. In all, it is estimated that Clonmacnoise was burned and plundered over thirty times, mostly by Irish and not Norse raiders. It is no surprise, therefore, that with the exception of the ogham stone nothing of the original monastic complex survives and only ruins of later constructions survive. In the reform movement of the 12th century, Clonmacnoise was not taken over by any of the "blow-in" religious orders from the continent and ceased to operate as a monastery.

The major historic monuments here include the remains of a cathedral, a castle (west of the visitor center), eight churches, two round towers, and a number of high crosses.

Although you are free to find your own way around the site, we strongly recommend that you orient yourself by watching the audio-visual presentation in the visitor center and that you take advantage of the excellent guided tours of the site available at regular intervals throughout the day. In addition to the monastic site, Clonmacnoise offers an exceptional visitor center with excellent exhibits, an audio-visual presentation, and tearooms; and at the far edge of the parking area there's a tourist information office with its own gift and book shop. [H/I 7/8] Clonmacnoise (090-967-4195) is open daily Nov to mid-Mar 10am–5:30pm; mid-Mar to May 10am–6pm; June–Aug 9am–7pm; and Sept–Oct 10am–6pm. OPW Heritage Card site.

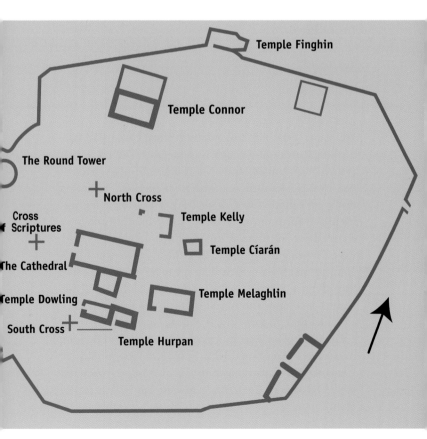

Side Site

Clonfert Cathedral

If you've developed a special interest in Brendan the Navigator, you may want to make a slight detour to visit the site of one of the two monasteries that he founded in Co. Galway. Nothing remains of Brendan's monastic complex, founded in 558 on the west bank of Shannon. What does stand here are the remains of a 12th century cathedral. It was originally cruciform, but today it's south transept is in ruins and its north transept is no more. It's one enduring boast is its Romanesque doorway, with six recessed orders, perhaps the finest of its kind in Ireland. A total of 15 carved human heads adorn the pediment, and more than twice that many animal heads surround the entrance. Clonfert today is nothing more than a hamlet, but if you are on the trail of Brendan, than you will find or sense his footsteps here. [H8] Located in the Hamlet of Clonfert, Co. Galway, 4.5 miles northwest of Banagher, Co. Offaly.

Option #1:

Bed and Board

We have two recommendations for lodging in the Mullingar area, from which you can reach Dublin airport (roughly 50 miles away) in an hour or so, though you would do well to consult your hosts regarding traffic at various times of the day. First, for a splurge, there's Mornington House in Multyfarnham, a short drive northwest of Mullingar (044-937-2191 www.mornington.ie) €€ CC a fine 17th-century Irish country manor house, made even more grand in 1896, providing a tranquil and lavish retreat in an idyllic landscape. Guests stay in style here, to say the least. They can also dine like royalty, if they so choose (restaurant €€€ CC). Your host and chef here, Ann O'Hara, is a member of Eurotoque, the European Community of Chefs, and she's working with her own homegrown and local ingredients. For a more modest but still attractive night's rest we recommend a peaceful country lodge, elegantly furnished with antiques including four-poster beds, overlooking Lough Owel. Lough Owel Lodge (044-9344-8714 www.loughowellodge.com) € CC is located in Cullion, just north of Mullingar and is signposted from the N4. The Ginnells, your hosts, do not serve evening meals, but offer an outstanding breakfast buffet each morning. You will not go wanting for restaurants in nearby Mullingar, just five minutes away by car.

Mullingar is a vital, appealing midlands town, and you will enjoy strolling its main street and scanning its menus. We recommend JP's Steakhouse (044-933-3620) at 28 Dominic Street for the best steak in Mullingar (and the area is known for its fine beef) €€ CC. If you're in the mood for more of a splurge and are willing to drive 6 miles or so outside of Mullingar, then we have the place for you. Crookedwood House (044-72165, www.crookedwoodhouse.com) €€ CC, a beautifully refurbished period Rectory beside a splendid 15th-century church overlooking Lough Derravaragh, has ambience, scenery, and award-winning cuisine. This may just be the finest restaurant in the midlands. At the very least it is a contender for the crown. And, if you can't bring yourself to go anywhere after dinner, Crookedwood House is now an inn with eight spacious bedrooms €€ CC. To find your way here take the R394 north out of Mullingar about 6 miles to Crookedwood Village. Turn right at the Wood Pub and proceed a mile and a quarter further to Crookedwood House.

Option #2:

Directions

For Skerries, take the M50 north around Dublin until you join the M1 north in the direction of Belfast. At junction 4, leave the M1 and at the roundabout take the 3rd exit and merge onto the R132 (signposted Skerries, Rush, Donabate). Follow signs to Skerries onto the R127 and eventually the R128. For Howth, take the M50 to its endpoint where it connects with the Malahide Road, the N23, until it comes to a T-junction at the coast road, turn right following signs to Howth.

Bed and Board

In Skerries [N7], you will find both bed and board at Redbank House, a landmark of hospitality in the village center. Redbank House, 6–7 Church Street, Skerries, Co. Dublin (01-849-1005 www.redbank.ie) €€€ CC. Redbank House abuts the Redbank Restaurant, which has won just about all the awards and testimonials any one board can bear. It all started with the restaurant, an eatery of considerable renown, particularly for seafood. You will eat like a king and sleep like a baby here; not a bad combination for the last night of your explorations in Ireland. Another winning combination is to stretch out for the night at The White Cottages (01-849-2231 www.thewhitecottages.com) €€ CC, sea's edge and a 10–15 minute walk from town, and to dine at prize-winning Stoop Your Head (01-849-2085 www.stoop yourhead.ie) €€ CC. If you arrive in Skerries with time left on the day's clock, look up Skerries Mills and/or Malahide Castle, two top nearby attractions or just stroll the harbor loop at sunset.

In Howth [N7], we also recommend a winning bed-and-board combination, right in the harbor—the King Sitric Restaurant and Guest House, East Pier, Howth, Co. Dublin (01-832-5235 www.kingsitric.com) €€€ CC. All eight guest rooms enjoy sea views. Another solid choice—less central, less costly, but with alluring extras—is the Deer Park Hotel Golf and Spa (01-832-2624 www.deerpark-hotel.ie) €€ CC, atop a low hill just outside the village of Howth just high enough to offer what H.G. Wells reputedly described as "the finest views west of Naples." The truth is, however, the rooms are a bit worn so the view from the inside surpasses the view of the inside. That said, the grounds are spectacular, so you won't want to be spending all your time in your room. One last option is the warmly welcoming, modern, and well touted Gleann na Smól B&B, Nashville Road, Howth, Co. Dublin (01-832-2936) €, just above the harbor—great value for money. Take Thormanby Road up from the village and turn left onto Nashville Road.

As you explore Howth Harbour, as you definitely should, you will find a string of great dining options along Harbour Road at the north side of the harbor. Survey the menus and their price-tags and make your own selection. You can't really go wrong here.

INDEX